Cardinal
Football

by Jim Bolus and Billy Reed
Foreword by Johnny Unitas

Sports Publishing Inc.
Champaign, Illinois

©1999 Billy Reed
All rights reserved.

Director of Prodution: Susan M. McKinney
Interior Design: Michelle R. Dressen
Dustjacket and Photo Insert Design: Terry N. Hayden
Cover Photo : David Klotz and George Thompson
Insert Photos: Kurt Vinion, David Klotz, and George Thompson

All interior photos courtesy of University of Louisville Archives

ISBN: 1-58382-048-5
Library of Congress Number: 99-68247

Printed in the United States.

www.SportsPublishingInc.com

Contents

Introduction by Billy Reed iv

Foreword by Johnny Unitas vi

1. The Bright New Era 1
2. Fred Koster: The Cards' First Superstar 5
3. The Loyalty of Ben Reid 9
4. A Rude Introduction to Big-Time Football 12
5. Frank Camp: The Cornerstone of the Cardinals 19
6. Otto Knop and his Blue-Collar Spirit 23
7. Into the Eye of the Hurricanes 28
8. The Legendary Skinny Kid from Pennsylvania 36
9. Lyles Helps Cards as Trailblazers in the South 59
10. The Colorful Lee Corso 70
11. Cards Climb to Nation's Top Twenty 77
12. Cards Gain Their Independence 81
13. Bold Schnellenberger Sets Cards' Course 86
14. U of L Builds Toward a Dream 92
15. From the Locker Room to the Field 97
16. The Dawning of a New Day 108
17. Appendices 114
    All-Time Year-by-Year Results 114
    All-time records, Coaching Records 116
    All-time Game-by-Game Results 117
    All-Time Letterwinners 124
    Year-by-Year Leaders 130
        Rushing 130
        Passing 131
        Receiving 132
        Scoring 133
        Tackles 134
        Punt Return Average 135
        Kickoff Return Average 136
        Interceptions 137
        Sacks 138
        Punting 139
        All Purpose Yardage 140
        Total Offense 141
    U of L All-Americans 142
    All-Time Bowl Games 143
    NFL Draft Selections 147
    Cards in the Pros 149

Introduction

When my longtime friend Jim Bolus died of a heart attack in May, 1997, he was in the midst of doing this book as a personal project. For Jim, who loved football almost as much as he loved the Kentucky Derby, it was a labor of love. A historian as much as a journalist, Jim loved to dig into dusty library files and yellowed newspaper clippings in search of fresh nuggets of information about games and players that were remembered dimly, if at all.

Sometime after Jim's death, I told Bill Olsen, then U of L's athletic director, and sports information director Kenny Klein that I would be happy to finish the job, if they so desired. After all, Jim and I were friends and colleagues for more than 30 years. Our relationship was cemented forever in 1972 when, as young reporters for *The Courier-Journal,* we shared two national journalism awards for our investigation of Kentucky's thoroughbred racing industry—a Sigma Delta Chi award for general reporting and a National Headliners Club award for investigative reporting.

So when Olsen and Klein responded in the affirmative, I was delighted. I figured that finishing this book would be the best way I could pay homage to Jim, the best person I've ever known. We were closer than brothers, talking almost every

day about things both personal and professional. I'll miss him as long as I live.

As I delved into this, our last project together, I was touched repeatedly as I pored through Jim's notes and files. It was almost like talking to him again. As a reporter, he was far more patient and fastidious than me. No detail was too small to escape Jim's attention. He was a nuts-and-bolts guy where I was more of a big-picture guy. But together we made a pretty good team.

I hope this book reflects both our teamwork and our affection for U of L football.

When I began covering high school football for the Lexington Herald in 1959, Jim was beginning his junior year at Louisville Male High. As a senior in 1960-61, Bolus was an All-State center and linebacker. He could have played for Frank Camp at U of L, but opted, instead, to cast his lot with Kentucky and new coach Charlie Bradshaw. That turned out to be a huge mistake. Shocked and angered by the brutal way Bradshaw treated his players, Bolus joined the mass exodus from UK that left Bradshaw with only 30 varsity players for the 1962 season.

Bolus returned to Louisville and enrolled at U of L. Although he gave up his football career, he never gave up his love of the sport. His negative experiences at

UK turned him into a staunch fan of the Cards. He was especially fond of the colorful Lee Corso, who succeeded Camp in 1969 and built U of L until it was good enough to have a 9-1 record in 1972.

In 1984, when I began writing in *The Courier-Journal* that U of L had a chance to hire Howard Schnellenberger, my columnist colleagues scoffed. I remember one of them coming up to me in the office and saying, "Billy, stop this —, you're making a fool of yourself." But I was confident in my sources. When Schnellenberger came to terms with U of L, Jim and I were both elated. We felt this represented a turning point for U of L, an irreversible commitment to striving to be a nationally competitive program. And, sure enough, it was.

My only regret for Jim is that he never got to see Papa John's Cardinal Stadium, the Cards' new home that opened in 1998. As somebody who followed the program from its days in Manual Stadium, Jim would have been thrilled to see the Cards settle into a state-of-the-art nest. At least, that's what I thought when I remembered him as I stood in the pressbox before the inaugural game.

This book was Jim's brainchild and most of the work is his. I just tried to fill in the gaps. I'm confident Jim would want me to say that we hope the book succeeds as a honest attempt to record an urban university's up-and-down struggle to find its niche in the world of big-time college football. We also hope it succeeds as a fitting tribute to all the athletes, coaches and administrators who have participated in that struggle.

From both of us, happy reading to everyone who loves Cardinal football.

Billy Reed
Louisville, Ky.
July 22, 1999

Cardinal Football

Foreword

To say University of Louisville football has come a long way is a huge understatement.

My journey to Louisville began with a car ride to the Pittsburgh airport in the fall of 1950. My high school coach, James Carey, was a good friend of John Dromo who was scouting a football game in Pittsburgh on this particular weekend. John asked him for a ride to the airport. Coach Carey brought me along and later assistant coach Frank Gitschier invited me down to the University of Louisville. I went down there and worked out for them with assistant coach Frank Gitscher and made the team. That's the way you had to do it in those days.

When I arrived at U of L in the spring of 1951, we really didn't have any facilities to speak about. We practiced right on the school property. Most of the athletes were housed in three Navy barracks. The basketball team had one, we had one and the Navy group had one as well. We practiced adjacent to the old Belknap Gym. Our lockers where inside the gym, and most of our games were played at Manual Stadium. At one time we only had eleven players on the team.

Many still considered U of L a basketball school. The football team wasn't very highly regarded and we rarely had over 1,000 people to watch a football game. My sophomore year, U of L decided it was going to try big-time football. Roy Mundorf came in from Georgia Tech as athletic director. At about the same time, U of L tightened up its academic standards, which caused us to lose several players, and that really disrupted the program.

Despite all of the trials and tribulations, it was a great experience. I'm grateful U of L and Coach Frank Camp gave me an opportunity to play and perform. After I began playing professional football and I was able to see some of the pro coaches, it dawned on me how far advanced Coach Camp was as far as his coaching ability and where his football mind was. We had run just about every conceivable offense at the University of Louisville and I always thought he was a lot smarter than most of the coaches I saw in the NFL. Not only did my experience prepare me for professional football, but I also got my education, which was my main reason for going to college.

Coach Camp had a profound impact on my career as a quarterback. I was on the run most of the time in the pocket, which was a bit of a drawback. I was drop-back passer, but I had to scramble and run a lot. However, the experience was very beneficial, in addition to the

fact Coach Camp was so knowledge-able about the game. I learned so much from him. He kept the program alive for many years when he practically had no scholarships to give.

The progression of Cardinal football over the years is nothing short of amazing. From Camp to Corso to Schnellenberger; from the win over Drake in the 1958 Sun Bowl to the monumental victory against Alabama in the 1991 Fiesta Bowl, a solid and sturdy

foundation has been laid by many great men who donned the Red and Black and gave their all for their school.

Now, U of L looks to enter a new era of football prosperity. After not having a true home field for many decades, the building of Papa John's Cardinal Stadium has propelled Louisville to the national forefront of college football.

Forty years ago, something of the magnitude of a 42,000-seat, on-campus stadium would have never been dreamed of. The new stadium is something I never would have believed. If somebody had bet me a million dollars to one I would

have said they were crazy because I didn't think it would happen at the University of Louisville. The stadium is a great place to play and is an asset to both the University and the community. Louisville football is a way of life for those who played there and who support the program. I think the program is beginning to prosper. The biggest thing you come away with is the camaraderie of the people who you played with and against in your career, not only in Louisville but also in your professional career. That always seemed to me to be something I took from the game, the people I met and people I played with. The game of football is still the game of football. It's getting knocked down, getting back up, getting knocked down again, and always getting back up.

As Cardinal football sits on the threshold of a new millennium, I know it will always face challenges and keep coming back stronger than ever. Today, more than any other, I'm proud to be a Cardinal.

—John Unitas

Chapter 1
The Bright New Era

Rising out of a former railroad yard on the south end of the University of Louisville's campus, the marvelous new red-brick football stadium symbolizes both the end of a journey, long and tortuous, and the beginning of a new era in which all things, including regular spots in the polls and bowls, are possible.

Called Papa John's Cardinal Stadium in honor of the Louisville-based pizza chain that made the largest single donation, the Cards' $63 million nest is what Athletics Director Tom Jurich calls, with only a modicum of exaggeration, "the nicest on-campus stadium in the country." It's not the biggest, with 42,000 seats, but the capacity can easily be expanded if and when the need arises.

Upon their first look at the new stadium, veteran Cardinal lettermen and longtime fans had to feel like pinching themselves, just to make sure they weren't dreaming. After all, from their first varsity game in 1912 (a 32-0 win over Transylvania), U of L had been forced to play its home games either in high school stadiums or minor-league baseball parks.

In retrospect, considering its lack of facilities, it's rather amazing that U of L has been able to recruit so many outstanding athletes through the years. Be-

gin with Johnny Unitas, who played for the Cards from 1952 through '55 before moving on to become the greatest quarterback in National Football League history. The list of former Cards who became household names in the pros includes Bruce Armstrong, Doug Buffone, Mark Clayton, Ernest Givins, Ernie Green, Tom Jackson, Joe Jacoby, Frank Minnifield and Otis Wilson.

One of the proudest chapters in the program's history came in the early 1950s, when U of L became one of the first predominantly white universities below the Mason-Dixon line to recruit blacks. Lenny Lyles, one of the university's first African-American players, went on to a great career as one of Unitas' teammates with the Baltimore Colts.

Yet, while helping every other state-supported university build an on-campus football stadium, the Kentucky General Assembly never saw fit to do the same for the university in the state's largest city.

From 1957 through 1997, U of L's home was the stadium at the Kentucky State Fairgrounds. Fine for Class AAA baseball, it was less than satisfactory for big-time college football, putting the Cards at a competitive disadvantage in

Cardinal Football

recruiting and scheduling that coaches Frank Camp, Lee Corso, T.W. Alley, Vince Gibson, Bob Weber, Howard Schnellenberger, and Ron Cooper fought valiantly to overcome.

With all due respect to the others, it was Schnellenberger, U of L's coach from 1985 through 1994, who did the most to bring about the new stadium. From the day he was hired, Schnellenberger, who coached Miami to the 1983 national championship, preached relentlessly about the need for a new stadium.

When Schnellenberger left U of L for Oklahoma after the 1994 season, the stadium still was a political football, spiraling perpetually in limbo. Then the project appeared dead when the state General Assembly, in keeping with its long tradition of ennui toward U of L, turned down the university's request for funding.

However, banker Malcolm Chancey spearheaded a grassroots campaign to get the money from corporations and fans. Acting on faith alone, the public put up its money to the tune of nearly $15 million. The drive got the over-the-top push it needed when John Schnatter, founder and CEO of Papa John's, pledged $5 million, the largest donation ever received by the U of L athletic department.

"It was actually a blessing in disguise that we got to build it ourselves instead of having the state involved," said associate athletics director Mike Pollio, "because we've been able to do some things and add some touches that the state might not have gone for."

The stadium's red-brick exterior blends perfectly with the clock tower, the Student Activities Center, and other buildings on campus. Even though it's brand-new, it has an old-time feel to it,

The University of Louisville faced in-state rival Kentucky on opening day at Papa John's Cardinal Stadium on Sept. 5, 1998.

sort of like the Camden Yards baseball stadium in Baltimore.

There are 7,000 parking spaces adjacent to the stadium, more than can be found at nearly all Division I programs. Inside, the seats all are red except for the black club-level seats below the pressbox and the luxury boxes. The university went for quality instead of quantity. The way the stadium is designed, U of L could have packed in more seats. However, in the interest of fan comfort, U of L opted for all chairbacks and more leg room in the aisles. In addition, special attention was paid to the needs of disabled spectators.

At the north end, the one nearest campus, there's a huge electronic scoreboard and TV screen for instant replays. Behind the scoreboard is the two-story building that houses the football offices, locker room, weight room, tutor-

ing areas, and the BellSouth Johnny Unitas Football Museum.

On the west side, it's possible to get an excellent view of Churchill Downs, home of the Kentucky Derby, from the 29 luxury boxes, the spacious pressbox, or the Brown & Williamson Club, a carpeted, climate-controlled pavilion that stretches the length of the stadium and is used year-round.

The field itself is Sport Grass, which combines a natural Bermuda grass turf with a below-the-surface system of synthetic elements to create a field that's far more durable than regular grass. It's the same surface used by the Green Bay Packers, the Baltimore Ravens, and the Cincinnati Bengals at their Georgetown College training camp.

As nice as it is, the stadium is only the centerpiece in Jurich's grand design for what he calls "Cardinal Park," an area

A view from the end zone in Papa John's Cardinal Stadium where the "Crunch Zone" fans hang out as some of the Cards' most rabid supporters.

4

Cardinal Football

between the stadium and the campus that will include a 70,000-square-foot fieldhouse, three football practice fields, a natatorium, a softball stadium, walking paths, and a track and field/soccer complex that will give U of L a 1½-mile billboard of verdant urban campus vitality stretching along Interstate 65.

"We get 35 million hits a year (from the interstate)," Jurich said. "We've got to market this as Cardinal Country and get our story out there. People in their cars and trucks will look over at Cardinal Park and do a double-take at how beautiful it is."

When the stadium's dedication game was held against Kentucky on September 5, 1998, Associate Athletics Director Mike Pollio was walking the field before the game when he received a cellular phone call informing him that his daughter, Lynn Hein, had just delivered his first grandchild, a girl named Haley.

"We opened the field at 1 p.m. and that's the time that will appear on her birth certificate," Pollio said. "That's pretty neat, don't you think?"

It was, indeed.

But the neatest part about the dawning of the new era was that U of L finally had a home of its own—a state-of-the-art home that should enable the Cards to recruit better players, draw bigger crowds, and schedule anybody it wants. And, of course, tailgate even more intensely (a national publication ranked U of L as the No. 2 tailgating school in the country.) It was a long time coming, but, as the saying goes, better late than never.

"This is the most spectacular college venue in America," said Schnellenberger at the dedication game, "and it's the most monumental thing to happen in this state since the Civil War."

That may have been stretching it a bit, of course, but it certainly was the most monumental thing ever to happen to U of L football, a perennially underdog program that, as we shall see in the following pages, has made more than its share of contributions to the colorful fabric of college football.

Chapter 2
Fred Koster: The Cards' First Superstar

Although the University of Louisville fielded its first varsity football team in 1912, nobody around the city took the sport very seriously until 1925, when first-year coach Tom King coached the Cardinals to an 8-0 record. Indeed, because of World War I, U of L didn't even play a varsity schedule from 1917 through 1920.

But in the "Roaring Twenties," when Red Grange was becoming a legend at Illinois and Notre Dame was becoming "America's Team," the Cards came up with a player who earned national attention.

His name was Fred Koster.

For a guy who was too small to compete in football at Louisville Male High School, Koster was a mighty big star at the University of Louisville. The Cardinals have had some fine athletes through the years, but not many who accomplished more on Belknap Campus than Koster. He did it all.

Fred Koster

As a 160-pound junior halfback, he led the country in scoring in 1926 with 124 points. An all-around athlete, he earned a total of 16 letters at U of L—four each in football, basketball, baseball and track.

In reviewing the 1925 football season, *The Thoroughbred* 1926 yearbook described Koster as "one of the state's greatest punters, passers and open field runners, and the best all-round athlete now attending the University of Louisville." The yearbook added that Koster expected "to enjoy his greatest football year" in 1926.

It was a very good year for him, that 1926 season. Koster will always be remembered in U of L sports annals for his 124-point production that season. He started the 1926 campaign in a big way, scoring 34 points in each of Louisville's first two games. He accounted for 56 points the rest of the season. Koster scored in all but the Centre game, a 6-0 loss, and the

Western Kentucky Normal contest, a 26-10 victory in which he played just a few minutes. The breakdown on his scoring in the 1926 season: 18 touchdowns, 10 goals after touchdown and two field goals.

U of L, captained by Jake Daugherty and in its second year under the direction of head coach Tom King, opened the 1926 season against Ogden College in Bowling Green, Kentucky. "After a hearty meal at the Helm Hotel, where the Louisville aggregation is staying, King sent the men to their rooms for a good night's rest," Jack Skeavington wrote in *The Courier-Journal*. "With the exception of Uncas Miller, end, who has a slightly twisted ankle received in a workout last Tuesday, the Cardinals are in good condition for the fray."

U of L walloped Ogden by a 79-0 score. Koster "starred with his long end

Fred Koster was a four-sport standout at U of L, earning 16 varsity letters in football, basketball, baseball and track.

runs, which he made on five occasions for touchdowns (and) earned four points on goal kicking," *The Courier-Journal* reported. His TDs included runs of 41 and 20 yards and a 17-yard pass from Marshall Espie.

In its next game, Louisville clobbered the Rose Polytechnic team from Terre Haute by 49-0 at Parkway Field. The fleet Koster scored his 34 points in this game the same as he did the opener—on five touchdowns and four goals after touchdown.

Later in the season, Koster demonstrated his versatility in Louisville's 25-12 triumph at Kentucky Wesleyan, which was then located in Winchester, Kentucky. He "was the whole show on offense," stated *The Thoroughbred* (1927), the U of L yearbook. "Fritz made all of the twenty-five points and was equally good on defense. The playing of Jim Blackerby and Harvey Mayhall was most outstanding. Harvey's line-plunges and Jim's remarkable generalship were praised on all sides. The playing of 'Long George' Barnett was the feature of the line. George performed as one inspired, he broke up passes, stopped Wesleyan runners before they started and was a demon in giving interference on the offense."

Koster wasn't listed in the probable starting lineup for the Wesleyan game.

In its advance story on the Wesleyan game, *The Courier-Journal* reported: "Fritz Koster, who has done most of the punting for the Cards this season, is, according to Coach King, 'just as good as he ever was.' Koster has been suffering from a hip injury suffered in the Centre game two weeks ago. Koster is a triple threat man, especially valuable in playing a team of the type of Wesleyan. He played for only a short time against the Teachers and with a two weeks' rest, the benefits of which are yet an unknown quantity, may display his usual fine game."

Koster played more than a fine game against Wesleyan. It was one of the greatest individual efforts by a back in U

Fred Koster became a respected football official, officiating in 12 bowl games.

of L's history. "Koster, severely injured in the Centre game two weeks ago and pronounced unfit to enter today's contest, played the whole game and made every score," *The Courier-Journal* said. "Three touchdowns, two goals from the field and one dropkick for the extra point after touchdown were the contributions of the Cardinal star, who played as if he were inspired. In the last quarter 'Fritz' eluded the whole Wesleyan team, skidded, side-stepped and ran seventy yards for a touchdown."

Koster wasn't the only member of his family making the news in that Wesleyan game. "A near-riot distracted the attention of the crowd at the Louis-ville-Wesleyan football game here this afternoon near the close of the third period, when Fred Koster, Sr., father of the Cardinals' star, was arrested for an alleged assault on a Wesleyan rooter," *The Courier-Journal* reported. "Mr. Koster, who was serving as one of the timekeepers, said that he did not strike the fan, but only pushed him away from Blackerby, who said the man had seized him by the neck when Jim was forced off the field to the Wesleyan stand.

"The charges against Mr. Koster were dismissed at the County Court tonight. Judge Lee Evans expressed much regret that the affair had occurred. The charge that Mr. Koster was bearing a concealed deadly weapon was termed ridiculous when Mr. Koster explained that his motion toward his hip pocket just after the brush on the field was for his handkerchief."

In U of L's season finale on Thanksgiving Day, Koster scored a touchdown in a 13-0 triumph over Southern College (Lakeland, Florida). That TD gave him a total of 124 points, four more than second-place Harry Wilson of Lafayette.

Koster participated in intercollegiate athletics five consecutive years at U of L. He lettered four straight seasons in basketball, starting with the 1923-1924 season, and four straight in football, ending with the 1927 campaign.

In basketball, Koster was a standout forward for the Cardinals. He twice led the team in scoring, averaging 10.0 in the 1924-1925 season and 8.0 in 1926-1927. He was Louisville's No. 2 scorer with a 5.3-point average in 1923-1924 and tied for the team's third-highest average (6.5) in 1925-1926.

Koster was quite a baseball player, too. He went on to play professional baseball for 10 years, including one season in the major leagues with the Philadelphia Phillies. Koster, an outfielder, also played for the Louisville Colonels and the St. Paul Saints in the old American Association.

Cardinal Football

Koster, who later served as an assistant football coach at U of L, went on to become a leading football official. He officiated in 12 bowl games, including the Sugar and Orange Bowls, and in 1969 was elected president of the Southeastern Conference Football Officials' Association.

When he died in 1979 at the age of 73, he was chairman and chief executive officer of Koster-Swope Buick. His survivors included his wife, the former Florence Schuler, whom Koster referred to as the "most wonderful girl in the world."

Fred Koster's scoring total in 1926			
Opponent .... *TD*	*GAT*	*FG*	*Total*
Ogden College .... 5 (Bowling Green)	4	0	34
Rose Polytechnic .... 5 (Terre Haute)	4	0	34
Xavier (Ohio) 1	1	0	7
Kentucky Wesleyan 3	1	2	25
Marshall 3	0	0	18
Southern College .... 1 (Lakeland, Fla.)	0	0	6
Total 18	10	2	124

Chapter 3

The Loyalty of Ben Reid

One day in 1927 University of Louisville football coach Tom King saw this 6-foot-3, 195-pound young man waiting for a trolley.

King, who knew a football prospect when he saw one, tapped the big fellow on the shoulder and asked, "Would you like to come out for my football team?"

"Sure would," replied Ben Reid—and thus was born a playing career for the Cardinals.

Reid earned three varsity football letters at U of L—one in 1928 as an undergraduate and two in 1930-1931 while attending medical school. Reid, a center who was co-captain of the 1931 team, holds the distinction of being the only medical student ever elected to the honorary society of Alpha Omega Alpha while playing for the Cardinals.

Reid was a stranger to organized football before he was spotted by King in 1927. He lived at 27th and Magazine, one block from Elliott Park (located at 28th Street, just north of Broadway). "We used to kick and pass the ball at the park," Reid recalled. But he didn't take part in any football games at the park. "I never played a game before I went to U of L," he said.

Reid, who graduated from Louisville Male High School in 1926, didn't play for the Bulldogs because he was busy carrying the old *Herald-Post* newspapers in order to earn enough money to pay his way through college.

Going out for the U of L team didn't mean that Reid received any financial assistance. "I don't believe they had any football scholarships in those days," he said.

Once he started playing for U of L, he also was a member of a local football team called Bonnycastle. "I played for Bonnycastle a couple of times," Reid said. "But Tom King made me quit playing for them. He was afraid I'd get hurt."

Reid talked about what football meant to him. "I sure did love it," he said. "If I ever made myself anything, it made me. Football's responsible for me. Football taught me to be tough and not to be afraid to be hurt any. I never got hurt bad enough to quit."

King, a Notre Dame graduate who coached U of L football from 1925 through 1930, made quite an impression on Reid. "He was a big influence in my life," Reid said. "His influence was great. He took care of everybody and took care of their troubles. He was the greatest coach who ever lived, as far as I'm concerned. Tom King was the greatest. He was the greatest man I ever knew. That's

amazing how Notre Dame has put out such great people like that."

Reid also has high praise for Jim Tom Robertson, captain of the 1928 U of L team. "Great boy, great man," Reid said. "Everything good you could say about him is true."

Of all his U of L teammates, Reid said if he had to choose one to go to war with it would be Robertson. "He was a tough player," Reid said.

Reid, born March 22, 1908 in Louisville, graduated from U of L in 1929 and from the medical school in 1933.

In 1931, the season he co-captained the Cardinals with Guy Schearer, the team finished with an 0-8 record. Actually, Louisville won two games that season (13-12 over Transylvania and 19-14

over Eastern Kentucky), but the team had to forfeit both after it was discovered that the Cards had used two ineligible players. "We were going to be a great team until somebody reported them as having played college football before for some other team in Kentucky," Reid said.

Recalling his career at U of L, Reid once told Jim Junot for a story in ScoreCARD: "Back in my day, we didn't have any separate defensive and offensive teams. We just went in there and played without getting out. If you had to go out with an injury or whatever, you had to wait until the next half to get back in. We also used to drop-kick the ball instead of holding it for a field-goal attempt."

As a center, Reid would spiral the ball back between his legs to the ball carrier. "We never handed the ball directly to the quarterback," he said. "We'd spiral it back to whoever was going to run the ball in the backfield."

If the play was going to the left, Reid would center the ball in that direction. And if it was going to the other side, he'd center it to the right. He'd center the ball "maybe three or four feet" ahead of the back—"and he'd catch up with the ball and start running. I'd have to lead him. One time I passed the ball to the left side when it was supposed to go to the right side, and I had to go back and pick up the ball myself and run with it. That was the strangest play I was ever involved in."

In 1935, Reid joined the medical staff at Saints Mary & Elizabeth Hospital in Louisville, and the only interruption in his tenure there came during World War II. Reid was in the service 3¹/₂ years, including 18 months in the Pacific as a surgeon in the Clearing Company of the 81st Division. "The toughest island on which I served was Peleliu," he said. "We had to give medical attention to the best of our ability under the worst possible conditions. Many times this was done under rifle and grenade fire."

Ben Reid (with shovel and hard hat) was on hand at ground-breaking ceremonies for Papa John's Cardinal Stadium on June 19, 1996.

Reid was awarded the Bronze Star in 1945 for his heroic achievement in connection with military operations against the enemy on Peleliu Island.

Returning home after the war, Reid resumed work at Saints Mary & Elizabeth Hospital. Reid was a busy doctor, and, by the time he had retired in 1989 after a career lasting more than half a century, he had performed approximately 60,000 surgical operations.

Reid has meant a great deal to the university. He was a longtime supporter of Cardinal athletics and was a founding member of the U of L Associates support group.

For all that he has done for U of L, the university hasn't forgotten him.

U of L designated December 23, 1981 as Dr. Ben Reid Night at the Cards' basketball game against Morehead State. "Your loyalty to Cardinal Athletics over the years has helped our efforts to build programs that today are nationally respected," U of L athletic director Bill Olsen wrote to Reid. "I offer a personal congratulations and my appreciation for your 'Cardinal Spirit' throughout the years."

Reid received the 1989-1990 Hickman-Camp Award. In a letter to Reid, U of L's Bill Olsen wrote: "Life affords each of us a lot of opportunities, and often being in the right place and having a lot of luck are important to how they turn out. You talked about how lucky you have been, but I really think we (U of L and our Athletic Department) are the lucky ones. The Hickman-Camp Award is the highest honor that we could pay you and is symbolic of what you mean to us. The Red Ruby and the Cardinal Eye are symbolic of the 'burning' loyalty and dedication you have given to our program and also of our appreciation for you and all that you have done for us. I know how lucky I have been to build on a rock-solid foundation that you played such a major role in helping Peck Hickman and Frank Camp establish. We love you and hope this expresses appropriately how much you mean to us."

Reid, who was inducted into the U of L Athletic Hall of Fame in 1990, has remembered the university. In 1988, he made a $350,000 endowment to the Ben A. Reid Sr., M.D., Chair of Surgery at U of L. And in 1996 he made a significant personal contribution to the Papa John's Cardinal Stadium project.

On June 19, 1996, it was only fitting Dr. Ben Reid, that 88-year-old gentleman, was among those participating in the stadium's ground-breaking ceremony. Without the Ben Reids of the world, those people who worked and perspired for the Cardinals back when football was struggling, the sport likely would never have survived on Belknap Campus.

Chapter 4
A Rude Introduction to Big-Time Football

Ten thousand dollars went a long way in 1928.

In a "Boosting Business Sale" at Myer Berman & Sons in Louisville, dresses (choice of crepes, satins and velvet trimmed) sold for $4.88, men's blue work shirts for 53 cents and men's handkerchiefs for 2½ cents. Prices at grocery stores included nine cents for a loaf of Grandmother's Raisin Bread and 10 cents for a can of kidney beans. De Soto Six automobiles could be purchased anywhere from $845 for the Faeton, Roadster Espanol, Sedan Coche and Cupe Business to $955 for the Sedan de Lujo—all prices f.o.b. Detroit.

Yes, $10,000 was a nice sum of money in 1928, especially for a university's athletic budget, although it would serve merely as pocket change for today's multimillion-dollar programs.

The University of Louisville football team received $10,000 for the 1928 Detroit game, but the guarantee came with a heavy price. The Cards not only lost the game to a mighty University of Detroit team but suffered costly injuries that sent the team reeling the rest of the season.

The Cardinals, with Tom King embarking on his fourth season as head coach, launched the 1928 campaign impressively enough, routing Eastern Kentucky State Teachers College 72-0 at Parkway Field. In going overboard in his account of this game, William Ray of *The Courier-Journal* declared: "Tom King put a team on the field that knew its onions, and it gave promise of being perhaps the best team that ever represented the University of Louisville."

Talented end Tommy Thompson was among the many Louisville standouts in this rout. He "lived up to all predictions," *The Courier-Journal* reported.

Tom King

"On the offense, he took out that tackle and on the defense he refused to be taken out by opposing backs, and nabbed his man every time."

Left halfback Bennie McDonald also starred, scoring four touchdowns, including a nifty 45-yard broken-field scamper in the fourth quarter. A plunge through the middle by Russ Hieronymus turned out to be not only Louisville's last touchdown of this game, but its last score of the entire 1928 season. Little could anybody imagine that U of L would be outscored 186-0 the rest of the season.

In hindsight, it's laughable that based off just one game these 1928 Cards would be heralded by *The Courier-Journal* as perhaps the best team ever produced at U of L—particularly in view of the fact that Eastern would be outscored 246-7 in losing all six of its games that season.

King had to know that his U of L team had a man-sized job on its hands the next week. Following its cakewalk against Eastern Kentucky, U of L went up against a Detroit powerhouse coached by Charles "Gus" Dorais. "His team was loaded," recalled Martin "Mike" Duffy, an assistant manager on the 1927 and 1928 U of L football squads.

It seems that Notre Dame was supposed to play Detroit early in the season, but Knute Rockne, the legendary coach of the Fighting Irish, was no fool. He wasn't keen on the idea of going up against Detroit.

Rockne, Dorais and King were all Notre Dame graduates. In 1913, Dorais, a quarterback, became Notre Dame's initial first-team All-America selection. Rockne, an end, was a third-team pick on Walter Camp's All-America team that season. In 1912, Dorais was Notre Dame's captain, an honor that Rockne held in 1913. Notre Dame went 7-0 in each of those two seasons.

Rockne took over the Notre Dame head coaching position in 1918. Pete O'Donnell, writing in the *Louisville Herald-Post*, noted in 1928 that Dorais had been a "Rockne pupil," since his playing days and that King "played at Notre Dame under Rockne and has been an ardent pupil at Rockne's summer coaching school every year the genial leader of the South Bend institution holds a summer grid session for coaches."

In 1927, Rockne's Irish had won out 20-0 over a Detroit team that in its previous game had given Army a scare before dropping a 6-0 decision. Notre Dame won national championships in 1927 and 1929, but sandwiched between those two seasons was a 5-4 record, the most losses ever for an Irish team in Rockne's 13-year career at the helm. Detroit, meanwhile, fielded a better team in 1928 than it had in 1927. Perhaps that combination in 1928—Detroit's rise to prominence and Notre Dame's one-season drop-off— spurred Rockne to place a call to King.

"Rockne called Tom King," Duffy recalled, "and said, 'Gus is loaded. Would you be able to find a way to have your Louisville team take our place?' Tom King said, 'What will we get?' Rockne said, 'Ten thousand dollars.' Well, that was more than they would get all season long."

Football guarantees these days, of course, are much higher than $10,000. But a lot of things have changed over the years in intercollegiate athletics.

Nowadays, football players have it a lot better than their predecessors did. The modern-day players are on full scholarship (including room, tuition and books). Moreover, with teams broken down into offensive and defensive units, the players have to play only half the game.

Times have changed.

In the old days, the U of L athletes weren't on a full ride and a good many of them, true all-around performers, played football, basketball and baseball. Certain athletes did receive aid in their tuition.

"Some guys got some help in their tuition," Duffy said. "I'm talking about Ray 'Bush Hog' McKinney, a fullback; Luther Tibbals, a guard; Howard Huff, an end, and (James) Tucker. They came up from Somerset. Guy Shearer was quite an

14

Cardinal Football

athlete. He was from Bluefield, West Virginia. I think he got his tuition free."

Not much help was free in those days, and the Cards headed to Detroit for their $10,000 guarantee. The U of L contingent, including assistant coach Ray Baer, traveled by rail on the B. & O. Pullman. "The trip up here was uneventful, only a few bridge games among some of the players being noticeable before

Ray McKinney

Coach King decided it was bedtime for his warriors ... " the *Herald-Post's* O'Donnell wrote from Detroit. "Coach King and his men were hustled into waiting taxicabs to the Wolverine Hotel, where the boys showed with knife and fork that they were as hale and hearty as ever. All the men, including the coach himself, did justice to a pleasing breakfast. Sight-seeing trips through the city known for its production of automobiles and also a glimpse of Canada, across the river, were the morning program."

The U of L players may have had fond memories of their sight-seeing excursions, but the game itself was something to forget. The Cards took a physical beating in a 46-0 rout at Detroit Stadium. Actually, Detroit could have defeated U of L by a larger score, but Dorais, showing mercy from the outset, started most of his reserves in this game. Only two Detroit regulars were in the lineup for the opening kickoff.

Detroit led 7-0 at the end of the first quarter and 34-0 at the half. Star halfback Lloyd Brazil, who was a 1928 second-team All-America selection by

Fred Turbyville, scored one touchdown against Louisville. "The Kentuckians were outclassed in every department of their play, but their fighting spirit repeatedly drew the plaudits of the 8,000 spectators," *The Courier-Journal* reported. The story added that the tackling of U of L's Austin Drewery "received much applause."

This was a Detroit team that was destined to go 9-0 and outscore its victims 267-27 in 1928. Brazil set school records that season for most yards rushing (1,393) and most yards total offense (2,230). He rushed for a school-record 209 yards in a 39-0 manhandling of Michigan State that season. *The Herald-Post* referred to "Brazil, Maloney, Vachon and Captain Connell" as "a backfield capable of coping with the best college elevens in the country. The quartet is a smooth-working bunch with speed and stamina to carry through. Their runs all favor the Notre Dame style of football, cutting in on end runs."

U of L's yearbook, *The Thoroughbred* (1929), declared that Detroit was "chosen by many critics as the outstanding college football team in the country."

No, Knute Rockne was no fool. Let Louisville play at Detroit. He'd take his Irish elsewhere.

U of L starters Dave Earl, a halfback, and LaRue, a tackle, were severely injured in the Detroit game. Also injured in this game was end Lawrence Wetherby with a sprained ankle.

The following week, U of L traveled to Chattanooga, "which was sort of a

redneck school," Duffy said. "They were just a rough, tough team. When you played them, you knew you were going to be in a battle. They were an independent team."

As was the case with Detroit, King was going up against another team coached by a graduate of his Notre Dame alma mater—Frank Thomas (a three-year football letterman for the Irish from 1920-1922).

Thomas' Chattanooga club crushed U of L by a 70-0 score before a homecoming crowd of 6,000 at Chamberlain Field. Kenneth Strong ran wild for the Moccasins, scoring six touchdowns. "Today's encounter was a listless affair, with penalties for Chattanooga and injuries to Louisville taking up a considerable part of the time," the *Herald-Post* reported. "It was dusk when the players and spectators wended their way from the field. ... The Cards were treated royally on their short visit to Tennessee, trips to Lookout Mountain and other historical places taking up the boys' time until game time."

Like the Detroit debacle, the Chattanooga game was a costly one for Louisville. Two more starters—McDonald (broken arm) and Thompson (fractured shoulder)— were lost in this game. So with the season just three weeks old, King had lost four starters and had to scout around for talent on campus. Well, talent might not be the best word. Bodies might be a better way of putting it.

"The next week Tom King had to go around to the U of L Playhouse— the theater—to get players to help fin-

Guy Shearer

ish the season," Duffy said. "He had to corral a bunch of those guys to help finish the schedule."

With the team crippled and in disarray, U of L struggled the rest of the season, although the scores were more respectable than the Detroit and Chattanooga blowouts.

"Resorting to an overhead game after failing to show any potential gains through the University of Louisville line, Jim Elam's Transylvania eleven scored three touchdowns, all via the air route, to hand Tom King's Cardinals their third consecutive defeat of the year by the score of 18 to 0 on the slippery Parkway Field gridiron," the *Herald-Post* reported.

The shutout defeats continued for Louisville.

In its next-to-last game, U of L suffered a 12-0 road loss to St. Louis University at Sportsman's Park. "The Cardinals played nice ball in this game and with a 'break' or two, might have outdone themselves to the extent of a win," declared *The Thoroughbred* (1929). "However, the 'break' never came, and once again the team was forced to admit defeat."

The U of L freshman team won one of four games in 1928, that victory coming by a resounding 52-0 over the Eastern Kentucky State Teachers College frosh at Parkway Field on November 23. Left halfback Ray "Bush Hog" McKinney was "elusive as a collar button," reported Tommy Fitzgerald of *The Courier-Journal* and scored five touchdowns, one coming on a 70-yard run and another on a 25-yard scamper. He

also kicked two extra points.

The next day the Louisville varsity, the last-place team in the Southern Intercollegiate Athletic Association, concluded its dismal 1928 season with a homecoming game against Marshall at Parkway Field. "The Cardinals, who will be able to start perhaps their strongest line-up since the disastrous Chattanooga game, will average about 172 pounds," reported *The Courier-Journal*.

Six U of L players completed their collegiate football career in this game—team captain Jim Tom Robertson, Ken Browne, Ford Fishback, Russ Hieronymus, future Kentucky Governor Lawrence Wetherby (who received his law degree from U of L in 1929) and R. J. Elsler Jr.

Only three players who started the disaster at Detroit—left end Browne, center Robertson and fullback Charles Spencer—were in the opening lineup for the Marshall game, which U of L lost 13-0.

"The final tilt was much like most of its predecessors," *The Courier-Journal* reported. "The Big Green backs of Marshall, spinning into an unbalanced line from deceptive formations and skirting the ends on reverse plays, drove their way through the black-shirted Cardinals for gain after gain throughout the fray, but chiefly in the first quarter, when they scored both their touchdowns. The ground-gaining superiority of Marshall accurately is indicated by the fact it made nineteen first downs to Louisville's two."

The Thoroughbred (1929), in a page on graduating athletes, had this to say about Fishback: "This lad came to U.L. from Notre Dame, after having been assured a position the following year on Rockne's famous eleven. 'The Albino' played regular guard for three years, being selected a member of the 'All-State' Team in 1926. He was also a member of the State Championship baseball team of

Lawrence Wetherby

Lawrence Wetherby, Kentucky governor from 1950 to 1955, was a two-year football letterman at the University of Louisville (1927-1928). A 1925 graduate of Anchorage High School, he enrolled at U of L as a pre-law student.

The Thoroughbred (1929), U of L's yearbook, said of Wetherby: " 'Chink,' 'Weth,' or 'W. Head,' it really makes no difference, as the boy answers to any of them, was the other end on the football team during 1927 and 1928. Wetherby is another lad who was not endowed by nature with a football carriage, but by perseverance and hard work won the respect of both his teammates and foes. During the past foot-

ball season he was injured, having severely sprained his ankle in the Detroit game. Nevertheless, even with the bad leg, he was a mighty nice little end. 'Chink' also was a member of the baseball team in 1928 and 1929, receiving his letter the latter year. He completes his law course in June."

Wetherby was a second baseman on the U of L baseball team. "My dad always told me if I wanted to be a baseball player to milk cows—that would make my wrists strong," he said.

Of the differences in college football, Wetherby said a half-century after his days at U of L: "The players are so much bigger and faster now. Why, I played on a first-class football team as a 165-pound end."

1927, playing both the infield and the outfield. Fishback graduates from the Law School in June, 1929 ..."

The yearbook provided the following writeup on Browne: "Brownie' was a regular end on the football team in 1927 and 1928. He was also a regular guard on the two State Championship basketball teams in 1927 and 1928. In 1927, 'Kenny' was selected as 'All-State' Guard on the mythical state team. Browne has been a power in Kentucky Collegiate athletics during the past two years and it is hoped that success will continue to follow him. He finishes his course at the Speed Scientific School in June."

And Elser received the following words of praise from the yearbook: "'Dick' played right guard on the football team for four years, being eligible in his freshman year for varsity competition because at that time the University had not entered the ranks of the S.I.A.A. Elser weighed but 150 pounds, so it is evident

that the boy has a lot of ability. One hundred and fifty-pound-college guards are not so easy to find. In his senior year, on the shipwrecked 1928 eleven, 'Dick' was compelled to play end, and be it said to his credit that his performance was as noteworthy at that position as it had always been while he played guard. Elser receives his LL.B. this June."

Generally when a new coach takes over a college team following a losing season, it takes time to rebuild the program. But in the case of King, he had needed no time elevating U of L to the heights of that 8-0 season in 1925. But instead of building on that foundation, King had the rug pulled out from underneath his program due to the academic casualties in 1926, and in 1928, three years after his arrival at U of L, the team had hit the depths of a 1-7 record.

King lasted two more years at Louisville, guiding the Cards to records of 3-5 in 1929 and 5-3 in 1930. Captain of the

In 1979, Earl Cox wrote in *The Courier-Journal:* "Actually, Wetherby was more closely identified with University of Kentucky football when he was governor because of his close friendship with Paul 'Bear' Bryant when the present great Alabama coach was at UK. Wetherby even did a lot of recruiting for Bryant, but they missed out on their biggest quarry, Flaget High quarterback Paul Hornung, who escaped to Notre Dame where he won the Heisman Trophy."

During Wetherby's tenure as governor, his administration built the Kentucky Fair & Exposition Center. Fairgrounds Stadium (later renamed Cardinal Stadium) was the home of the U of L football team for 41 years (1957 through 1997).

1930 team was Tommy Thompson, one of the greatest athletes Louisville ever produced.

King, a versatile coach, also directed U of L's basketball, baseball and track teams as well as serving as athletic director. As head of the athletic department, he was a one-man operation with assistant coaches. King even taped players' ankles before games.

"Tom King was a fine gentleman," Duffy said.

Where the football fortunes dropped off after King's initial success, he coached the U of L basketball squad to the Southern Intercollegiate Athletic Conference championship of Kentucky in the 1927-1928 and 1928-1929 seasons.

Not coincidentally, King's departure as the Cards' coach came a year after Dr.

Raymond Kent became the president at U of L. "Dr. Kent was more interested in social services," Duffy said. "He was opposed to intercollegiate athletics, but he would condone intramural athletics. I remember well when he was named president, Tom King heard from Knute Rockne, who told him to leave U of L, that Kent was not a football man. He didn't believe in it."

King spent much of the rest of his career at Michigan State University. He was an assistant football coach for eight seasons (1933-1940). From 1950-1956, he was dean of students.

After retiring in 1966, he and his wife returned to Louisville, where this highly respected former Cardinal coach died in 1972 at the age of 76.

Chapter 5

Frank Camp: The Cornerstone of the Cardinals

The loss of Tom King sent U of L football into a long, deep spiral of mediocrity. From King's departure after the 1930 season to Frank Camp's arrival before the 1946 season, the Cardinals only had one winning season—the 5-2-1 record posted by Coach Laurie Apitz's 1939 team. For U of L, the Great Depression was a period of de-emphasis. While UK was building its future, joining the fledgling Southeastern Conference in 1933, the Cards spun their wheels against schedules that included such regional opponents as Transylvania, Georgetown, Centre and Hanover.

This era wasn't devoid of stars. Players such as Lewis "Sonny" Bass (1940-42), Tom Carroll (1941-42), James Caulfield (1938-40), Norbert Elbert (1939-41), Tom Giannini (1930-33), Charles Hampton (1937-40), Charles Isenberg (1940-42), Tom Leahy (1936-39), Melzar Lowe (1933-36), William Slider (1938-39), and William Threlkeld (1934-35) represented the Cards with great distinction. But varsity football simply wasn't a priority. In fact, from 1943-45, U of L didn't field a varsity team because of World War II.

But when the Cards resumed a varsity schedule in 1946, they had a new coach, Camp, who would spend the next 23 years taking the program to a new

Frank Camp quickly molded the Cardinals into a winner in his first season at U of L in 1946.

Coach Frank Camp (front left, seated) talks with members of his 1947 team that produced a 7-0-1 record.

level of respectability. A graduate of Transylvania College in Lexington, Camp had spent 16 years coaching high-school ball in Hodgensville, Glasgow, and Henderson.

Here's what U of L's 1946 game program said of Camp:

"Frank Camp, U of L's "atom-bomb" head coach, is a native Kentuckian, was a three(sport) letterman in college, and in 16 years of coaching has an outstanding record of 102 wins, 35 losses, and four ties.

"During his college days at Transylvania, he was captain of the football and basketball teams, and played quarterback and tailback on the football team. His diminutiveness has proved no handicap to him in coaching as his teams have won several conference championships, and he was selected as coach of the West All-Stars in 1942 in this annual high school classic. In addition to foot-

ball, he has tutored basketball, baseball, and track.

"A rigid disciplinarian, he has no time for an athlete who will not keep in top condition...He is not in the habit of losing games, and does not expect to change his ways during his first attempt at collegiate ball. He is non-commital over the prospects of his team, but it is generally believed he has assembled the best material in U of L history."

It wasn't easy, though, as this report in U of L's homecoming program reported:

"He (Camp) had no schedule, very little equipment, and only a few players. President Jacobsen had stated (in 1930) that football would be played on a "subdued basis," which means any number of things to some and absolutely nothing to others. For a time, it was feared that U of L would lapse into its old ways (after Camp was hired) and not try to keep the

newly won prestige it had gained through several very fine basketball teams.

"In less than two months, the former Transy star made it plain that he

Frank Camp (center) and assistant coaches J.D. Dunn and Clark Wood brought the Cardinals to respectability.

was going to have a winning ball club at U of L. He scraped together a schedule which was absolutely the best anyone could have done under the circumstances. The majority of the teams had been consistent winners over the Cardinals in the pre-war days. During the summer months, Camp "beat the bushes" for players, and when the first practice was called, 110 responded. This number was at least twice the number who had ever turned out for football, and gave an indication that Louisville might win a few games..."

The 1946 Cards were captained by left guard Vince Lococo, who was returning from a stint with the Army Air Force in World War II. The line included center Lloyd Redman—whose son, Bob, and grandson, Chris, would go on to play for the Cards—and rangy end Jack Coleman, who was to become an All-American basketball player and the star of the Cards' 1948 NAIB champions.

Camp installed the new "T" formation instead of the single-wing that many colleges still were running, and he picked Frank Gitschier, a product of the Pennsylvania coal fields, to be his quarterback. According to a U of L media guide, "Gitsch has no superior in his ability at handling the ball from the T formation. He is a magician behind that line when it comes to faking and handing off, and when the situation demands it, he is a fine passer, possessing those rare qualities of accuracy and coolness which all fine passers must possess."

The Cards were underdogs in their season opener against Evansville on the road, but captured a 13-7 victory. Their touchdowns both came in the second quarter, both on passes to Coleman.

Wrote Larry Boeck in *The Courier-Journal:*

"Evansville, whom many observers believe to be the toughest on U of L's schedule this year, probably gave the tipoff to what Card fans can expect the rest of the season. Tonight's triumph may be the first step on the long road back to gridiron prowess."

He was right.

At season's end, Camp's first team had a 6-2 record, which was only U of L's second winning season since 1930. The Cards shut out Wittenberg (19-0), Georgetown (20-0), and Union University (25-0). Their only losses came to Western Kentucky (20-19 in Bowling Green) and Eastern Kentucky (28-7 in Richmond).

Larry Boeck and Norb Elbert "squared off" on the U of L campus in 1941.

22

Cardinal Football

Quarterback Gitschier, who would go on to have a successful career in the FBI, said in a 1996 interview the 1946 team may have been Camp's greatest coaching job because of the way he meshed youngsters with war veterans to build a winning team.

Proving his rookie year was no fluke, Camp guided the Cards to a 7-0-1 record in 1947, the only blemish being a 7-7 tie at St. Joseph's. It was the university's first unbeaten season since 1925, but U of L wasn't playing at a high enough level to merit a bowl invitation.

On February 27, 1948, U of L became a charter member of the Ohio Valley Conference, which also included Evansville, Western Kentucky, Eastern Ken-

Frank Gitschier

tucky, Murray State, Morehead State, Tennessee Tech, and Marshall. In the league's first season, the Cards slipped to 5-5, but Camp wasn't deterred in his drive to upgrade U of L football.

The 1949 season was the first in which U of L played its home games in duPont Manual Stadium instead of Parkway Field. Here's how the 1949 media guide described the Cards' new nest:

"It has a seating capacity of 17,000, but on several occasions another 10,000 persons have jammed the field. It has a new lighting plant which was completed three years ago, at which time the stadium was rededicated as a living war memorial to the boys who lost their lives from Manual in World War II. The engineer that installed the new lighting system claims that it has more candle power per square foot than the nationally famous Soldiers Field in Chicago.

"The Louisville followers are glad that they finally have a regular football field to play on rather than the baseball park that they have been using for the past two years."

Playing against a beefed-up schedule, the Cards went 8-3 in 1949, their only losses coming to Miami (Florida), Xavier, and Southern Mississippi. For the third consecutive year, they were led in rushing by Tom Lucia, who gained 800 yards on 115 carries.

Suddenly the Cards were flying high, leading a lot of Louisville-area high school stars to begin considering U of L as a viable option for their college careers. One of them was Otto Knop, a lineman from St. Xavier who would become a Cardinal immortal.

Tom Lucia was the Cards' leading rusher in three straight seasons.

Chapter 6
Otto Knop and his Blue-Collar Spirit

Anybody who knows the difference between an X and an O realizes the value of linemen.

An absolute truism of football is that the game is always won and lost in the line, and when Otto Knop was at the University of Louisville, he excelled at his skills as a center and linebacker.

Just how good was Knop?

Well, Clark Wood, who was a U of L assistant for 18 years, said Knop was "the most outstanding offensive lineman" he coached.

Knop's contributions can best be measured by the belief of legendary University of Tennessee football coach Gen. Robert Neyland that one good blocker was worth three ball carriers. Knop wasn't just a good blocker—he was a great one.

Linemen traditionally are overshadowed by backs or ends, but that wasn't the case when Knop was knocking heads on the football field. He earned the most valuable football player awards at Louisville St. Xavier High School in 1948 and at U

Otto Knop

of L in 1952, quite an achievement for a man doing his work in the trenches. Moreover, as a standout player on the 1955 Bolling Air Force Base team, he received the game ball from its national service championship victory. Knop's teammates on that Bolling Air Force Base squad included such stars as 1953 Heisman Trophy winner Johnny Lattner and Minnie Mavraides, both from Notre Dame.

Knop was an all-around athlete at St. Xavier, lettering in football, basketball, swimming and track. He earned All-City recognition in 1947 and 1948 and was a second-team All-Stater in 1948. He also was state champion in the shot put.

One newspaper account in 1947 said the following about the St. X standout:

"Otto Knop does everything. The quiet, likeable St. Xavier junior has played three positions in the line and three in the backfield, and to hear his coach, Ray Baer, tell it, he's great any place you put him.

"Right now the St. Xavier center isn't

doing much of anything but taking care of a wrist broken in the Bengals' opener and keeping himself in shape to play more football. Knop, a 16-year-old 170-pounder, began his football days as a fullback but played both right and left half before an emergency in the line made a tackle of him last year. He began this season as a center but filled in at guard one day to plug a hole. His versatility has Baer afraid to miss a practice for fear that on returning he'll find Otto coaching the club.

"The 'one-man team' paradoxically has found his injury of some benefit—he has learned to center the ball with one hand and intercept passes on defense the same way. 'It's really helped my coordination,' he pointed out."

In a game against Manual, St. X was hit with a 15-yard penalty after referee

Jim Beirsdorfer threw a penalty flag on Knop for piling on against Harry Jones.

Knop protested the call, telling Beirsdorfer: "Why, I wouldn't hurt him (Jones); he's my buddy."

Beirsdorfer smiled and said: "He may be your buddy, but it's still 15 yards."

Knop, a rugged competitor, made his presence known at U of L in a big way. He played in every game in his first season on Belknap Campus in 1949 and did so well that one U of L coach declared he was "the best freshman linebacker I believe I've ever seen."

Following a 19-7 loss to Xavier in Louisville's sixth game of the 1949 season, one story said: "Roses to Otto Knop, the freshman linebacker for the Cards, who turned in a stellar performance against the Muskies last Saturday. Otto was consistently pulling down the opposing backfield men after they had broken through our forward wall. The public-address system at DuPont stadium announced Otto's name so often that many of the spectators wondered where (head coach Frank) Camp had been hiding this boy all season."

Going into Knop's sophomore season, a U of L coach talked about the player's defensive instincts. "He just has that sense which tells him where the play is coming, and he sticks his head in there and stops it," the coach said. "I believe he smells the spot."

As a sophomore in 1950, Knop received honorable mention on The Associated Press Little All-America team, and the following season he earned similar honors on the United Press team. In 1952, he was U of L team captain and a Collier's Little All-America first-team selection. The Cardinals' 1952 media guide said of Knop: "One of Louisville's top candidates for national honors is this veteran center from Louisville. A regular since he came to Belknap Campus, Otto will be the top offensive center, and see plenty of service at the linebacker spot.

Center Otto Knop earned the praise of many at a position that is often overshadowed by others.

Cardinal Football

Definitely one of the key men on the squad."

Among the highlights of his career was his overall play in one of the most memorable games in U of L's football history—a stunning 13-13 tie in 1950 against heavily favored Miami. In helping to spark the U of L defense, he recovered a fumble that led to the tying touchdown late in the game.

Of that game played in the Orange Bowl, Knop once told Louisville sportswriter Tev Laudeman: "I think it was a combination, for us, of being up for the game and being an underdog. Sometimes that makes you play to extremes and do what people don't expect you to do. And our coaches did an outstanding job of getting us fired up. They really had Miami well scouted."

Knop went his entire career at U of L without an injury until he broke his right arm just before halftime of his next-to-last game, a 34-20 homecoming victory over Eastern Kentucky in 1952. "Through his four years of front-line duty, he'd miraculously escaped injury, especially considering his almost 60-minute service in every game as center on offense and linebacker on defense," wrote Baxter Melton of *The Louisville Times*.

Knop played on the Bolling Air Force Base team in 1954 and 1955 and was team captain in 1955. Bolling won the national service championship in 1955 and was runnerup in 1954.

Following the service, Knop was an assistant coach at St. X from 1956 to 1959. During that time, the Tigers captured two state championships (1956 and 1957) and put together a 32-game unbeaten streak.

A man who loved the game of football, Knop was elected president of the Kentucky Chapter of the National Football Foundation and Hall of Fame in 1968.

For all that he achieved on and off the field, Knop was honored by his alma maters. He was a member of the first

class of inductees in St. X's Athletic Hall of Fame (1985) and was selected to the U of L Athletic Hall of Fame in 1979 in its second induction class. In 1985-1986, he was the first recipient of the Hickman-Camp Award, the highest honor bestowed by U of L's athletic department.

On the football field, Knop had a way of making things happen, and that ability carried over into his business life as an interior designer. Knop worked 20 years for Hubbuch in Kentucky, becoming a senior vice president and a director for the Louisville design firm. In 1977, he founded Knop Family Inc., a Louisville design firm for which he served as president until his death in 1987.

He also was successful in other business ventures. He was the developer and owner of Apple Valley Resort on Lake Cumberland. He also had ownership interests in the Lakeview Garden Apartments (at the time the biggest apartment complex in Louisville), Breckinridge Square Apartments, Breckinridge Inn Hotel, Holiday Inn Rivermont at Zorn Avenue and Poplar Level Terrace Apartments.

Knop was a four-year football letterman at U of L (1949-1952), and three of his sons also earned football letters for the Cardinals—Otto Jr. (1976-1979), Brian (1978) and Kurt (1980-1981). Another son, Eric, lettered in basketball at Xavier.

Otto Jr. had the unique experience of going up against his father in the 1979 U of L varsity/alumni spring football game. In the unusual format of this game, former U of L players, backed up by varsity third- and fourth-stringers, knocked heads with the Cardinals' first and second teams in a full-speed battle. Otto Jr. was a middle guard, and his father was a center—and they squared off against each other on a couple of series.

Many of the ex-players weren't up to seeing all that much action, but the elder Knop was. The 48-year-old former lineman played the entire first half on offense and afterward received the Most

26

**Cardinal
Football**

Courageous Award. "My dad was out there for blood," said his son.

Otto Jr. is a chip off the old block.

It seems that his father wasn't bashful about mixing it up in extra-curricular activities on the football field, and neither was Otto Jr.

In a rugged 1951 game, Otto Sr. was one of four players (two from U of L and two from St. Bonaventure) ejected.

Twenty-five years later, in Otto Jr.'s very first game at U of L, he was involved in a fight against Mississippi State. Never mind that he was just a freshman and that the game was over and that U of L head coach Vince Gibson and his assistants were trying to hustle the players off the field. Never mind any of that stuff. Otto Jr. had seen two Mississippi State players jump on U of L center Ron Heinrich and began to beat on him on the sidelines after the final play of the game. The Louisville coaching staff corralled all of the players—except for one—and herded them to the locker room. The lone exception was none other than Knop, who instinctively ran to the rescue of his teammate. His helmet was knocked off, which was not the best thing to happen in a fight. "I grabbed my helmet and started swinging it to protect myself," Knop recalled. "There were fans that were kicking me—besides all the football players. And then the next thing I know is Vince Gibson tackles me and gets me off the field— just basically almost tried to carry me off the field. I had a couple cuts on my head where I had gotten hit pretty hard. And

Following his playing days, Otto Knop had a successful career in interior design.

Ron Heinrich, he got out of it. I got hurt worse than he did in the fight."

Afterward, Otto Jr. said he "was real upset. The coaches were yelling, 'You can't do that in games.' They were real mad at me."

His father, who attended every game in his son's four-year career at Louisville, was there to try to calm down Otto Jr.

Otto Knop Sr. was always there for members of his family—whether it be on the football field or any phase of their lives.

"His love of family, his country and his loyalty to our university and our athletic programs are character traits that helped empower him to achieve the highest level of success as an athlete and as a leader in our community," said U of L athletic director Bill Olsen.

Others spoke in glowing terms of Knop, who was inducted into the Kentucky Athletic Hall of Fame in 1994.

"Otto was one of the finest persons I have ever had the pleasure of being associated with and knowing during my lifetime," said prominent Louisville attorney Frank E. Haddad Jr.

Wood, the longtime U of L assistant, said he remembered Knop for his leadership qualities. "He was highly respected by all of his teammates," Wood said.

U of L needed players of Knop's qualities during this important phase of its football development. As Wood said, U of L had "resumed football in 1946 after the end of World War II. Though we had a limited budget and a limited number of players, the outstanding performance of a few enabled us to move the program to such a level that we tied the University of Miami in 1950 at the time they were ranked in the top 10 in the country. Otto played a major role in moving our program to a respected level within a few short years."

Nick Odlivak, a University of Kentucky man, also was lavish in his praise of Knop. In 1994, Odlivak recalled that he first met Knop at St. X at Broadway

and Second Street in 1948. Wildcat coach Paul "Bear" Bryant "asked me to drive him to Louisville on a recruiting trip, as he wanted Otto at UK," Odlivak said. "However, Otto decided to stay in Louisville to help his parents. Consequently, he went to U of L, which was the university's good fortune.

"I am the permanent president of the 'Bear Bryant Boys' Reunion Group," Odlivak added. "Our group voted to install Otto as an honorary member in our organization, the only person bestowed that honor. I always referred to Otto as a man's man."

"Otto's success was not limited to football," said Frank Gitschier, who was a U of L senior in Knop's freshman season of 1949. "He was a very good student, parent and husband. His ability in the business world is well documented, and his contributions to charities were numerous. Otto Knop was a man who lived life to the fullest."

Johnny Unitas also was quite familiar with the many contributions that Knop made during his life. "He was a great competitor and leader, both on and off the field and in the classroom," said Unitas, who took snaps from Knop in 1951 and 1952. "Otto was of high moral character and was constantly concerned about his fellow man. He was always someone you could count on when the going got tough."

Quarterback Johnny Unitas took snaps from Knop two seasons (1951-52).

The going got especially tough with Knop near the end of his life, and yet he kept on demonstrating the fighting spirit by which he had always lived. "The greatest example of how much my father loved his family was his battle with cancer," said Eric, one of Knop's eight children. "The doctors gave him one to six months to live, and he fought it for two years. At the funeral, Frank Gitschier said something that has stuck with me since. He said, 'Otto Knop is a winner. The only thing or person that could beat Otto was God himself—and Otto gave Him a hell of a fight.'"

Chapter 7
Into the Eye of the Hurricanes

The 1951 *Thoroughbred,* the University of Louisville yearbook, led off its section on athletics with a photograph of a group of "pallbearers" carrying a "casket." The caption read: "Dean Walker mournfully leads the gloomy funeral procession for the old dead U of L school spirit. In the black casket being carried to its final resting place, lay its charred and scorched remains. At the Homecoming Bon Fire a new vibrant school enthusiasm was created from the ashes of the departed one. Inspired with the new born loyalty and zeal the students cheered the Cardinals to victory after victory."

Well, "victory after

victory" was stretching it a bit (at least on the football field), because the 1950 U of L team won only three times on its 10-game schedule. Six games resulted in losses, and then there was a tie.

No, then there was THE tie. The tie heard all around the football world.

That tie—a 13-13 battle against a heavily favored University of Miami team—ranked higher than any victory that U of L achieved in the 1950 season. Indeed, an argument could even be made that the 13-13 tie ranks higher than any victory in the history of Cardinal football at that time.

Yes, it was that big.

U of L students "laid to rest" the old school spirit while a new enthusiasm was born.

First, some background.

Little did anybody on Belknap Campus know that the seed for this tie was planted the previous month when Purdue traveled to South Bend, Indiana, and ended Notre Dame's 39-game unbeaten streak by a 28-14 score. The following week Miami pulled the rug out from under a Purdue team that figured to have a letdown. "A rugged University of Miami team ignored touted Purdue's press clippings and gave the Boilermakers a 20-14 pasting before an unhappy crowd of 32,000," Gene Hollingsworth wrote in *The Courier-Journal*.

Football is a game of emotion, a game of peaks and valleys. Following its conquest of Purdue, Miami won its next three games by wide margins, and by the time its encounter with U of L came around—on Friday night, November 10 in the Orange Bowl—the Hurricanes were flying high. This team could look back on its upset of Purdue as a major achievement, and the week after the U of L game Miami was scheduled to go to Florida. No way could Miami take Louisville seriously, particularly after having whipped Purdue, the conqueror of Notre Dame.

Miami entered the U of L game with a 6-0 record. The Hurricanes, ranked ninth by the Associated Press and 12th by the United Press at the time, were striving to find their place in the collegiate football sun. "Miami, for years, played a small schedule and on the occasions it stepped into the big time, it got its ears pinned back," Warren Koon of *The Louisville Times* wrote before the game. "It began a struggle toward the big time, the same as the University of Louisville is trying to do, only Miami put its oar in a little earlier."

Miami, favored by 28

Dan Rivenbark

to 33 points over Louisville, was coached by Andy Gustafson. So popular was the Hurricane coach that one school booster said, "Gus could be the governor of the state today if he chose to run."

The Hurricanes had their sights set on the Orange Bowl game on New Year's Day. U of L had no such aspirations—not with a 3-4 record.

Credit goes to shrewd head coach Frank Camp and his staff for preparing the Cardinals for this game. First of all, the game was on a Friday, and U of L practiced on Sunday of that week, which automatically got the players' attention. "They thought, 'Hey, this has got to be something special. We don't practice on Sunday,'" recalled Frank Gitschier, a U of L assistant at that time.

Secondly, and most importantly, the Louisville coaches were banking on exploiting Miami's offensive tendencies. "Their offense was typed," Gitschier said. "They ran certain kinds of plays first, second and third down. Coach Camp did the greatest sales job on a group of kids you've ever seen in your life. They went down to Miami a 33-point underdog, and they knew they were going to win the game. We sold those kids on 'We've got the formula. We got the secret. We know what they're doing. We know how to beat this team. We're going to play this defense on first, this defense on second and this defense on third.' We had three defenses that were the strength against those kind of plays on first, second and third down."

There was one catch, though. Miami star quarterback Jack Hackett was out with an injury. "We were all worried that the second-string quarterback wasn't going to run the offense the same way," Gitschier said. "But we gambled anyhow. We

Bob Bauer

played different defenses on first, second and third downs, and Miami's offense was so typed that the second-string quarterback ran the offense the same way that the first-stringer did."

With second-string quarterback Jack DelBello at the controls, Miami completed only four of 16 passes for 43 yards.

Miami led 7-0 at halftime. The Cardinals tied the score 7-7 in the third quarter before the Hurricanes moved ahead 13-7 in the fourth. U of L then scored a touchdown in the late going, and with the stunned crowd of 28,824 watching in silence, Dave Rivenbark's extra-point kick with 1:15 left went through the uprights, and the Cards momentarily thought they were leading 14-13. Except a penalty was called by head linesman Jim Armistead.

There seemed to be confusion over the reason for the penalty. Something was said about U of L having only 10 men on the playing field, which was not an infraction in itself as long as there were seven on the line of scrimmage. And for years the story would be repeated that Louisville was offsides on the play, which wasn't the case. After the game, referee Howard Ector explained the infraction, saying: "We counted the men,

and there were only 10 men on the field. There were only six men on the line of scrimmage. An offensive team must at all times have at least seven men on the line of scrimmage. The important point is that there were only six men on the line."

At any rate, Rivenbark had to attempt the extra point again after U of L was penalized five yards, and this time he was unsuccessful on his kick.

Forty-six years after this game, we asked Bob Bauer to recall the costly penalty that was called on him on the first extra-point try that would have won the game for the Cards. Bauer, who lined up at right end, was the U of L player who should have been on the line of scrimmage—but wasn't. If you had been in Bauer's shoes that evening, chances are you could have done exactly what he did.

"I always had a fullback lined up behind me," he recalled, "and I always had a ritual of just reaching around after I took my stance and patting him on the knee. When I reached around to pat him on the knee, he wasn't there."

Kenny Day, the fullback who normally lined up behind Bauer, had been injured, and in such a situation a backup was called on to fill in for him on the extra-point team. But backup Harold Striegel failed to show up, and there was Bauer confronted with a problem. The fullback was supposed to be lined up off his right leg in order to pick up anybody that would rush from the outside. "In my mind," Bauer recalled, "I'm thinking, 'Well, they can block that kick.' So I raised up and asked Dave Rivenbark to call timeout. He looked at me and just kept on going.

"Well, Miami saw there was nobody behind me, and they overloaded on my side. The only thing I figured that I could do was take a step backwards and then when the snap signal came just throw my body parallel so they'd kinda run over me—which I did. But when I took that step back, I took myself off the line of scrimmage. And that was the penalty—

only six men on the line of scrimmage. I took myself off the line of scrimmage, and the rule states that you must have seven men on the line of scrimmage."

Was it a good call by the official? "Oh, yes," Bauer said. "I definitely took a step back (before the ball was centered)."

Apparently, in the excitement of the moment, U of L failed to communicate on the sidelines in order to get a replacement in the game for the injured Day on the original extra-point attempt. "It was Ken Day's job to go in there or get somebody in there," recalled Clark Wood, the longtime U of L assistant. "The backup said Ken never notified him or told him to go in. It was a mix-up. Everybody was so darned excited, I'm not surprised."

Nowadays we've become spoiled by instant replays, but in 1950, technology wasn't so sophisticated, and it wasn't until the Tuesday night after the game that Louisvillians had the opportunity to watch filmed highlights of the 13-13 tie. Excerpts from the game film were shown on WAVE-TV with narrating by Camp and sportscaster Don Hill.

Any doubts about the official's call were removed when the films revealed that U of L clearly had just six men on the line of scrimmage.

Even though the penalty cost U of L the triumph that it richly deserved, the 13-13 tie was a moral victory if there ever was one.

The Courier-Journal reported that the Cardinals "outplayed the Hurricanes almost from start to finish. Their brilliant defensive display never let the Miamians' vaunted passing and running attack get into high-gear long enough to do

the devastating damage it was supposed to accomplish."

Afterward, Camp said: "We told them the defense, and they made it work. The boys played their hearts out for us."

Camp provided five reasons that led to what was described as the Cardinals' "greatest hour in gridiron history."

(1) Defense. After the game, Camp told someone connected with Miami: "Last year you beat us (26-0 at Louisville) on wide stuff, outside runs and end passes. This year we were set for that on defense, and when you tried it again, we stopped it."

(2) The telephone communications between Clark Wood in the press box and another U of L assistant, J.D. Dunn, and the quarterbacks on the field. Louisville players credited Wood for "knowing what Miami was doing and what we had to do."

(3) The strong defensive work of guard Chuck Asher and linebacker Otto Knop. In the secondary, Rivenbark, Day, Carl Repass and Bill Karns were constantly breaking up Miami passes.

(4) The contributions of substitutes. "Camp used 35 players, the most he's

Chuck Asher

Otto Knop

ever used in a single game and every one came through, particularly an unheralded halfback named Bob Aspy," *The Louisville Times* reported. "Aspy and sub fullback Bill Pence banged the Miami line into submission."

(5) The running of Jim Williams and Tom Lucia.

Lucia, the team captain, made a great run for the Cards' vital last-quarter TD. He caught a swing pass in the flat and, despite having four Miami defenders around him, went all the way on a 29-yard scoring play.

The Louisville Times reported that "typical of the spirit" was Repass, "who incidentally was hurt late in the game after turning in a whale of a game. Carl said he needled the Miami backs into helpless fury by saying after each tackle, 'If that's the best you All-Americans have to offer, send us some ball players. Can't you guys run any better than that?' "

Carl Repass

In addition, Louisville did an outstanding job on Al Carapella, a Miami tackle who went on to play professional football for the San Francisco 49ers (1951-1955). "He was a great defensive lineman," Gitschier said. "Our guys really took care of him."

The U of L players were befriended around town by Miamians. "After that game, the Miami people really took us to heart," said Bauer, who turned in a top defensive effort at end against the Hurricanes. "We went out that night and ate and ran around the town and never had to spend a penny. They treated us so well down there. Any nightclub or any restaurant we went into, they saw us with our U of L stuff on and they joked that everything was on the house.

Bob Aspy

"By tying that ball game, we got to stay another day," Bauer added. "So we had quite a celebration."

The press saluted U of L for its accomplishment.

"I've never seen a better display of just downright guts than the Louisville boys put up," wrote Ted Smits of the Associated Press. "They played it to the hilt and deserved everything they got."

"Saturday's games developed several upsets," Earl Ruby wrote in *The Courier-Journal*, "but none to touch the staggering 13-13 tie the University of Louisville fought with Miami Friday night. Oddsmakers for the betting sheets, usually the most accurate of all, regarded the Floridians such prohibitive favorites that they refused to even quote odds. Said one, 'That game ranks with the Army-New Mexico and Harvard-Princeton games as strictly no contest.'"

"It is a tribute to Frank Camp that he managed to keep the spirit of his boys at a high keel despite disappointing setbacks, especially the one to Houston," Marvin Gay wrote in *The Louisville Times*. "Some of the fans were beginning to complain. They'll now be among the first to climb on the Camp bandwagon. All along, I've maintained Camp had done wonders with the material at hand."

These U of L players were heroes back home and were treated like kings upon their arrival by chartered plane at Standiford Field. A crowd estimated at between 5,000 to 6,000 roared "as Camp led his band of 38 Cardinals from the plane," Jimmy Brown wrote in *The Courier-Journal*. "They had just scored the nation's top upset of the week and one of the biggest of the season. From Camp, down to the last player, manager and sports writer aboard the plane when it landed, the huge turnout was a delightful surprise. True, some well-wishers were expected to be on hand, but apparently the Cardinals hadn't yet realized the magnitude of the achievement and the upheaval it caused in the old home town."

As he looked from the plane window, U of L tackle Maury Wolford said: "It sure makes you feel wonderful, just like winning the ball game all over."

A parade of motor policemen, fire wagon and horn-blowing motorists made their noisy way to Belknap Campus, where the noise and hoopla continued with a spirited pep rally.

On the Wednesday after the Miami game, an appreciation dinner, complete with turkey, was held in the Brown Hotel's Roof

Bill Pence

Garden to honor the team. Timing for this dinner couldn't have been worse. It didn't take Sigmund Freud to realize the psychological impact of interrupting the team's routine in midweek to toast a recent victory—especially when a dangerous opponent such as Washington and Lee was coming to town for a Saturday game. *The Louisville Times* was waving a red flag. "The affair is well-meant and the players deserve it," Warren Koon wrote, "but close observers feel that eulogizing over the Miami game may tend to make the players forget their fracas Saturday and spend their last good practice day, tomorrow, thinking of the past performance. We hope not, but it's possible and it's happened before. One of the things, we feel, which helped U.L. in its stunner with Miami was a huge luncheon held last Friday, just before the game, in which Miamians, fans and writers, expounded at great length on the prowess of the Hurricanes in past performances. It was duly reported in the press and served the purpose of bringing the fighting spirit of the Cards up while tending to leave the Miami players with the feeling 'we've been great in the past, don't worry about this game.' "

Approximately 250 people attended the dinner. Admission price was $3. Dr. John W. Taylor, the retiring U of L president, warned the players "to leave their Miami clippings behind in the Washington and Lee game." The dinner was held "with a healthy respect for the invading Generals," reported *The Courier-Journal*.

But still the idea of holding an appreciation dinner during the season is not the best way of keeping a team in the right frame of mind. The Cards were praised by Louisville mayor Charles Farnsley, U of L Associates president Jimmy Stewart and William Duffy, the university's football coach back in 1915 and 1916.

"This might sound funny," Farnsley said, "but I think it's a good thing for a university to have an outstanding football team. It helps the university raise money for better teachers as well as making for a better school."

Duffy, paraphrasing the poem "Casey At the Bat," put a Cardinal twist on the verse. He said the tie against Miami "partly wiped out the four defeats

Tom Lucia scored on a 29-yard Swing pass vs. Miami.

34

Cardinal Football

the Cards have suffered this season—a win over Washington and Lee would do the rest."

"They gave everybody a watch," Gitschier recalled. "It was the damnedest thing you've ever seen."

During practice sessions for the Washington and Lee game, the coaches had to deal with the problem of bringing the team back down to the planet Earth.

Maurice Wolford

"We're still up in the clouds," Gitschier recalled. "Our kids' feet aren't even touching the ground. I know all week we weren't reaching them. We knew we weren't reaching them."

One of football's basic psychological theories is that what goes up must come down, and this U of L team would be in for quite an emotional letdown the first half against Washington and Lee. George Barclay, the Washington and Lee coach, declared that his high-scoring Generals "will gain ground on any team in the country." Washington and Lee's clever Gil Bocetti was as good as any split T quarterback in the country. The Generals brought a 6-2 record into this game.

If the Cardinals were having trouble getting their game faces ready for Washington and Lee, it wasn't because they weren't warned—by their coaches and by the media—about this team's strength.

On the morning of the game, a story by Earl Ruby read: "The Washington and Lee football team meeting the University of Louisville here this afternoon is probably the greatest in school history, thinks Cy Young, alumni secretary. Cy played on two Southern Conference championship teams (1914-15) and has seen most of the school's top squads. 'These boys today would have given my teams a good licking,' he said, 'on basis of

depth alone. The starting team might have been more rugged in those days, but there was no depth. Our 1915 team lost only one game, by a scant margin to Cornell, national champion. We sent only 15 men on that trip.'"

"The Cardinals, despite their amazing upset tie with Miami, are counted one-to two-touchdown underdogs on some oddsmakers' sheets against the Southern Conference leaders, and will have to hump all the way to gain another upset," reported *The Louisville Times*.

Some 10,000 fans turned out for the game and watched U of L fall behind 20-0 at halftime. "It took Louisville's Cardinals two quarters to forget their Miami press clippings yesterday at duPont Stadium, but when they did they put on a stirring rally that fell short just five points as they lost 33-28 to Washington and Lee," Jimmy Brown wrote in *The Courier-Journal*.

The Generals' tough Walt Michaels, who would go on to make four Pro Bowl appearances in his 10-year career with the Cleveland Browns, rushed for 65 yards on 11 carries from his fullback position. He scored 15 points on two touchdowns and three extra points.

Losing to this Washington and Lee team was certainly no disgrace. These 1950 Generals likely were the best football team in the school's history. They compiled an 8-2 record during the regular season and finished the year ranked 18th in the United Press poll and tied for 18th in the Associated Press poll. The losses in the regular season came to archrival Virginia 26-21 and at Tennessee 27-20. Tennessee ended 1950 ranked third by UP and fourth by AP, and losing to the Volunteers after outgaining them in total offense is ranked by many at the Lexington, Virginia, university to be the best game ever played by a Washington and Lee team.

Washington and Lee, the 1950 Southern Conference champion, gained its only major bowl berth that season. With Michaels missing the game due to

an appendectomy a week earlier, the Generals lost to unbeaten Wyoming 20-7 in the Gator Bowl on New Year's Day, 1951.

As for Miami, the Hurricanes came back after the U of L tie to win 20-14 at Florida, followed by victories at home over Iowa 14-6 and Missouri 27-9. On New Year's Day (1951), Clemson scored on a safety in the fourth quarter to edge Miami 15-14 in a hard-fought Orange Bowl game at the site of U of L's memorable battle earlier that season.

Miami, which had a final 1950 record of 9-1-1, was ranked 15th in the final AP poll and 13th by UP. Of the Hurricanes who played in the U of L game, five were 1951 National Football League draft choices and two were selected in the 1952 pro draft. These Hurricanes had a good offense, averaging 22.8 points in their 11 games. Their lowest output came against Louisville. Only three opponents—Purdue and Florida with 14 each and Clemson with 15—scored more than 13 points against Miami.

Knop, the bruising U of L lineman, later recalled that while he competed in service football with the Bolling Air Force Base, a couple of Miami players were on his team. "They said we had the hardest-hitting team they played," Knop said.

That was a hard-hitting team, that 1950 U of L club. It finished its season with a 3-6-1 record, hardly anything to inspire poetry, but the 13-13 tie with Miami is a game that will live forever in the annals of Cardinal football history.

Nearly 6,000 fans greeted the Cardinals at the airport after their monumental tie against Miami in 1950.

Chapter 8
The Legendary Skinny Kid from Pennsylvania

❞❞ Everybody knew that with Johnny Unitas it was just a matter of time," recalled Bob Bender, who also was given the starting call for the second half of the 1951 St. Bonaventure game. "Everybody who played on that team—I don't care who he was—knew Unitas was the greatest thing that ever hit Louisville."

U of L sports publicist Les Moise capitalized on the quarterback's reputation by distributing cards the next season that said: "See Unitas Pass Saturdays."

"There was a time when the publicity department at the University of Louisville put a sign outside the stadium to advertise its games with a come-on enticement that read: 'See Unitas' Pass.' An unrefined prankster took the 'P' away from 'Pass' and the sign became an embarrassment," once wrote John Steadman, sports editor of the *Baltimore News-American.*

Those fans who turned out to watch Johnny Unitas pass during his four-year career at U of L (1951-1954) saw quite a show. He was the best—Johnny U.

That name—Johnny Unitas—is famous throughout the football world, but back in 1950, not a single coach at Louisville had ever heard of this player. U of L's recruiting of players wasn't as advanced in those days as it is now, and one day in the fall of 1950, head coach Frank Camp told his assistants: "I want you coaches to go out and talk to your players, because next year we're going to need a quarterback and we're going to need a center."

Frank Gitschier, who coached the U of L freshman team along with Joe Trabue, proceeded to ask the members of the frosh to inform him of any quarterback or center prospects that they might know.

Two freshmen who had played in the B League in Pittsburgh approached Gitschier and told him about a quarterback whom they had competed against in that high-school league. "Hey, there's a kid who plays at St. Justin," they said. "His name is Unitas."

That was the first time his name was mentioned at U of L.

Camp instructed Gitschier to begin corresponding with Unitas. It so happened that John Dromo, who had been

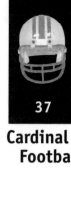

hired originally to coach the U of L freshman basketball team, also assisted with the Cards' football squad at the beginning of his career at Louisville. In the fall of 1950, Dromo went to Pittsburgh to scout Miami, an upcoming U of L football opponent. Dromo knew Unitas' high school coach, Jim Carey.

The way U of L head coach Frank Camp once recalled the chain of events, Dromo called Carey, who asked if it would be all right to bring Unitas to the Pittsburgh-Miami game. "He was trying to sell us on John at the time," Camp told U of L graduate student Rick Cushing in a 1980 oral history project. So Unitas attended the game for his first contact with a member of the U of L athletic department.

In the final analysis, it was Gitschier's perseverance that paid off in the recruitment of Unitas, whom the U of L coaching staff had never seen on films.

Gitschier, who hailed from Sharon, Pennsylvania, was planning to go home to visit his parents at Christmas time in 1950. Prior to that trip, Camp asked Gitschier what he thought of Unitas.

"Coach, this guy can throw the ball," Gitschier said. "There isn't any doubt about that. I've made some calls, and I've written letters to some of the coaches up there that I know, and they said, 'Yeah, this kid has some potential.'"

"Well, you go up there and see him," Camp said. "You visit with him, and if you like what you see, offer him a scholarship."

Keep in mind that U of L wasn't the only school going after Unitas. He had tried out at Notre Dame but wasn't offered a scholarship. He didn't pass a rigid entrance examination at the University of Pittsburgh. Indiana University initially had shown an interest in him but then stopped recruiting him.

Gitschier saw Unitas for the first time on his trip home during the Christmas holidays in 1950. Unitas' mother, Helen, whose husband was dead, had to work hard to raise three children at their home at 345 Williams St. on the north side of Pittsburgh.

Gitschier dropped by the home and had a talk with Mrs. Unitas. He didn't promise her that John would become a football hero at U of L. He didn't tell her that someday a U of L dormitory would be named in honor of her son. He didn't predict that John would go on to stardom as a pro. He didn't say that Unitas would become a household name in football.

No, Frank Gitschier didn't say any of those things.

"The only thing that I will promise you," Gitschier told Mrs. Unitas, "is that I will see that he gets to Mass on Sunday and he'll graduate. That's all I'm going to promise you. We'll give him room, board, books and tuition, and if laundry money is still in effect, he will get laundry money."

And that's how Johnny Unitas was recruited by U of L. Louisville signed him to a football scholarship because (a) other schools either weren't interested in

NFL Hall of Fame quarterback Johnny Unitas was recruited by Notre Dame, Pittsburgh and Indiana among others before landing at U of L.

him or couldn't land him for whatever reasons, and (b) the persistant Gitschier kept writing to him and telling him that Louisville wanted him.

When Unitas entered U of L, he was on academic probation because he failed to pass the entrance examination. He was permitted to carry 13 hours at the beginning until he proved that he could handle college work—which he did his first semester. Afterward, he was on a

Coach Frank Camp (left) knew Johhny Unitas had a lot of potential when the future NFL Hall of Famer cam to U of L's campus.

full academic schedule and graduated in four years.

Not only did Unitas handle the academic side of college life, but he also handled a conglomeration of formations and systems and series in U of L's playbook. An athlete with a good head on his shoulders, Unitas called all of his plays during his career at Louisville. If you've ever seen the U of L playbook that Unitas had to memorize during his days on Belknap Campus, you'd know that he was one smart quarterback.

1951 SEASON

Louisville's Cardinals started football practice yesterday in weather that was almost too hot for baseball, golf or even swimming. Despite the extreme discomfort, Coach Frank Camp managed to welcome 18 lettermen, 17 graduates from last season's frosh, and some 40 freshmen. The quarterback slot is a repeat of last year's dilemma there. Bill Karns, Jack Browning and John Shelton alternated last season. With Shelton shifted to left half, the battle now is among four men, Karns, Browning, and sophomores Jim Olmstead and Bill Campbell.
— *The Courier-Journal*
September 2, 1951

UNITAS, JOHN: Rangy 6-3, 175-pound freshman from Pittsburgh. Although a yearling, he's looked exceptionally good at passing and ball handling and, with a season under his belt, could be a top man.
—1951 U of L media guide

Media guides at times have been known to exaggerate, and in the case of Unitas, he wasn't 6-3 and he didn't weigh 175 when he first came to U of L. "He was about 5 foot 11, and he weighed 135-140 pounds, and he had bow legs," Gitschier recalled.

Camp recalled that Unitas was about 6-1, "but he had the big hands, big feet, lean and had a lot of potential. This is the reason, I think, some of the schools weren't interested in John. He was too small. He weighed about 145 pounds at that time. I would say John Unitas was probably the first quarterback ever put on weights. I started him on a weight program, punch the punching bag, jumping rope. John picked up weight—about 185 pounds by his sophomore year.

"He was tough. Tough boy. John wanted to play. He always wanted to play pro ball, and he didn't mind working. And John would listen to you. John came in the summer before he started in

school and worked at Brown & Williamson. He stayed there at the university. At that time, you could work with the coach, so I spent a couple hours with him every day during that summer working on throwing the football, certain fundamentals. I've always said he had to be a great boy to stay here at the university in the summer and do nothing but work and throw a football, because at that time U of L didn't have many dormitories—didn't have many people on campus. He convinced me then that he wanted to play."

Unitas would continue to build himself up with the weights during the off-seasons, and by the time he left the Cardinals after four years, he had put some muscle on his bones and was built solidly enough.

The 1951 media guide suggested that Unitas would develop into a top man after a year's experience, but Camp couldn't wait a full season for Unitas. The Cards won their 1951 opener but then dropped their next four games. The first of those defeats came 39-7 at the hands of a Boston University team sparked by quarterback Harry Agganis, "The Golden Greek." The left-handed Agganis led a Boston University passing attack that completed 15 of 21 aerials for 227 yards against Louisville.

Agganis, a tremendous athlete, set a Boston University record for passing that season with 1,402 yards. His team finished 1951 ranked 18th in The Associated Press poll, and Agganis received the Bulger Lowe Award as New England's outstanding football player. Following college, Agganis went into professional baseball and played the 1953 season with the Louisville Colonels of the American Association, hitting 23 homers, driving in 108 runs and batting .281. He went to the majors the next season, playing for the Boston Red Sox. Sadly, this great athlete died in 1955 at the age of 25. Death was said to have been caused by "a massive pulmonary embolism."

When Agganis played football against U of L in 1951, a crowd of 10,000 turned out for the game at Manual Stadium. In Unitas' career at U of L, interest and support in the program would decline. Little did the football fans of the area realize that they had an opportunity to see a young man who would go on as a professional to gain acclaim as the greatest quarterback in the history of the sport.

When Unitas first reported to U of L, he was a raw rookie who didn't know a lot about the fundamentals of the quarterback position. He had played football at St. Justin, a small Catholic high school in Pittsburgh. Gitschier, a four-year letterman at U of L (1946-1949) himself, had to learn the fine art of quarterbacking when he first came to Belknap Campus. Camp taught Gitschier how to play quarterback. Having learned from one of the game's most brilliant offensive minds, Gitschier in turn imparted his knowledge to Unitas and coached the young man at quarterback throughout his four years at Louisville.

Unitas had to be taught the basics of the quarterback position.

Early on in practice that season, Unitas was flipping his wrist over on his passes and wobbled the ball like a dying duck. One day the coaches had a meeting.

Unitas got his first extensive action in the fifth game of his freshman year at St. Bonaventure.

"Hey," Camp told Gitschier, "your boy's not doing so good. You've got to get him squared away. He's not throwing that ball right. Work on his fundamentals."

Gitschier continued to work with Unitas, to develop his skills, to tutor him—and by the time the St. Bonaventure game was approaching, Camp was thinking in terms of starting this freshman quarterback who was coming into his own.

Back when Unitas hadn't been faring so well in practice, Camp referred to him as "your boy" in his comments to Gitschier. Now it was a different story, and one day at a coaches' meeting, Camp told Gitschier, "Our boy Unitas is looking a lot better."

Gitschier still laughs at that recollection.

As U of L was preparing to meet the St. Bonaventure University Indians on October 27, it was reported that Unitas, who had played only sparingly that season, would start the road game. "By starting Unitas, Camp indicates he plans to use more passes than the Cards have used in any of their previous games," Jimmy Brown wrote in *The Courier-Journal*. "Heretofore, Unitas alternated at the signal calling spot with sophomore Jim Olmstead."

But it wasn't until halftime, with the Cards trailing 6-0, that Camp decided to make some changes, the most important being Unitas receiving the starting call for the third quarter. All this youngster did was go out and complete 11 straight passes during one stretch. Three of his completions went for touchdowns—two to Roy Pugh and one to Karns. His third TD strike put the Cards ahead 21-19, but St. Bonaventure came back to win the game 22-21 on a field goal in a disputed windup.

The main focus of this story was the way St. Bonaventure won the game. Following an incomplete pass by the home team at the end, U of L players celebrated, thinking the game was over because the clock showed no time

remaining. However, it was ruled that time indeed did remain, and Walt Czaja, who had missed two extra points earlier, booted the game-winning field goal. The timekeeper said that there were still three seconds left, which only meant that the Cards would return the kickoff to no avail.

The Louisville Times reported that St. Bonaventure ran four plays after 15 seconds appeared on the clock. "Coach Camp sent me in with 45 seconds showing on the clock to find out the exact time left," Bill Pence said afterward. "When I asked the head linesman about it, he said, 'One of those fellows over there is keeping it,' and pointed to the other officials. When I asked to go over and see him, he said, 'Come on, let's play ball,' and started the game again. I'm still trying to figure how seven plays were run with 45 seconds showing on the clock."

The controversial finish was the obvious way for any sportswriter to lead off an account of that game, but history would tell us that the story on that Oct. 27 afternoon—the real story in the total scheme of things—was the birth of

Unitas, an ninth-round NFL draft selection, was released by Pittsburgh before starring with the Baltimore Colts.

a college quarterback, the unheralded Johnny Unitas.

Yet in *The Louisville Times'* follow-up story the Monday after the game, Unitas' name was mentioned just once—and well into the story, at that. The significance of Unitas' contribution still hadn't sunk in with the media.

Of Unitas' performance, Camp said afterward: "We weren't going anywhere without him, that's for sure. And if he keeps throwing the way he did against St. Bonaventure, he'll do us a lot of good."

St. Bonaventure was quarterbacked by Ted Marchibroda. "The only quarterback who has looked any better against us all year is Harry Agganis of Boston University," Camp said afterward, "and he had a lot more protection than Marchibroda did."

There were some touches of irony in this game. As fate would have it, Marchibroda later would alter the course of Unitas' professional career. In 1950 and 1951, Marchibroda played at St. Bonaventure, and after the football program was dropped there, he transferred to the University of Detroit, where he led the country in total offense in 1952. A first-round draft choice of the Steelers in 1953, he played one season of pro ball there before joining the Army. When he returned to the Steelers in 1955 from military camp, the team decided there was one too many quarterbacks on its roster and, in what proved to be one of the worst moves in the history of all sports, released rookie Unitas, a ninth-round draft selection. The Steelers gave Unitas $10 for bus fare from their training camp to get him home. With their first baby on the way, Unitas and his wife could use the $10, so he kept the money and hitchhiked home. The irony continues in that the Steelers' training camp was at St. Bonaventure, the site of Unitas' first stardom in collegiate football

In 1955, Unitas played sandlot football in Pittsburgh for $3 a game "and the right to take a cold shower" afterward.

The next season he signed on with the Baltimore Colts, and the rest is history. It was after Unitas retired that Marchibroda coached the Baltimore Colts from 1975-1979 and later in Indianapolis from 1992-1995 after the franchise moved there. And when Baltimore gained a new franchise in the National Football League beginning in the 1996 season, it was Marchibroda who was named the head coach of this team called the Ravens.

A week following the St. Bonaventure game, U of L faced another player who would later cross paths with Unitas in the pro ranks—Alex Webster. The 6-foot-3, 210-pound Webster was a tailback in North Carolina State's single-wing attack. He was a talented player, but U of L benefited from a tough defense, Karns' 81-yard punt return and the weather to upset the Wolfpack 26-2 before some 1,000 brave fans who turned out in four inches of snow, 19-degree cold and a 40-mile-an-hour wind at Manual Stadium. N.C. State didn't come dressed for the occasion. "They wore short sleeves and real thin jerseys," Bender recalled.

This was the first time that U of L and N.C. State met in football, and it wouldn't be until 43 years later that the two teams would play each other again. During the week of the 1994 contest, Webster recalled that frigid game back in 1951. "When we left Raleigh, it was about 80 degrees," Webster told Bill Woodward of *The News & Observer* (Raleigh, North Carolina) "We had light-weight uniforms, and there was snow all over the place when we got there. I just remember freezing my tail off."

Actually, the game should be remembered for better reasons than Webster freezing his tail off. First and foremost, it should be remembered as a monumental victory for the Cards. Putting that game in perspective, Marvin Gay of *The Louisville Times* wrote: "One of the glorious pages of University of Louisville football history, maybe the most glorious, was written last night in the snow and cold of Manual Stadium. The

42

Cardinal Football

band of U.L. faithful, some 1,000, was cold outside but warm in, as the Polar Bears of Frank Camp defanged the Wolfpack of North Carolina State, 26-2. It was most popular and just that this victory, one that will be discussed years hence, was achieved before the most loyal of the loyal. Those of faint heart, and cold feet, stayed away."

This game originally was scheduled for Saturday afternoon, November 3, but in order to avoid conflicting with the University of Kentucky's homecoming contest against Miami (Florida), it was switched to the previous night. Acting athletic director John Heldman said the bad weather cost U of L's Athletic Association "between $6,000 and $8,000." The low gate receipts didn't begin to cover such expenses as a guarantee to N.C. State, stadium personnel and a $1,000 rental fee. "We can't blame fans, though, for not coming out in that kind of weather," Heldman said. "But we wish more could have seen the great game our boys played."

The victory snapped a four-game Cardinal losing streak.

Babe Ray

Houston assistant coach Bob Evans, who scouted his team's upcoming game against U of L, was impressed by powerful Cardinal fullback Jim Williams; Babe Ray, who played his finest game; rangy sophomore end Mike Dewald, a defensive standout, and Unitas. The young U of L quarterback completed only one of 10 passes, but his receivers, with their cold fingers, had trouble catching the ball. "That quarterback can throw," Evans said. "He was hitting his receivers on the button."

Karns' punt return qualified for a spot on a highlight film. "Bill Karns, a converted quarterback, busted the game wide open when he took that punt, faked three State boys into the stadium seats, then followed beautiful

downfield blocking," Marvin Gay wrote. "He reversed his field twice, and the whole operation was a thing of beauty."

Of the N.C. State players, Elmer Costa, a 1950 All-America tackle, "easily was the best of the invaders' linemen," reported *The Louisville Times*.

As for Webster, he carried the ball 11 times for a net 67 yards and completed only five of 16 passes for 90 yards. He was hurt in the early going and was removed from the game in the fourth quarter after being hit hard.

Webster "was the best single-wing tailback I ever saw," said Gitschier. "He'd take that ball on the direct snap and he'd start to his right and he'd fake that ball to the fullback and he'd put the ball behind his back. We'd never seen anybody do that before. Then he'd kinda trickle out in the flat. Shoot, he had the ball. He was a helluva tailback in the single wing."

Webster later played professionally for the New York Giants and combined with Frank Gifford to form one of the best halfback combinations ever. As a pro, Webster would meet up with Unitas and the Colts in some memorable battles, including Baltimore's 23-17 overtime triumph on December 28, 1958 for the NFL championship, a game that is still considered the greatest in the history of professional football.

"What made the difference in this ball club?" University of Louisville football coach Frank Camp asked of nobody in particular inside the locker room following a 1951 game against visiting Houston.

"That Unitas," replied junior fullback Bill Pence.

"You mean to tell me, Pence, that one man, a freshman, did it. How?"

John Unitas did it with talent and leadership, with poise and confidence.

Unitas turned in many splendid performances at U of L, and one of his best came in the Cards' upset victory over Houston before a small crowd of 3,000 at Manual Stadium.

Jim Williams was a powerful fullback in the backfield with Unitas.

Jimmy Brown wrote in *The Courier-Journal* that Unitas, "gambling and throwing passes with the aplomb of a Las Vegas, or Monte Carlo veteran, pitched Louisville's Cardinals to their second upset win in a row, a surprising 35-28 victory over Houston's rugged Cougars. The gangling, 19-year-old freshman twice came up with all-or-nothing plays at duPont Stadium that would have left him the goat had they failed. Both paid off, one breaking a 21-21 tie early in the fourth period, and the other wining the game for the battling Cardinals, who were 19-point underdogs. Unitas was the difference in the two teams."

For the day, Unitas completed 12 of 19 passes for 240 yards and four touchdowns.

One of his TD strikes came on a fourth-and-two on the Houston 40. With the Cougars expecting a run, Unitas tossed a scoring pass to Dave Rivenbark. Unitas, although just a

freshman, demonstrated his leadership in a big way on that play and showed his teammates who was in charge. "Unitas called for a pass, and I checked signals," said Pence, whose 15-yard run had been a big play in the Cardinals drive that reached the Houston 40. "I told him I could make two yards anytime—if not, there was no use for me to be out there. And he told me, 'You run the ball when I call your signal, and I'll call the plays.'"

Unitas promptly hit Rivenbark for the touchdown.

Later, from his seven-yard line, the daring Unitas dropped back into his end zone and fired a pass to Babe Ray, who caught the ball on the U of L 40 and went all the way, outrunning three defenders, on a 93-yard scoring play. "That's when he made a believer out of me," Pence told Camp, the U of L coach.

He made believers out of everybody

Unitas played a year with the NFL San Diego Chargers in 1973 before retiring.

who was watching him do his thing.

Unitas would have had a fifth touchdown pass against Houston, but an apparent 35-yard scoring strike in the end zone to John Shelton was nullified due to a pass interference penalty against the U of L receiver. "... interference was called on Shelton, despite the fact he caught the ball nearly six yards from the Houston defender," Brown wrote in *The Courier-Journal*.

All in all, Unitas put on a passing clinic against the Cougars.

"If Coach Frank Camp is smart, he'll take Unitas, enclose him in a cellophane bag and put him away with the Cardinals' uniforms for safekeeping over the winter," Brown wrote. "They better not let anything happen to this boy. He's the most colorful player to hit Louisville in a long time."

Houston, which began playing football in 1946, went 5-5 during the regular season and then won the Salad Bowl 26-21 over Dayton on New Year's Day (1952). Four members of this team were honorable mention All-America, including Gene Shannon, who finished the season ranked fourth among NCAA rushers with 1,036 yards.

Against U of L, Houston rushed for 279 yards, but the Cardinals mixed up their offense with 127 yards on the ground and 240 in the air.

1952 SEASON

There is no comeback like the comeback of a champion. Battered to the floor and forsaken by everyone but himself, he rises from defeat and returns to action with a new enthusiasm to conquer all before him.

That is, in essence, the story of the 1951 University of Louisville football team. Badly battered in the early season by four consecutive losses and forsaken by all but themselves, the coaches and a few faithful followers, they swept to victory in the last four games of the season making the greatest comeback in the history of

the University.

Probably no name in the "comeback kids" register is any more well known than "the kid from Pittsburgh," Johnny Unitas. Leading a downtrodden team back to victory with his superb passing and fine field generalship, Unitas is one man who makes the future football picture bright.

— 1952 Thoroughbred
(U of L yearbook)

Sixty-three University of Louisville gridders began their annual fall labors in sweltering weather yesterday at Belknap Campus. And as a squad that included 35 freshmen and only six seniors met Coach Frank Camp, the veteran mentor, who is starting his seventh season at the U.L. helm, immediately labeled inexperience as his biggest worry. ... Especially high on Camp's list are quarterback John Unitas, center Otto Knop, fullback Jim Williams and guard Jack Valvo.

— The Courier-Journal,
September 2, 1952

An optimist would look at the season prospects of the University of Louisville Cardinals as bright, but a pessimist can find a million loopholes. The guy with the bright outlook would point to quarterback Johnny Unitas, who, as a freshman last year, took over the vital signal-calling spot and led the Cards to four consecutive victories. His teammates don't call Johnny "Mr. Sparkplug" for nothing.

—1952 U of L media guide

Contrary to the high hopes expressed by Bob Bender, contrary to the U of L yearbook's thought that Unitas was the one man who made the future football picture bright, the sport would not go forward during this great quarterback's next three years with the Cardinals.

Just when the U of L football faithful thought it was safe to test the big-time football waters, the school's board of trustees pulled the rug out from under the athletic program. Dr. Philip G.

Davidson, no great lover of football, had become the U of L president in 1951, and on January 6, 1952, the board of trustees decreed a reduction and limitation to the university's own financial responsibility to football and other intercollegiate sports. The new policy called for U of L to give aid to athletes in the form of tuition only. In addition, athletes were to receive no preference in the awarding of scholarships.

U of L president Dr. Phillip Davidson lowered athletic aid and tightened academic standards in 1952.

In previous years, the university had provided room and board, along with tuition, to the athletes. Under the 1952 trustees' edict, no assistance beyond tuition could come from the school's general funds. Included in the general funds were gate receipts from games.

Davidson was quoted as saying: "I wouldn't call it a de-emphasis program. It amounts to this: The university is going as far as it feels it can go financially for athletics. It's now up to the community. After all, the university is a community project."

As it turned out, 15 to 22 players on the team would no longer meet higher academic standards imposed by U of L and were taken off scholarship. "These guys would have been eligible at any other school," Bender said. "So it made it very tough."

Unitas and Bender were among the dwindling number of full scholarship players remaining. "We got books and tuition and $25 a month," Bender said. "Some got $15, but the maximum you could pay at that time was $25."

Earl Ruby, sports editor of *The Courier-Journal,* tried to look at the negative news at U of L in a positive way. "The University of Louisville placed its athletic program on solid ground when it decided to limit grants from the general fund to tuition only," Ruby wrote. "Eventually most schools will have to come to this same decision if football, with its multiple platoons, is to survive. There are enough jobs in Louisville for all the football players who really wish to work in their spare time, and plenty of University Associates to line them up. It will be the task of the new athletic director, Roy Mundorff, to get them all together."

But, of course, the task at hand was an impossible mission.

This U of L team suddenly was decimated, and Camp found himself in the same position that Tom King found himself following his unbeaten season of 1925 and that Laurie Apitz found himself during his entire time at Louisville. And that position wasn't conducive to winning football games. U of L simply wasn't competing on a level playing field with its opponents, many of whom were rolling right along with scholarships and funding and support—the whole works.

Dr. John W. Taylor, the previous U of L president, had wanted major-league football, and with Mundorff having been brought in from Georgia Tech as athletic director, such teams as Tennessee, North Carolina State, Boston University and Florida State were put on the schedule. "They had a lot more people on scholarship," Bender said. "Then you could have 110, plus about 30 walk-ons."

Once Davidson's regime decided to de-emphasize football, Camp was in a no-

win situation. The Cards had a big-time schedule but didn't have enough big-time players to compete on that level.

Unitas recalled that the situation was so bad during spring practice one year "we had to scrimmage one side of an offensive line at a time because we didn't have enough people."

U of L opened the season with two victories—19-12 over Wayne State and 41-14 at Florida State—to extend its winning steak to six games. Unitas put on a passing clinic against Florida State, completing 12 of 13 aerials in the first half and 16 of 21 for the game. He threw three touchdown strikes in that game at Tallahassee.

The convincing 1952 triumph over Florida State was not a harbinger of things to come in U of L's series with the Seminoles. The '52 Florida State team simply wasn't very good. Louisville's 41-point total was the highest ever scored

against a Seminole team, a record that would be eclipsed four games later that season by Mississippi Southern's 50-point eruption. Florida State, which played its inaugural season in 1947, went 1-8-1 in 1952.

The rest of the 1952 season was essentially a struggle for the Cards, who won only one of their remaining six games and finished with a 3-5 record.

One of those losses came by a 29-25 score at Memphis State, a wild game in which Unitas completed 17 of 30 passes and threw for three touchdowns. The quick-thinking Unitas improvised on a screen pass to avoid a loss on one play. "We were in one of those spread-out formations," Gitschier recalled. "He was going back to pass, and the defense blitzed him—which was not unusual—and a guy had wrapped his arms around him and pinned his arms to the side. John just took the ball and flipped it behind his back to Jim Williams, who was out to the left. Williams took the ball down the field for a huge gain. John was so adaptable to what was happening."

(The 1952 Memphis State game wasn't the only time in Unitas' football career that he tried one of those behind-the-back passes. Pro Football Hall of Fame lineman Merlin Olsen once said of Unitas: "This is a very special man, a man who means a great deal to me—Johnny Unitas, the finest quarterback I ever played against. His leadership ability and his ability to stay cool in a crisis were remarkable. But I guess I remember him best because I lined up across from him so many times, and he always seemed to find a way to win, even when you thought you had him cornered. I can remember once there were four of us right on top of him, arms outstretched. No way he could throw a pass. He just flipped the ball behind his back to one of his running backs, who promptly ran for a first down.")

In the Cards' next-to-last game of the '52 season, a 34-20 homecoming triumph over Eastern Kentucky, Unitas

Unitas' supporting U of L cast was diminished in 1952.

completed seven of eight passes but played only a minute in the second half due to an injured shoulder. In the season finale, Unitas saw action for only four plays, one of which resulted in a touchdown pass. Louisville was clobbered 55-26 in that contest at Mississippi Southern, which gained its ninth straight success following a 20-6 season-opening loss to Alabama.

1953 SEASON

Even in defeat the name of Johnny Unitas had resounded through the crowd, and many teams were stifled by the "kid from Pittsburgh." His superb quarterbacking and great passing won him praise from every team we played, for as one newspaper put it 'Unitas We Stand, Divided We Fall' must be U of L's motto.
  —*1953 Thoroughbred*

"Football, a controversial subject at the University of Louisville these past few years, started its 1953 stand at the Belknap Campus institution minus much of the predicted gloom. First, an imposing squad of 55 candidates reported to Coach Frank Camp to start drilling for a nine-game schedule that includes mighty Tennessee, plus such strong foes as Xavier, Cincinnati and Chattanooga. ... Seventeen lettermen were among the group that reported for two workouts in oven-like temperatures. The veterans were led by John Unitas, now a junior after ranking high in the nation's passing statistics as a Cardinal freshman and sophomore. Around this gangling, 185-pound pass master, Camp will build practically his entire hopes for success this season."
  — *The Courier-Journal,*
     September 2, 1953

What makes an All-American?
A backfield man must pass, he must run and block, he must punt, he must play defense ... this year John Unitas will do all those things. Last year with the platoon system in play, Unitas stuck to of-

Unitas wore number 16 at U of L—the lone number retired by the Cardinals—and No. 19 as a professional.

fense. Despite the fact that Louisville only played an eight game schedule, and in two of these John made little more than a token appearance because of an injured shoulder, he still finished among the top ten (according to NCAA statistics) of the nation's passers.
  —*1953 U of L media guide*

Unitas had a chance to transfer to Indiana University before the start of this season. Back when he visited Notre Dame following his high-school football career, he tried out under the supervision of assistant coach Bernie Crimmins, who later became the head coach at Indiana. Crimmins had been impressed with Unitas at the Notre Dame tryout, but the player's size was against him. "I was about 5-11, maybe 6 foot, and 135 pounds," Unitas recalled, "and he was concerned about me being hurt and injured."

So Notre Dame decided not to give Unitas a chance to play for the Irish.

Cardinal Football

Crimmins, who took over as IU's head coach in 1952, made a call to Unitas after his sophomore season. "He said he'd like to talk to me about transferring from the University of Louisville to Indiana to play for him," Unitas said.

The transfer would be contingent on whether he would have one or two years of eligibility remaining. The Big Ten subsequently ruled that Unitas would be eligible for two years.

Unitas talked with his mother and his high-school coach about Indiana's proposal but decided against leaving U of L. "No, I'm not going to do that," Unitas said. "Coach Camp was nice enough to bring me down here and give me a full scholarship. I can't do that to someone who's having some problems here with the program. I'm here for the four years."

Unitas considered transferring to Indiana when funding to the Cards' program was diminished, but chose to remain at Louisville.

Life always has its twists of fate, and in this particular situation it was ironic that Crimmins, while at Notre Dame, had turned down Unitas, and now Unitas, at U of L, was turning down Crimmins.

Louisville won its season opener in 1953 and then lost the rest of its seven games on the schedule. The Cards were outscored by a staggering 291-77 that season.

One of Louisville's defeats in 1953 came by the whopping score of 59-0 at Florida State, which was quarterbacked by none other than Lee Corso, a future U of L head coach.

Unitas is best remembered this season for his contributions in a loss. A 59-6 loss, that is.

Louisville, with its de-emphasized football program, had no business on the same field with Tennessee. "Although the Volunteers aren't the powerhouse of

former years," Jimmy Brown wrote in *The Courier-Journal*, "they expect the clash to be nothing more than a breather. Coach Harvey Robinson's work all week has been with his reserves as he plans to give his regulars, some of whom are injured, a rest before next week's North Carolina tilt."

U of L coach Frank Camp praised his team's spirit and attitude before it departed for the game. "The fact we're playing Tennessee seems to make no difference to them," he said. "It has just been another week of football practice for us."

Football players are confident by nature, so it wasn't surprising to read some of the pre-game quotes from Louisville's players.

"They pull on their uniforms the same way we do," said junior lineman Bob Bender.

Said senior tackle Bill Lively: "The bigger they are, the harder they'll fall."

"It'll give us a chance to beat one the best teams in the country and avenge all of our four losses," said sophomore guard Jack Meade.

The quotes made for good reading, but Louisville had no chance in its crushing defeat at the hands of the Volunteers in that October 24 game at Knoxville.

Unitas was a one-man show. In spite of weak protection, he completed nine passes, including six of 10 in the first half, and rushed for 52 yards. He scored the Cardinals' lone touchdown, punted and returned kickoffs and punts for more than 100 yards. On defense, he was constantly making tackles.

"Unitas played probably the best game of his U.L. career," Brown wrote in *The Courier-Journal*. "He was the chief Cardinal on offense and was outstanding on defense. When he was hurt while run-

ning to the Tennessee 16-yard line in the final period, he came off the field with an ovation from the Tennessee stands."

Unitas scored U of L's touchdown on the first play of the fourth quarter when he deceptively kept the ball after faking a pitchout and charged up the middle on a 23-yard run.

The Tennessee defense came after Unitas throughout the game, and never once did he flinch. He kept hanging in there under the tremendous pressure. Unitas is known for his great passing ability, but in those days he was an excellent safety as well. Fierce competitor that he was, he played both ways most of

his career at U of L, unless he was injured.

Against Tennessee, Unitas made so many tackles that he couldn't even raise his arms after the game. His jersey and shoulder pads had to be cut off.

In the *Knoxville News-Sentinel*, Bob Wilson wrote: "The Volunteers .. dominated the game, but John Unitas, Louisville's lanky quarterback, stole the show. Hailed mainly as a passing star, the 6-1, 185-pound Unitas was a terrific performer in all departments against the Vols.

"He not only directed the Cardinals' attack brilliantly, but passed expertly,

Before moving on to NFL stardom, Unitas not only served as the Cardinals' quarterback but also punted, played defensive back, and returned punts and kickoffs.

punted well, ran like a halfback, kicked off and tackled like a demon."

Wilson added that in the fourth quarter, the "battered and bruised" Unitas "was helped off the field as the spectators saluted his gifted and courageous play with an ovation that resounded across Loudoun Lake."

Robinson paid a special tribute to Unitas, calling him the best quarterback the Volunteers had seen that season. Among the quarterbacks who had lined up against Tennessee in 1953 was Mississippi State star Jackie Parker.

"That Unitas does the best job of sliding up and down the line, or the belly play or almost anything," Robinson said.

The game itself was a rout, but the statistics weren't quite that lopsided. Tennessee had a 22-16 advantage in first downs and outrushed the Cards 375-194. Louisville freshman Don Boyd, who reeled off a 41-yard run, was the game's leading rusher—82 yards on 11 carries. With Unitas at the controls, U of L held a slight edge in passing yardage, 96-95.

In the fourth quarter, Tennessee fourth-stringer Ray Martin intercepted a pass on his goal line and returned it 100 yards, still ranking as the longest touchdown return on an interception in Volunteer history.

The Volunteers just had too much manpower. Bender, who played offensive tackle and defensive end, recalled that he didn't have a picnic against Tennessee. "I could have sold popcorn in the stands because they two-timed me, constantly double-teamed me," he said, "and I had a little time after being knocked in the stands to sell a few boxes of popcorn."

This Tennessee team, which finished the 1953 season with a 6-4-1 record, boasted Darris McCord, a 1954 All-American tackle who played for the Detroit Lions from 1955 through 1967.

Gen. Robert Neyland, whose long and highly successful tenure as Tennessee's head coach had ended in 1952, saw Unitas in that 1953 game— and he liked what he saw. "Gen. Neyland

never had a lot to say good about anybody—he wasn't that kind of a person— but he did make some very complimentary remarks about Unitas' courage," Gitschier said.

In its season finale, Louisville suffered a 20-13 homecoming defeat to Eastern Kentucky, which was led by Roy Kidd's three touchdown strikes and two interceptions of Unitas passes. A crowd of 2,500 watched the game at Parkway Field.

In the third quarter, Unitas intercepted a Kidd pass on the Eastern 30 and led the Cards on a short drive for a touchdown that came on a nine-yard pass to end Clarence Smith.

Kidd, a Little All-America quarterback in 1953, became the Eastern Kentucky head coach in 1964 and carved out a superb record. The winningest coach in Ohio Valley Conference history, he directed the Colonels to Division I-AA national championships in 1979 and 1982.

More than 40 years after going against Unitas in that U of L game, Kidd recalled: "When we played them, it was obvious that he never had a lot of protection. Mechanically, he was really outstanding. He had a good arm and he had a great touch on the ball, too. A lot of guys can throw it hard, but some of them can't lay it out there on a little flat or a short pass or a little screen or something like that. Some of them have got good strong arms and can hit the deep ball and the deep sideline, but then when it comes to the little touch, good quarterbacks have got to have a little touch to it where they can lay it out there a little softer, and he could do those things."

1954 SEASON

The de-emphasized University of Louisville football team of 1953, made up mostly of freshmen and a few returning lettermen, played one of the toughest schedules in the school's history. It included such teams as nationally ranked Tennessee and Cincinnati and the future

powerhouses of Florida State and Chatta-nooga. The record book reads nine defeats and only one win, but this does not tell the complete story, for some of these games could easily have gone either way and in many cases it was a lack of experience and reserve power that cost the Cardinals a game.

The switch from two platoon to sixty-minute football, plus some injuries at critical times kept the team always at a low potential since the lettermen, along with the freshmen, were short on experience in playing both offense and defense. Yet, led by the superb passing and pass defense of John Unitas (Mr. Football), and the fine line play of such stalwarts as Dick Kovanda, Jim Hollowell, Bob Lichvar and Bob Bender, the Cardinals never seemed to give up trying to get back in the win column.

—1954 *Thoroughbred*

"University of Louisville football coach Frank Camp scanned his work roster again. 'I know I've got some if I can just find 'em,' he joked. The lost 'items' were seniors, of which U of L is in extremely short supply. 'Let's see,' continued Camp, 'We have exactly five seniors—quarterback John Unitas, fullback Don Purcell, center Miles Kozubik, tackle Dick Kovanda and guard Reggie Bethea. As you will notice, Unitas is our only senior back.'"

— *The Courier-Journal*,
September 2, 1954

UNITAS, JOHN ... senior ... Mr. Football for University fans ... called Mr. Sparkplug by players for his leadership in 1951 when he led the Cards to victories over W & L, N. C. State, Houston and Mississippi Southern ... a great field general .... solid defensive man ... has no peer as a passer ... Louisville's candidate for All-American, All-Southern or all anything ... great professional prospect ... called last season by Tennessee Coach Harvey Robinson 'the best QB I saw this year' ... Against Tennessee Unitas was never better, he completed nine passes, ran for 52 yards, scored Louisville's only touchdown, punted, returned kickoffs and punts for over 100 yards, and made so many defensive tackles it was amazing ... But the Tennessee game was only typical of Unitas who in his three years of college football has a statistical passing record of: 203 completions in 392 attempts, good for close to 3,000 yards and 24 touchdowns and a completion percentage of 52 percent ... Louisville lets Unitas stand on his record.

—1954 U of L media guide

Unitas, one of five seniors still around from the 1951 freshman group of approximately 40 players, was captain of the 1954 team, which managed to win three of its nine contests.

An interesting game in U of L's football history came this season against Florida State, which was in the process of building its football program. The game

Dick Kovanda

Jim Hollowell

Bob Lichvar

52

**Cardinal
Football**

was interesting because two Seminole lettermen on this team were Corso (who intercepted six passes that season) and Vince Gibson, each of whom later would serve as U of L head coach. Another player on this Florida State roster was Buddy Reynolds, otherwise known as Burt Reynolds. Yes, the Burt Reynolds that many have grown to love on the movie screen.

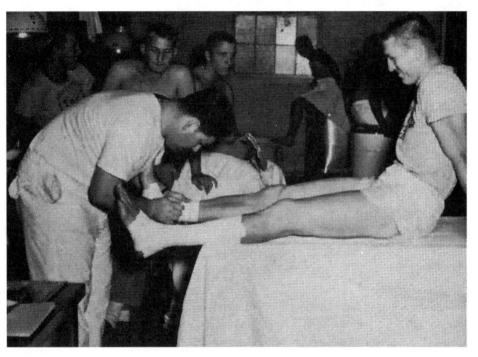

Injuries hurt Unitas as a junior, but his toughness and courage under fire were among his best attributes.

This game originally was scheduled for Parkway Field but was switched to Manual Stadium after the Louisville Colonels, the AAA affiliate of the Boston Red Sox, earned a berth in the Junior World Series.

"Florida State, striving for a place in the national football sun, and Louisville, seeking the shade of more modest competition, meet at 2 p.m. today at Manual Stadium," Johnny Carrico wrote in *The Courier-Journal*.

This game was a mismatch. With Reynolds scoring one touchdown and running back Corso kicking one extra point and substitute guard Gibson recovering a fumble and intercepting a pass in the first half, the Seminoles rolled to a 47-6 victory. "After yielding a quick touchdown to the invaders, Louisville lashed back with Johnny Unitas pitching the Cards to a tally," Carrico wrote. "The valiant play—both offensively and defensively—of the oft-injured quarterback was the chief source of entertainment to the scarcely 1,000 partisans in the stands."

Florida State won eight and lost four in 1954. One of the losses came by a 47-20 score to Texas Western in the Sun Bowl.

More than 40 years later, Corso was asked what he remembered about Unitas. "Aah, he was sensational until the poor guy lined up and we went after him," Corso replied. "He didn't have anybody."

Corso added that after U of L whipped Florida State in 1952 "they lost all their good players." Football, of course, is a team sport, and with no supporting cast, Unitas couldn't be expected to win games all by himself.

On November 5, 1954, the day before the Cards' final home game of the season, Carrico wrote the following in *The Courier-Journal*: "Despite misleading ru-

"Louisville's famed passer, John Unitas, is scheduled to start for the first time this season after a siege of injuries," sports editor Bill McGrotha wrote in the *Tallahassee Democrat*. "Two years ago, when the Kentuckians thrashed the Seminoles 41-14 at Tallahassee, Unitas was the whole show, completing 16 of 21 passes. However, last year, he was able to complete only one of three as FSU rolled to a smashing 59-0 triumph.

"FSU Coach Tom Nugent makes no bones about the fact he's worried about the slender star. 'Louisville will be tough with Unitas back,' Nugent said. 'That boy will give our pass defense its first real test. If it isn't ready, we should find out this weekend.'"

mors, U.L. football isn't in bad financial shape. There's a pretty good chance that the Cards will finish close to the black despite an unsuccessful season. There are two main reasons why U.L.'s football outlook is improving. First, the day of the costly guarantees are gone, along with heavy travelling expenses. Secondly, the Cards own their own park now (Parkway Field) and are free from the burden of rent.

"Camp faced an almost impossible job with the Cards this year. Of the 34-man travelling squad, 21 are FRESHMEN. You just don't win games with inexperienced youngsters. If the present personnel remains, Camp can look forward to rosier prospects next season. And too, U.L. is expecting the return next year of two of the finest tackles ever to perform for Frank—Jim Wolf and Maurice Wolford. Both are playing service ball now."

Tickets for Unitas' last home game were $2.50 for boxes, $2 for lower grandstand, $1.50 for upper grandstand and $1 for general admission. The 2 p.m. game was broadcast by WINN, with Jim McIntyre at the microphone.

Unitas threw one touchdown pass in the Cards' 24-0 homecoming victory over Morehead before what *The Courier-Journal* called "a "ridiculously small crowd of 1,600."

Unitas' last game for the Cards

ended in a 20-6 loss at Eastern Kentucky. "John Becker, Jack Meade and Nunzio Tisci were stand<u>out</u>s in the Louisville defense along with the heady Unitas," reported *The Courier-Journal*. Eastern had a fine team, going on to win the Tangerine Bowl 7-3 over Omaha to complete an 8-1-1 season.

The injured Unitas was hampered enough during his final season at U of L that he didn't even lead the team in passing yardage. In 1954, he completed passes good for 527 yards, second to Jim Houser's 560.

1955 SEASON

Graduation will claim only three of the starting eleven (twenty-two might be more correct), Miles Kozubik, Dick Kovanda, and John Unitas, the hardest of all to lose. For the last four years John has been a leader and an outstanding performer for Cardinal teams.
—1955 Thoroughbred

Unitas finished his career at U of L with 245 completions in 502 attempts for 3,139 yards and 27 touchdowns. The Cards had a winning record in only one of his four seasons—5-4 in 1951, the year following the monumental 13-13 tie against the University of Miami. Louisville's record his final three seasons was 7-18, years in which the program was just struggling to stay alive due to the administration's de-emphasis of the sport. Many of the starters during his years at U of L were non-scholarship players. Certain Louisville players hadn't even been starters on

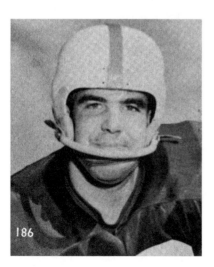

Jim Wolf

Maurice Wolford

their own high-school teams. That's the kind of personnel that surrounded Unitas for all too much of his career at U of L.

Yet despite the lack of support from the administration, Unitas made the most of his opportunity at U of L.

What made Unitas such a supreme player—both as a collegian and a professional? "His courage was the greatest thing about him," Gitschier said. "He stood in the pocket, and his courage was unquestioned. He would just stand in that pocket, and, with all that violence and mayhem going on around him, he would stand there and eat his lunch before he threw the ball."

Unitas learned how to stay in the pocket while at Louisville, and it was second nature for him to do so as a pro.

Along with courage, Unitas had talent. He had a great arm and could hum a down-and-out pass 25 yards like nobody in U of L history.

Unitas also had a tremendous desire to be successful. "He had a drive within him to be as good as he could be," Gitschier said. "You could call him cocky. He was so confident."

Unitas also was good at listening. "Let me tell you something," Gitschier said, "you told him something once, that was all. He had a helluva memory."

All of these qualities paid off for Unitas as a professional. Starting in 1956 and continuing until late in the 1960 season, Unitas threw at least one touchdown pass in 47 straight regular-season games for the Colts. Since Unitas also threw scoring passes in both the 1958 and 1959 NFL championships, his streak actually reached 49 games. This remarkable accomplishment is likely the nearest achievement to an unbreakable record in all of sports.

Unitas won numerous honors during his professional career. In three seasons (1959, 1964 and 1967), he received the Bert Bell Trophy (presented by the Maxwell Club) as the NFL's Player of the Year. He played in 10 Pro Bowl games (1957, 1958, 1959, 1960, 1961, 1962, 1963, 1964, 1966 and 1967) and was named that game's most valuable player three times (1959, 1960 and 1963). He was a member of the all-league teams (both Associated Press and United Press Interna-

Among Unitas' NFL records that will be difficult to break is his string of throwing at least one touchdown pass in 47 straight regular-season games for the Baltimore Colts.

tional) in five seasons—1958, 1959, 1964, 1965 and 1966. Named the "Player of the Decade" for the 1960s, he was inducted into the Pro Football Hall of Fame in 1979.

The standard by which all great quarterbacks are compared, Unitas was voted the quarterback for the 50th anniversary All-NFL team. And in 1994, he was one of three quarterbacks selected on USA TODAY'S 75th anniversary All-NFL team.

Looking back on his football education at U of L, Unitas once said: "I feel that Coach Camp and his theories and his coaching were far ahead of any professional coach that I played for—as far as his ability and the kind of system he used. We ran the regular backfield, we ran the spread backfield, we ran trips, we ran the flood formation, we ran the double wing formation here at school. We had the one-back guy, the single back, the fullback. Jim Williams was a tremendous fullback. He could go inside or outside with great speed. So we used him to the nth degree, but we also had a tremendous passing game because we had good receivers and Coach knew the passing game in and out. He was so far advanced as far as his overall technique of doing things and his overall offensive thinking."

U of L hasn't forgotten Johnny Unitas. On April 14, 1975, dedication ceremonies were held in the naming of Unitas Tower, a campus dormitory. Moreover, Unitas is a member of the U of L Athletic Hall of Fame, and his jersey number—16—was the first one ever retired in Louisville's football history.

Unitas Tower, a U of L campus dormitory named in the Hall of Famer's honor, is just one tribute the Cardinals have made to their legendary alumnus.

No story about Johnny U. would be complete without mentioning the fact that he has never forgotten his football roots.

Unitas developed a lifelong bond with Frank Gitschier, his quarterback coach at U of L. When Unitas was inducted into the Pro Football Hall of Fame, he asked Gitschier to be his presenter.

Gitschier, a man with a genuine love for the game of football, has been instrumental in the success of the Johnny Unitas Golden Arm Foundation. Unitas has appeared annually at the Frank Camp chapter's annual Scholar/Athlete Awards Dinner and the Johnny Unitas Golden Arm Award Presentation in Louisville. Since 1987, more than $200,000 in college scholarships has been raised for youth leagues, high-school football players and college walk-ons in the area.

Unitas, who has brought national exposure to the chapter, is a popular figure at the dinner, wearing a smile and shaking hands enthusiastically with each recipient—from the peewee league all the way up to the winner of the Johnny Unitas Golden Arm Award, which goes to the country's top senior quarterback. You can look far and wide, but you'll never find a more approachable football legend than Unitas.

A leader on the playing field, Unitas has carried the ideals of football forward into its relations with his community and his fellow man.

Johnny Unitas' U of L Passing Stats			
Year ..... Comp.	Att.	Yards	TDs
1951 46	99	602	9
1952 106	198	1,540	12
1953 49	95	470	3
1954 44	110	527	3
Totals 245	502	3,139	27

The Johnny Unitas Golden Arm Award is presented annually to the nation's top senior quarterback by the Frank Camp Chapter of the Unitas Golden Arm Foundation.

Unitas stands next to the statue in his honor located in the end zone of Papa John's Cardinal Stadium.

Unitas and his son John, Jr., look at the display case devoted to the NFL Hall of Fame quarterback in the BellSouth Johnny Unitas Football Museum.

Chapter 9

Lyles Helps Cards as Trailblazers in the South

For the first time, FSU was playing against a team with Negroes in its lineup. Three of them—center Andy Walker, halfbacks George Cain and Leonard Lyles—were starters.
— *Tallahassee Democrat*
   October 3, 1954

It was news in 1954 when black football players first emerged on the Southern collegiate scene. News enough that the paragraph mentioning Andy Walker, George Cain and Lenny Lyles appeared as high up as the sixth paragraph in the account of Florida State's 47-6 victory over the University of Louisville.

U of L is believed to be the first predominantly all-white university in the South to use black football players.

The stage was set for black players on Belknap Campus after Louisville Municipal College, the Negro branch of U of L, was closed at the end of the 1950-1951 academic year. With its closing at Seventh and Kentucky streets, the integration of all of U of L's academic units took place in 1950 and 1951. U of L thus became the first Southern university to break the racial barrier and admit black students to the university.

In 1955, Woodrow M. Strickler, then vice president at U of L, said in an address to the 10th National Conference on Higher Education in Chicago: "It must be admitted that the fall months of 1950 were viewed with some trepidation with the appearance of Negroes on the campus, in the classrooms and cafeterias and with their participation in all activities of student life. In no instance, however, did the presence of a Negro student cause any reaction or difficulty. The university has endured many emergencies during the past five years, but none of these emergencies has had a basis of racial conflict."

In his address, Strickler noted that Kentucky was a border state "with social relationships which sometimes follow those of its Northern neighbors, but which more frequently are typical of the culture of the Southern states. Segregation prevails in railroads, in parks, hotels, restaurants and in other places of group gatherings. Public schools have been segregated since their establishment."

In an oral history interview with U of L graduate student Rick Cushing in 1980, longtime Cardinal coach Frank Camp recalled that after Louisville Municipal College closed and U of L became integrated, "then the black athletes were

eligible. So we did start recruiting (them) as soon as they told us that this was legal and that this is what we should do. It didn't make any difference to us because of their color. It was whether a man could play. We went out to get Lenny Lyles."

Asked if there was any resistance in the community to integrating football, Camp replied: "I would say there was very little. We always have some voices in that aspect. I thought the university did an outstanding job. The colored people in the community did a great job in helping us recruit Lyles and any of the top boys we wanted.

"We had problems. They'd call us names and things like that, but we didn't pay much attention to that. I think this a great adjustment that the blacks had to make—quit listening to a lot of chatter and going out there and do their job. And this is what they did. They got out there and played. I told them I had been called all kinds of things when I was coaching ... they were just words and didn't mean a thing—just get out there and forget about it and do what they were supposed to do. And I think the attitude of the community is what helped us a lot."

Camp said the black players recruited by U of L "were outstanding young men, and they could play. It wouldn't have done any good if they couldn't. It wouldn't make it grow as fast as it did. You had to take the top young men if we wanted to see the thing adjust, and this is what we tried to do."

Clark Wood, an assistant football coach at U of L for 18 years, was one of the keys in

Clark Wood

the recruitment of Lyles. The U of L coach even tried his hand at watering the grass in his visits to the Lyles home in the projects. "Coach Wood used to come and talk with me, and he indicated that if I would come out there, they would bring on three more black athletes," Lyles said. "He'd talk to my mother. She'd be trying to keep our grass growing, and he'd take the hose and water the yard and try to convince her to let me go to the University of Louisville."

Lyles and Wood are friends and sometimes play golf together. But back when he was being recruited by U of L, Lyles didn't want any part of Wood. "I used to hide from him," he said. "I'd see him coming, and I'd take off because I didn't want to talk with him. I didn't know him, and, of course, this big, blond guy coming around and talking to me about the University of Louisville, I just wasn't too sure."

U of L eventually did land Lyles, but it took some work from the black community to help pull off this recruiting gem. Reporting on the opening practice session of the 1954 season, *The Courier-Journal* informed its readers that "the Cardinals received a welcome addition" late that day when Camp learned that Lyles planned to join the team. There was much more to this story than that brief mention in the last paragraph.

It seems some problems had arisen in U of L's recruitment of Lyles. "Several incidents happened, and I kind of changed my mind and was a little concerned about going to U of L, being a black athlete coming out of the urban area and going to a school that never had black athletes before," he recalled in a recent interview.

One of the incidents would have made any black athlete stop to think about stepping foot on Belknap Campus. Lyles said that while he was being recruited by U of L, he was told: "Well, now, boy, you can't come out here and be expecting to go with these white girls.

Don't expect to come out here and start that."

Lyles' reaction?

"I said, 'Whoa, whoa. I got a girl-friend. That ain't my intent. I'm coming to play football and get an education.' But that was said to me, and I won't tell you who said it because it would be em-barrassing. I didn't understand why one would even bring that up. I had not even been around white girls or anything like that. When that was said to me, I didn't know what that meant. So that was just one of the things, I guess, that would make you apprehensive when you've not had the experience of going to an inte-grated university or high school. But, at any rate, that was part of my introduc-tion, and that bothered me a tad. But I overlooked that and went on and came back and got a scholarship."

He had to be persuaded to take the U of L scholarship. Lyles actually had slipped out of town and traveled to Lin-coln University, an all-black school in Jefferson City, Missouri. Dwight Reed, who coached the Louisville Municipal Col-lege football team from 1946 through 1949, was the Lincoln coach. "I'd been around black people all my life, and Lin-coln looked good to me," Lyles said.

"U of L got a little concerned about that after they found it out," Lyles added. "They said, 'We need to get Lenny back because we've offered three more scholarships to George Cain, Clyde Bingham and Andy Walker. If we're going to do this and integrate our team, we need Lenny. He was the one that we wanted to head up all this.' U of L went around, I think, and talked with Frank Stanley (editor and publisher of *The Lou-isville Defender*), and my coach and some others and sent them out there to get me. Dan White (a Central assistant foot-ball coach) and a couple of his friends came out and picked me up and brought me and enrolled me in the University of Louisville. I had not signed a grant-in-aid with Lincoln University at that time.

Dwight Reed was out of town. I think Dan White and Dwight Reed kinda lost friendship over that because they came out and picked me up when he was out of town."

So Lyles returned to U of L. "I don't know if that was a heavily publicized situation," he said, "but we shook hands and I felt a little more comfortable. They said, 'We really need you here because we're going to bring in these other three black athletes if you go here.'"

In 1954, the timing was right for blacks to play football at U of L. The uni-versity was in-tegrated, and, after a two-year period in which the football pro-gram couldn't award scholar-ships during a de-emphasis of the sport, Camp and his staff were per-mitted to once again give scholarships in 1954. Camp was the per-fect man to be at the helm at U of L. This gentleman coach was color blind when it came to athletes. And Lyles was the per-fect person to help break the color bar-rier. He was a tremendous athlete, and the other two black freshmen on the team—Cain and Walker—were outstand-ing football players as well.

Lyles also had been recruited by In-diana University. "I did go up there and look around a little but, but I was in awe

Lenny Lyles (left) and Ken Porco were teammates on the Cards' 1957 team that posted a 9-1 record and won the Sun Bowl in El Paso, Texas.

62

Cardinal Football

because it was so big, and I never played in a place that huge before. And I was a little frightened."

Lyles added that while he was at Indiana on a recruiting visit he was advised by Hoosier football player and track star Milt Campbell, a gifted black athlete who would win the 1956 Olympics decathlon championship, not to attend the Bloomington university. "He said, 'You don't want to come over here. They'll just wear you out. They'll make you run track and football and use you up.'"

Lyles was an end with jet-like speed from Louisville Central High School. In his senior season of 1953, Central upended Flaget 13-7. Lyles, who caught touchdown passes of 54 and 90 yards against Flaget, received the John E. Miller trophy as the most valuable player on Central's 1953 team.

At U of L, Lyles was converted to halfback. Cain was from Middletown, Ohio, and Walker hailed from Birmingham, Alabama. Another black, Clyde Bingham, also was among the four black freshmen at U of L in 1954, but he didn't stay with the Cardinals.

Walker initially reported in 1954 to Kentucky State, an all-black school. "Coach (George) Edwards and I didn't get along, and I decided to come on down here to give it a try," he said.

Walker said he practiced at Kentucky State for about three weeks. "I hadn't really signed any papers," he said. "I only had a partial scholarship up there. Off season, the football players had to work. They couldn't afford to give full scholarships like the big universities could.

When I heard all of that, I came on down here."

Walker, Lyles and Cain had full scholarships at U of L.

The first black athlete at U of L actually came along two years earlier—Lawrence "Bumpy" Simmons, a three-year letterman at Louisville Central High School and captain of the Yellowjackets' 1951 team.

Simmons, a mid-term graduate of Central, enrolled at U of L in January 1952 and participated in spring practice that year. He saw brief action in the last quarter of the Cards' 19-12 triumph over Wayne State in their season opener of 1952.

In a story appearing in *The Louisville Times* after the Wayne State game, Simmons said savvy of the players was the major difference between the high school and collegiate ranks. "At first it seemed like I was being trapped all the time, but I'm doing a little better now and I hope to get better all the time," he said.

The newspaper added that the 191-pound freshman lineman "also pointed out the heavier weights in college pigskin personnel."

Camp was quoted as saying Simmons had "a world of potential. We haven't really had too much chance to watch him in game action yet, so I'm hoping he won't think he's on the spot out here and just play to the full of that potential."

W.L. Kean, the head coach at Central, said Simmons "was a great team leader for us. We used him at tackle on offense and as a linebacker on defense. We couldn't have had a finer representative out there."

For some reason, Simmons didn't remain with the U of L team.

"He never told me why he left," Wood said, "but he used to come back and see Coach Camp all the time. So it wasn't anything that we did. We weren't responsible for him leaving."

Lenny Lyles was among the first African-American football players at U of L.

Lyles, however, said that Simmons suggested to him that he might not want to attend U of L. "All of us at Central certainly wanted to see Bumpy make it because we knew he was a great athlete," Lyles said. "I felt like he could make that team out there. I don't know what kind of problems he was having, but obviously being the only black player trying to participate and win a spot couldn't have been easy. I understand that from situations where when you're the only one or only two or whatever, oftentimes it can be made quite difficult—for whatever reasons that might be. So Lawrence kind of said, 'You may not want to go to the University of Louisville. You may want to go someplace where you can feel a little more comfortable and make a contribution and be accepted.' We never understood why it didn't work out."

The black football players came along at U of L before high schools were integrated in the area. In 1956, *The Courier-Journal* reported: "Louisville Male High School has jumped the gun on integration. On the practice football field ... white and Negro youngsters have been grunting, groaning, and sweating side by side since August 20, although registration won't be until next Wednesday and Thursday. ... Other City and County high schools are reported also to have jumped the integration dates on their football fields."

As a sign of the times, certain white coaches originally were skeptical of black football players. Ignorantly, these coaches thought blacks didn't want to hit, an implication that they didn't have the heart for the rugged game of football. Those coaches came to realize soon enough that the black players would run and block and tackle—and rock and sock—with anybody.

In 1957, Lexington Dunbar became the first all-black high school admitted to the Kentucky High School Athletic Association. That same year *The Courier-Journal* reported that Paul McPherson of Manual and David Baker of Male "will be

the first Negroes ever to play in the Thanksgiving Day game. Both are standouts."

In 1959, Manual's sensational halfback, Sherman Lewis, became, in the words of *The Courier-Journal,* "the first Negro to make All-State in football."

U of L's first black basketball players were Sam Smith, Wade Houston and Eddie Whitehead, who began their varsity eligibility as sophomores in the 1963-1964 season.

Camp, who died in 1986, was ahead of his time in recruiting blacks.

In his advance story on U of L's 1954 season debut, *The Courier-Journal's* Johnny Carrico wrote: "Frank Camp has sprinkled his opening lineup liberally with sophomores and freshmen. The yearlings are Leonard 'Bones' Lyles and George Cain, a pair of halfbacks who will be the first Negroes ever to win a starting assignment on a U.L. team."

Walker, who cracked the starting lineup at center after four weeks with the Cardinals, had an outstanding freshman season and was named to Dayton's all-opponent second team.

Times were much different in the '50s, and the U of L blacks encountered certain problems that would never happen today.

Andy Walker

Something as routine as a pre-game meal could present problems with blacks on the team.

U of L players from that era —white and black alike—remember a pre-game meal incident at Parkmoor Bowling Alley. "All of our teammates were sitting at a long table," Lyles recalled. "And as we walked in the door, we started up there, and (someone) said, 'No, no, no. You all go in the back.' They sent us all the way to the back—could hardly see us. I saw our teammates had their heads down. I

Cardinal Football

know they didn't like it, but they understood what was going on."

Lyles added that the U of L coaches—Camp, Wood and assistant J.D. Dunn— "came back to sit with us. It was so far back you couldn't see us. But we got through that. No one raised any hell."

Walker recalled that when he was preparing to sit down at a table with the white players at Parkmoor, "a man ran up to me and said, 'Oh,

George Cain

no. You don't sit here. You sit back there.' I got upset, but I didn't really show it. It affected me some because that was the first time I ever ran into something like that. I was raised in the South, but I never had really run into discrimination because everyone knew their place."

And then there was the time that U of L, on its way to Richmond for a game at Eastern Kentucky, stopped off for a pre-game meal at a Frankfort restaurant, where the team had eaten in previous years. Wood called the restaurant's proprietor in advance "and told him we had some blacks players and we didn't want any incident. 'Oh, we won't have any trouble.'"

Talk, of course, is cheap. "When I went up there, I noticed he was pulling the shades down in front and ushering everybody out of the building. He came up to me and said, 'The black players have to eat down in the basement.' I said, 'Well, you set "x" number of seats because the coaches will eat down there

with them.'

"People would get scared," Wood added. "The closer the time came to doing it, then they'd get scared about what people would say."

U of L's blacks didn't receive the best of treatment at certain universities, including Eastern Kentucky, Murray State and Western Kentucky.

"Mainly, the thing we didn't like was piling on and tackling out of bounds," Wood said. Lyles and Cain sometimes would be tackled five or 10 yards out of bounds, but the officials "were afraid to call" a penalty, Wood said.

Wood recalled that the situation became bad enough at Eastern that Camp called Eastern Kentucky president Dr. William F. O'Donnell "and told him what kind of treatment we had been receiving up there—that some of the fans were calling names and bad stuff like that. He told Coach Camp, 'Well, come on up here; it won't happen anymore.' The president met us out on the field before the game, and he said, 'I've told my people how to act, and I expect them to do it.' Well, we did not have any incident at all—no tackling out of bounds, no ugly words and stuff like that."

Wood said that Murray "was even worse" than Eastern. "They never changed," he said. "They were terrible."

"Eastern and Western were always tough," Lyles said, "but I recall at Dayton, Ohio, the guys came over and said,

'Lenny, we wanted to test you this game. We tried to put it to you as best we could. We tried to see what you were made out of.' I said, 'You did a good job. I want you to know that.' They were hitting pretty hard and staying with you and gang-tackling and that sort of thing."

Recalling the treatment that the black players received on the football field, Cain said: "It got a little bad, but it didn't get too bad because our teammates were good at making sure none of that went on too much. But it happened—the twisting and the gouging and the spitting and the name-calling."

So did hitting "under the pile and out of bounds," Cain added. "But we overcame that. Our team rallied around us, and we were a unit. The coaches and the players tried to shield us from a lot of that crap that was going on back in those days. A lot of those players back then were from other parts of the country where that kind of crap wasn't going on, and they couldn't imagine that it was happening. They'd never seen anything like that before. But I'm not one to dwell on the past and the bad things. There were a lot of good things happening."

Cain remembered what Camp said. "He used to tell us to hit 'em where it hurts the most—and that's to score on 'em."

Lyles put a big hurt on Eastern in 1957 by scoring three touchdowns—on runs of 67, 54 and 28 yards—in a 40-14 victory at Richmond.

Like Cain, Lyles remembers that his "teammates stood up for me. They took care of me pretty good. We had some great guys. Kenny Porco blocked for me, and we had Gil Sturtzel, Les Houston, Mario Cheppo and others. We had some good guys on the team. Dale Orem was my quarterback. He was always good to me. He believed in me."

Orem was the quarterback of U of L's outstanding 1957 team. In the 1954 freshman season for Lyles, Cain and Walker at U of L, Johnny Unitas was the team's senior quarterback. Lyles, Cain and Walker, during their four-year career at U of L, played on three teams with winning records—7-2 in 1955, 6-3 in 1956 and 9-1 in 1957. The 1954 team, which was young and inexperienced, went 3-6.

Racial problems weren't restricted to the football field.

Lyles recalls a track meet at Eastern Kentucky in which the mood of the crowd went from downright nastiness to one of admiration and respect. "I ran the 100, and people up in the stands called me nigger and black and onionhead," he said. "So I won the 100-yard dash. Anything you can think of, they were calling me. So I came back and ran the 220. I smoked everybody in that one. And then I came back and anchored the quarter-mile relay, and I won that one. Then I came back and did the long jump. Before I got out of there that day, there was applause.

"So I have to say, even though there were some tough times and times that shouldn't have been, I think my presence certainly changed the behavior of some of the fans that were there because I guess they recognized, well, the guy ran and he did it fair and he beat our people, so I guess he's all right."

Mario Cheppo

Few, if any, of these incidents were reported by the media.

Actually, the presence of blacks at U of L wasn't a major story in 1954. Nowadays, the media would be all over such a historic story, but the appearance of black football players at U of L surprisingly enough (at least, by today's standards of judging news) didn't receive that much attention from the newspapers, which suited Wood just fine. "I don't think publicity like that helps you a whole lot," he said.

Lyles received publicity for his feats on the football field. Hailed as the "Fastest Man in Football," he set individual game records for most points (24) and most yards gained rushing (247) in 1955 against Toledo. He established season records for most points (132 in 1957), most yards gained (1,207) and most total yards gained (1,345). For his career, he set individual U of L records for most times carrying the ball (394), most yards gained rushing (2,780), most total yards gained rushing and passing (2,925) and most points (300).

Lyles scored 42 points as a freshman to lead all collegiate scorers in Kentucky. He tied Centre's Gene Scott for the state scoring championship in 1955 with 84 points, thanks to a huge effort in U of L's season finale, a 33-13 victory over Toledo. Lyles "put on one of the best one-man shows in Louisville football history," Carrico wrote in *The Courier-Journal*. "The 195-pound Louisville Negro, the fleetest human being in Kentucky, barreled for four touchdowns and missed a fifth by only a yard."

In 1957, Lyles was a Little All-America and scored 132 points, tops in the country.

As a track star, he was clocked in 9.4 seconds for the 100-yard dash and 20.6 seconds for 220 yards, both blazing times.

When it came to running with the football, Cain had plenty of ability himself. He returned a kickoff 100 yards against Eastern Kentucky in his 1954 freshman season. As a sophomore, he scored three touchdowns against Xavier, including kickoff returns of 85 and 95 yards.

In Louisville's 34-20 triumph over Drake in the Sun Bowl on January 1, 1958, Lyles was injured in the early going and didn't return to action. Carrico wrote that Cain, "overshadowed by Lyles for four seasons," played "first-rate football, especially on defense. His shadowing of Drake's top scorer, end Jerry Mertens, contributed strongly to the win."

Cain scored 54 points and rushed for 523 yards in 1957.

George Cain, a teammate with Lyles for four years, shined in the 1958 Sun Bowl.

Freshman runningback Ken Porco was hoisted on his teammates' shoulders after running for 119 yards against Drake in the Cardinals' 1958 Sun Bowl victory.

Wood, who calls Lyles "the best all-around halfback" in U of L history, said speed and size were the player's strong points. "You get people sometimes who really are complete football players," Wood said. "We've had a few of those. Even back in the days when we went both ways, probably 90 percent of the people were stronger in either offense or defense. But we had Leonard Lyles and Ernie Green (a black who played at U of L from 1958 through 1961) and George Cain—and they were equally good on both. "

Lyles played for the College All-Stars in their 35-19 victory over the Detroit Lions in 1958 and went on to spend 12 seasons (1958-1969) in a standout National Football League career. A first-round draft choice, he was a running back on the Baltimore Colts' 1958 NFL championship team. He went to the San Francisco 49ers for the 1959 season, playing running back there his first season and cornerback in 1960. He returned to the Colts for the final nine years of his career, all as a cornerback.

When Lyles was with the Colts in his rookie season of 1958, he was one of seven blacks on the team. In his final pro season in 1969, he was one of 12 blacks on the Colts' squad.

Football was a big part of Lyles' life, but there were other lessons he learned along the way at U of L. Looking back on his classroom days in college, Lyles said: "Some teachers didn't think I should be there. I had one teacher—I won't give you his name—but he thought I should go back and work. He didn't think I should be in college. Then there were some teachers who were helpful. Mrs. Riley Emberger (a professor of English) knew I had kind of a weak background in English and some other subjects, and she worked with me. She was probably one of the reasons that I was able to get my degree and get through the University of Louisville.

"Because of Mrs. Emberger, I was strengthened very strongly, and I was certainly grateful for her support and help," he said. "She told me what I needed. She said, 'Here's what I can do. Here's what you've got to do. And if you do that, you'll improve in your English and so forth.' She stuck by me, even after I left U of L and went to pro football, if she caught me making a talk on television, she'd write me a note and say, 'Mr.

68

**Cardinal
Football**

Lyles, I heard you and you did an excellent job and I want to thank you. I see you did learn something at the University of Louisville." She was always pretty proud of me, and I'd always go back and see her after football season when I came back from Baltimore."

Les Shively, the former longtime alumni secretary at U of L, remembers Lyles working a part-time job in his office. "Lenny was very shy when he came out there," Shively said. "He'd be sitting there, and I'd say, 'What did you say, Lenny?' He'd say, 'Didn't say anything, Mr. Shively.' I'd say, 'Well, why not? And he'd say, 'Well, every time I open my mouth, you correct me.' "

Lyles improved his grammar dramatically—"Oh, God, did he ever," Shively said. "He's a great guy."

Walker, described in the 1957 U of L media guide as "the Mister Quiet" of the team and "Louisville's outstanding postwar line backer," tried out for the NFL's Chicago Cardinals in 1958, and after a two-year stint in the service, he returned for another attempt to earn a spot with that franchise, which had moved to St. Louis. "I stayed till the last cut each time," he said. "They had a quota system at that time—only so many blacks on the team—and I was always the odd man out."

Walker, who had been an All-Army center and linebacker while playing military football in Germany, also tried out for the Buffalo Bills of the American Football League in the early 1960s. The Bills wanted to put him on their taxi squad, but Walker declined that

Andy Walker

offer and left the team. "I couldn't say whether it was the quota system," he said in explaining why he didn't make the Bills' team.

Walker, a physical education teacher at Westport Middle School, has been with the Jefferson County school system for 28 years.

Cain, has been associated with the Long John Silver's chain for 27 years and runs a restaurant at 34th and Broadway.

Lyles, has his hand in various businesses. He is the sole owner of Lyles Plaza, a shopping center located between 26th and 28th streets on Broadway, and in partnership owns Lyles Mall across the street. He also is a partner in Concessions International of Louisville. In addition, Lyles owns real estate property on Chestnut Street and has a small consulting company called Lyles Enterprises Inc.

These three men were trailblazers back in the mid-1950s. They were all talented four-year football lettermen who graduated from college and were inducted into the U of L Athletic Hall of Fame. Their contribution to U of L should never be underrated.

Lyles was asked if he was glad he went to U of L.

"Absolutely—for a number of reasons," he replied.

One of those reasons is the relationship he developed with certain people at U of L—teammates such as Kenny Porco and Mario Cheppo and Frank Otte and assistant coach Wood. "Those relationships mean a lot to me," he said.

Lyles said that his relationship with Wood, who was also the U of L track coach, "transcended him recruiting me. He stood up for you, and he was there. Coach Wood was pretty close—and still is. You can bet if something takes place and you look around, he's going to be there with you."

Reflecting on his days at U of L, Lyles said: "Once it worked out and I have to say all in all and with the frustrations—I don't want to say racism, but a lack of understanding because of the

Cardinal Football

times that we were in—I probably would go through that again because I've had a great career and I've done well here in Louisville. I don't have any regrets, but I have a lot of memories and a lot of tales to tell.

"I feel real good about all that happened. I feel good about the university and my experiences. And there were all kinds of experiences. Some were unpleasant, some were very, very exciting and some of the relationships were just fantastic. It was like peaks and valleys. But it was like life during that time."

Finally, a review of black players at U of L wouldn't be complete without referring back to the first time that Florida State played against blacks in 1954 against U of L.

As a matter of curiosity, we called Florida State to find out when the first time a black played for the Seminoles.

Well, it happened in the season opener of 1970, exactly 16 years after Lyles, Cain and Walker played against the Seminoles.

J.T. Thomas was the first black to play for Florida State.

He started in his first game, a 9-7 victory for Florida State at Tallahassee.

Oh, yes, who was Florida State's opponent in that game?

None other than the University of Louisville.

Chapter 10
The Colorful Lee Corso

Lee Corso was unconventional as the Cardinals' head coach from his first game.

The door slammed shut behind him. His players, beaten when victory was so near, sat in silence. Some cried. Some bowed their heads, figures of frustration. The University of Louisville football team lost yesterday, 31-21 to Cincinnati. Coach Lee Corso had to tell them why.

"Give me your attention," he said. He spoke loudly. He paced in a small circle, hands stuffed in his pockets. "All I have to say ..." He stopped. His voice was no longer strong. Suddenly, he was a man choking back a sob. "All I have to say is that I'm proud of you guys. We tried, we did everything we could and ..."

He stopped again. He put his hands on his knees and dropped his head. He couldn't talk. He stood that way in the center of the room for maybe 15 seconds.

Horace Jones, a tackle, threw down a Pepsi-Cola can. The clatter of the can on the concrete floor filled the room. Corso didn't notice it. He started pacing again, his ripple-soled shoes leaving tracks as he walked in and out of the Pepsi spilled across the floor.

Corso took up his speech again. He rambled. He told his players that Wichita State

was next. He told them they could still win the Missouri Valley Conference championship. He told them to forget the short-lived fight near the end of the game, that it was nothing, just a symbol of their frustration. By now, Corso was shouting again.

"Now, when you go out of this dressing room and get on that bus, I want every one of you to have his head up. We did our best. I tell you this, I'm going out of this dressing room and I'm going on that radio and tell them we did our very best."

— Dave Kindred,
The Courier-Journal
November 9, 1969

Cincinnati was U of L's homecoming opponent in Lee Corso's first year as head coach of the Cardinals. The colorful and dynamic Corso had brought to U of L a lot of enthusiasm and imagination. Besides that, like his predecessor, Frank Camp, he knew offensive football, and he put an exciting team on the field.

The U of L job was the first head coaching position for the 33-year-old Corso, who previously had served as an assistant coach at the Naval Academy. In the minds of certain people, U of L assistant and longtime successful high-school coach Paulie Miller should have been named to replace Frank Camp, but the powers-that-be at U of L thought otherwise, and Corso was the man chosen for the job.

After the Sun Bowl team of 1957, the Cards had embarked upon an 11-year period of so-so football that eventually led Camp to retire after a 5-5 record in 1968. As has been the case throughout its history, these U of L teams featured some excellent individual talent. Savage linebacker Doug Buffone, for example, went on to an excellent NFL career (1966-80) with the Chicago Bears, and tackle Ken Kortas, a 1964 first-round draft pick by the St. Louis Cardinals, enjoyed a six-year career with the Cardinals, Pittsburgh Steelers and Chicago

Ken Kortas

Doug Buffone

The spacious Brown & Williamson Club provides comfort and class on game days and for a host of special events throughout the year. The B &W Club runs 100 yards in length and 20 yards wide and provides direct access to the club seating area within Papa John's Cardinal Stadium.

A view from the Papa John's Cardinal Stadium Press Box, with the Cards' practice fields in view at the upper left. Over 100 media can be accommodated in the main seating area of the box, which also features 11 working booths and a press lounge area.

Inside one of the 29 private suites located on the fourth and fifth levels of the stadium.

tory. Ron Shanklin, a future pro player with the Pittsburgh Steelers (1970-1974) and the Chicago Bears (1975-1976), caught one TD pass for the winners. "We were just finally overpowered by a team that has some really great football players," Corso said after suffering his first loss at U of L.

HOMECOMING: A FIGHT OUT OF FRUSTRATION

Cincinnati, coached by Ray Callahan, scored three touchdowns in the final 9½ minutes to overcome Louisville 31-21 before a homecoming crowd of 10,361 at Fairgrounds Stadium. Cincinnati quarterback Albert Johnson (who would play seven seasons for the Houston Oilers in the pro ranks) drew the pregame raves, but it was unsung Jim Ousley who brought Cincinnati back from the dead. Ousley came off the bench to lead the Bearcats to three of their four second-half touchdowns. The visitors' final TD came with just 35 seconds left when U of L let Johnson, who had returned to the game to run out the clock, slip through for a 30-yard touchdown. Many of the fans began to leave, but the action still wasn't over. A fight broke out with 13 seconds to go, instigated by Bouggess and Cincinnati's Mike Crangle and then mushrooming into several other skirmishes before order was restored.

Bouggess was the only player ejected from the game. He deserved the rest, anyway, after picking up 130 yards, including a 30-yard TD scamper, in 27 carries.

Bouggess explained the fight this way: "This end (Crangle) was throwing fists and calling me names during the game. I held it back as long as I could. I was keyed up a lot for this game; I really wanted to win it. At the end, he hit me on the chin at the start of the play, and when the play was over, I went after him."

Bouggess jumped on top of the 6-foot-5, 230-pound Crangle, and U of L's 170-pound split end, John Copeland, piled on the Cincy end, too.

"All I know," Crangle said, "is that he (Bouggess) was pass-blocking, and he threw an elbow at me the first time. I told the referees about it, but he started swinging the second time. I just backed off, and he grabbed a hold of my shirt and that No. 14 (Copeland) jumped in."

Cincinnati end Jim O'Brien, whose last-minute field goal would lift the Baltimore Colts to the 1971 Super Bowl title over the Dallas Cowboys, kicked one field goal and four extra points against U of L.

THROWING IN THE TOWEL—LITERALLY

In its next-to-last game of the season, U of L traveled to Memphis State to face an angry group of Tigers.

With a bagful of tricks in its repertoire, U of L was hoping to spring a mousetrap of surprises on Memphis State. There was only one minor problem for the Cardinals: Memphis State was not a mouse. A bull was more appropriate—and a scorned one at that. Louisville was facing a Memphis State team that was riled up by the fact that it wasn't going to a bowl game.

Lee Bouggess, an All-Missouri Valley Conference selection at defensive end in 1968, was moved to running back under Corso and gained 1,064 yards as a junior.

**Cardinal
Football**

Memphis State, 4-0 in the MVC and 7-2 overall as it prepared for its season finale, was on the threshold of securing its second consecutive all-winning season in league play in its drive for conference title No. 2. But little good all that had done for the Tigers. Despite high hopes, they weren't chosen to participate in any of the bowl games.

The U of L-Memphis State game was designated the "Appreciation Bowl" by Memphis mayor Henry Loeb, who was in sympathy with the team's plea that it should have been invited to a bowl.

Corso, meanwhile, promised to seize upon his team's situation as an overwhelming underdog by unloading some surprises. "We've got some changes for this game," Corso said on the eve of the battle after sending his squad of 37 players through a light workout in Memorial Stadium. "I will say this much. We're go-

Corso kept his sense of humor in a tough loss at Memphis by tossing in a towel late in the game.

ing to do some things differently against Memphis—and what we do differently will be noticeable to everybody in the world."

Up until that point of the 1969 season, Corso had tried 20 times for the yardage on fourth down instead of punt-

What else might Corso have up his sleeve? He wouldn't elaborate, but he did say this much: "When the other team has superior material, you gotta do things, take chances when you wouldn't take chances before. You can't be conservative. If you haven't gotten the big prize before, you might as well go for it in an all-out effort. The whole thing might backfire on you and you might get beat worse than if you had played it conservatively. But what the hell's the difference? You never got it before anyway."

U of L had never gotten the big prize before against Memphis State, losing all seven of their previous meetings.

Corso clearly was a man shooting for the moon against Memphis State, but he didn't even get off the launching pad. And, at the end, he wound up throwing in the towel.

From the opening whistle, when the chant, "Go to hell, Liberty Bowl, go to hell," rang out from Memphis State's cheering section and Francis Ayandele's onside kick to start the game fell short of going the required 10 yards, one thing was obvious:

It was going to be a long, long day for Louisville.

A merciless Memphis State team mauled the Cards by a 69-19 score before 18,344 blood-thirsty fans.

Many U of L players and coaches were miffed because Memphis State took two time-outs in the last 25 seconds to rack up its 10th and last TD. Despite the piling-it-on antics by Memphis State, Corso managed to smile to the bitter end. In the closing seconds, he yelled for a towel. Handed one, he jokingly threw it in the general direction of Memphis State coach Bill "Spook" Murphy.

The story of that towel-throwing incident has been embellished through the years. It has even been reported that Corso walked all the way out to the middle of the field and waved the towel at Murphy. But truly, Corso waved the

towel from the sidelines, not the center of the field. It is doubtful that many people who were still left in the crowd even noticed it.

At any rate, Murphy obviously didn't see the "surrender" signal as he kept his first team in. And, afterward, he claimed:

"I feel real bad about the score. I didn't want to call those time-outs. The players on the field were doing it. What Louisville ran into today was a real mad, un-

Bill Gatti

happy football team. I couldn't stop my players from running up the score."

Quarterback Rick Thurow, who scored that last TD on an 18-yard run with 12 seconds left, confirmed that Murphy wasn't responsible for the timeout. "Our linemen were calling the time-outs," he said. "Coach Murphy didn't want that at all."

All Corso would say was: "I'm not mad at them, really. Did I look mad after the game?"

Indeed, Corso took the defeat gracefully as he raced across the field and shook hands with Murphy at the game's conclusion.

As an aside, Corso later said that he was glad Memphis State missed the extra point after its final touchdown. He said a score in the 60s sounded better than one in the 70s.

Corso had hoped to catch the Tennessee team off guard with some changes. He instructed soccer-styler Ayandele to try two onside kicks (Mem-

phis State, however, wound up with both), and in the second quarter the U of L boss successfully gambled on a fourth-and-two-inch situation at the Cardinals' 24.

"We gotta go for it," Corso said, with Memphis State leading 14-0 at the time. "If we don't do something soon, we're gonna get killed."

U of L got killed anyway, the score zooming out of control so quickly that it was useless for Corso to rely on other ploys.

Memphis State set two school records and tied three others in the rout. The school records were set in touchdown passes (five) and total yards of offense (659). Records were equaled in first downs (37), passing first downs (17) and touchdowns (10).

Stars on this Memphis State team included quarterback Danny Pierce, lineman Bob Parker, wide receiver Preston Riley, defensive back Steve Jaggard and defensive back Jerry Todd, all of whom were selected in the 1970 NFL draft. Pierce ran for one TD and threw three scoring strikes against U of L.

TURKEY DAY IN TULSA

Just five days after the Memphis State debacle, U of L played at Tulsa in a Thanksgiving Day game. P.T. Barnum never had anything on Lee Corso when it came to gimmicks, and for this game the U of L coach had a turkey paraded to midfield for the pre-game coin toss.

Larry Ball

Horace Jones

Lee Bouggess, who suffered a painfully jammed toe in the Memphis State game, didn't practice prior to the Tulsa game. But once the game started, he responded with 171 yards in 28 carries, including two touchdowns, in a 35-29 victory that ended Louisville's season with a 5-4-1 record. "I'd give my leg for the team," Bouggess said. "And I almost did."

As hard as Bouggess played, U of L's bruising fullback, Bill Gatti, gained even more yards—175 on 15 carries, all in the second half.

Afterward, the U of L team deposited Corso in the shower, and the coach said: "I've never been associated with a team that had more determination and character. I also haven't seen many teams that wanted a game more than this one. I just feel very, very happy."

On the plane returning to Louisville, Corso said: "I'm drained emotionally. But this is better than the Army-Navy game when we (Navy) beat them. We had to beat them (Tulsa) at their place, and we had just been beat 69-19 and we'd never beaten them in their park in the history of the school. And we had a chance at a winning season."

With only four days to prepare, the U of L staff had worked hard for this game. The tired Corso turned to his lovely wife and said, "Betsy, remember Sunday when I worked from 10 in the morning 'til two the next morning? Was it worth it?"

"Yes, it was," she replied.

TALENT GALORE ON 1969 FRESHMAN TEAM

U of L had some fine football players on the 1969 team, including Larry Ball, Lee Bouggess, Bill Gatti, Horace Jones and Cleo Walker, all of whom would go on to play professional football.

Still, Corso needed to strengthen the Cards' roster. So he and his young staff went out in the first year and recruited an excellent crop of freshmen, who were ineligible for varsity play in those days. In 1967 and 1968, the U of L freshmen won only one of six games and were outscored 184-106 by their opponents.

But the 1969 baby Cardinal team was loaded with talent and opened its season with a 21-13 victory at Dayton, which had walloped the U of L freshmen 62-20 the previous season. "The kids went out under trying circumstances and never gave up," said U of L frosh coach Roy Terry. "The game was played in 80-degree weather, and we have a squad of only 24."

The U of L freshmen, boasting such future varsity standouts as Tom Jackson, John Madeya, Larry Griffin, Gary Barnes, Tony Burdock and Tom Martin, won their other two games in the 1969 season—40-6 over Southern Illinois and 22-7 over Vanderbilt.

Help was on the way.

Chapter 11
Cards Climb to Nation's Top Twenty

Date: September 27, 1969.
Score: University of Kentucky 10, Mississippi 9.
Headlined quote from UK coach John Ray:
  "We're on our way."
Comment overheard on Belknap Campus:
  "He didn't say which way."

Ray was in his initial season as UK's coach, and following a 58-30 loss at home to Indiana in his first game at the helm, the Wildcats pulled off that fluke one-point upset victory over Southern hero Archie Manning and his Ole Miss teammates at Lexington.

That triumph was the high point of Ray's otherwise unsuccessful tenure at Kentucky. In the four years that Ray coached Kentucky, his teams managed just 10 victories against 33 losses. UK obviously went the wrong way under Ray.

Meanwhile, down the road at the University of Louisville, head coach Lee Corso was taking the Cardinals in the right direction. His team improved from 5-4-1 in his first season (1969) to 8-3-1 in 1970, followed by records of 6-3-1 in 1971 and 9-1 in 1972.

Up until 1970, Louisville wasn't in Kentucky's league in football, with the exception of 1925, when the Cardinals outscored their opponents 133-2 en route to an 8-0 season. In the post-World War II era, Louisville benefitted from superb coaching from Frank Camp and turned out more than its share of top players, but the U of L football program as a whole didn't have the fan support and financial backing and tradition that existed at Kentucky. UK simply had more good football players than Louisville did. But Corso and his staff were able to recruit some fine talent, and for three years (1970, 1971 and 1972) Louisville had the horses to compete with the Wildcats. With Louisville's football fortunes improving and Kentucky struggling under Ray, make no mistake about these facts: (a) UK would have had its hands full with the Cardinals in the 1970 and 1971 seasons, and (b) the 1972 U of L power unquestionably was better than the Wildcats.

Corso's 1970 team, which opened the season with a 9-7 loss at Florida State, was Missouri Valley Conference champion and tied Long Beach State 24-24 in the Pasadena Bowl. His 1971 club ended a season-opening 0-0 tie on Vanderbilt's one-yard line. His 1972 team was Missouri Valley Conference tri-champion.

While at U of L, Corso dearly wanted to play Kentucky. But UK didn't seem to

think such a game was a good idea.

"I challenged them to play us," Corso said in an interview. "And they said they couldn't play us because there was not enough room on their schedule. Well, then one year comes along and all of a sudden there's an 11th game on the schedule. I said, 'Perfect. How about the University of Louisville and Kentucky.' And they said, 'Well, we can't play Louisville.' I said, 'Why?' They said, 'We can't play because we need to make money.' So I said, 'I'll tell you what I'll do. I'll bring the Louisville team over there, and you can keep all the money. We will take nothing. I will pay out of my pocket for our expenses—the bus, the pre-game meal, anything. I'll pay for everything. That means you can make all the money.' And they said, "A-ba-ba-ba-a-ba-ba, well, we can't do that because we've got to play a nationally renowned team.' I said, 'Okay.' So they signed Villanova. And I said, 'Oh, that was a big one. That's a nationally known team. I thought it was a football game—not a basketball game.'

"So I tried and tried and tried to get them to play, but they didn't want to play because we were very, very good and probably superior to them in every area."

The interviewer told Corso he would have beaten the Wildcats in 1972.

"Aw, it wouldn't have been a contest," said Corso.

Instead of facing U of L, the Wildcats defeated lowly Villanova 25-7 in their forgettable season opener. This was a Villanova team that won only two of 11 games all season. U of L, meanwhile, finished the season cracking the top 20 in the polls—16th in The United Press International and 18th in The Associated Press.

Corso was right. In 1972, it wouldn't have been a contest between Louisville and Kentucky. With better personnel, a vitalized coaching staff and the psychological advantage of facing the state university that was usually played up over Louisville on the sports pages, the Cardinals had everything that it took to put a whipping on those 1972 Wildcats.

That 1972 bunch ... Corso's finest team

Ask Corso to comment on that 1972 team, and he'll reply: "There were no apparent weaknesses. Everything we did, we did it to perfection. It was extremely talented. That was the finest football team that I had. The only other one that could compare to it was the Indiana team in '79 (which went 8-4 and outscored Brigham Young 38-37 in the Holiday Bowl). That was a sensational team, too. But I think the '72 team had more spectacular players—like (Tom) Jackson and (Marty) Smith and Reggie Brown and Richard Bishop, Howard Stevens, (Larry) Griffin, (Tony) Burdock,

Gary Barnes

Howard Stevens

(Gary) Barnes, Steve Reese. Those guys could play. The whole defense practically went to the pros."

Jackson, that great U of L linebacker, was selected on the 1972 Walter Camp first-team All-America squad. All told, running back Stevens was named to five All-America second-team units that season. Those two U of L stars both were named to the 1972 Associated Press All-America second team. Three other U of L players received AP All-America honorable mention in 1972—tight end Barnes, center Frank Gitschier III and quarterback John Madeya.

Louisville landed eight players on the 1972 All-Missouri Valley Conference first team—Barnes, Reese, Gitschier, Madeya and Stevens on offense and Jackson, team captain Tom

John Madeya was a three-time All-Missouri Valley Conference quarterback for the Cardinals.

Martin and Joe Welch on the defensive unit.

Jackson and Madeya were All-Missouri Valley Conference selections three straight seasons.

The 5-foot-5 Stevens, who transferred to U of L following his sophomore season at Randolph-Macon, was named the league's Offensive Player of the Year for the second straight season and became the first back to rush for more than 5,000 yards as a collegian.

Jackson led a strong U of L defense in 1972. The Cardinals ranked first in the country in both rushing defense (allowing 82.1 yards a game) and total defense (202.5 yards per game).

UK, which was anything but an offensive juggernaut, wouldn't have figured to score much against these Cards. After all, in the 1972 season, the Wildcats were shut out three times and managed only one touchdown in three other games.

TOM JACKSON: MR. EVERYTHING

How good was Tom Jackson? "Best I ever saw," Corso replied. "Best player I ever coached. He was the finest linebacker I ever saw play the game from a coach's standpoint. He was better than anybody I coached against, either. Those guys at Ohio State—(Randy) Gradishar, (Tom) Cousineau—and some of those others at Michigan, they were good, but this guy was better than any of them.

"He had fantastic quickness—unbelievable quickness. And for about 225 pounds, he was strong. He just never missed. He never missed a guy. He was tough. He could run. He was everything."

Freshmen weren't eligible in 1969, Jackson's first season at U of L, but once he started playing on the varsity in 1970 he made a sudden impact. In the 1971 U of L media guide, Corso said of Jackson: "He's just a great football player. There's not a better linebacker in the country. He's big, strong and fast, and he loves to hit."

Jackson was honored as the Missouri Valley Conference Player of the

80

Cardinal Football

Year in 1970 and 1972. Following his senior season, he played in the American Bowl and Blue-Gray games.

Jackson went on to play 14 professional seasons with the Denver Broncos (1973-1986). "TJ" made three straight Pro Bowl appearances (1977-1979) and was named first-team All Pro in 1977 and 1978. His teammates named him Denver's defensive Most Valuable Player in 1974, 1976 and 1977 and the Broncos' most inspirational player six straight seasons (1981-1986). When he retired from the Broncos, he was tied with Gradishar (called by Woody Hayes "the best linebacker I ever coached at Ohio State") for most interceptions by a Denver linebacker—20.

In 1992, Jackson was inducted into the Broncos' Ring of Fame, which honors players and administrators who played major roles in the franchise's success. The Ring of Fame is on the facade of Mile High Stadium's east stands.

In 1994, Jackson was inducted into the Kentucky Athletic Hall of Fame, and in the program for that dinner, he was quoted as saying: "Lee Corso wanted to see me do well, do things on the football field, allow my skills to be honed and seen. It was probably the basis for the good things I came in contact with in my professional career.

"I'll always believe the team we had as juniors and seniors is as good as it's ever gotten at U of L. ... if you ask me who I think is the best team that ever played there, I lean toward the John Madeyas and the Howard Stevens, and what they were able to accomplish in their time."

Tom Jackson and Lee Corso

Chapter 12
Cards Gain Their Independence

On November 19, 1977, late in the third quarter of U of L's football game against Indiana State, athletics director Dave Hart ducked into the training complex at Fairgrounds Stadium to return a call from the Independence Bowl committee in Shreveport, Louisiana. At that moment, the committee was meeting to decide the opponent for Louisiana Tech in the December 17 game. At the same time they were fighting Indiana State on the field, the Cards were battling East Carolina on the bowl committee's note pads.

"What's the score up there?" asked bowl committee chairman Ed Powell.

"Twenty-four to seven Louisville," said Hart.

Vince Gibson guided the "Red Rage" Cards to the 1977 Independence Bowl.

"Are you going to win?"

"Well, I guess."

"You've got the bid if you win," said Powell.

With only seconds remaining in what turned out to be a 27-16 Cardinal win, public-address announcer John Tong told the crowd that U of L had accepted the bowl bid, touching off a party on the Cardinal bench that carried over into the locker room.

"Oh, man," said nose guard Jeff Henry. "Shreveport! Shreveport! I can't believe it! A bowl game! That's good seafood country down there and I love seafood, so I can't wait to get there."

For coach Vince Gibson and his team, the bowl game seemed to be certification of U of L's re-

Cardinal Football

building effort, and never mind that the Independence Bowl wasn't exactly on the same level as the Orange or Sugar. After Lee Corso bolted U of L for Indiana after the 1972 season, the Cards went 5-6 and 4-7 under T.W. Alley. Among U of L fans, unrest was rivaled only by apathy, leading Hart to fire Alley and bring in Gibson, who had generated national at-

Otis Wilson

tention while coaching quarterback Lynn Dickey at Kansas State in the late 1960s.

"When we were considering Vince, there was, frankly, some apprehension because he had been on probation at Kansas State," Hart said. "That ruined their program out there. Vince felt bad about it and told us, 'Once you get your fingers stung reaching for the cookie jar, you don't do it again.' I think he's done a super job. We have a well-run, highly or-

ganized, disciplined football team."

At K-State, Gibson built his promotional campaign around "Purple Passion." At U of L, it was "Red Rage." And for awhile, it worked. In their first three seasons under Gibson, the Cards went from 2-9 to 5-6 to the Independence Bowl team's 7-3-1 heading into the Shreveport showdown against Louisiana Tech. Alas, however, the team came up short in the university's third bowl appearance.

It was a funny sort of game for the Cards, one full of big plays and lousy plays and enough missed opportunities to make Gibson feel as old as Gen. Omar Bradley, the Independence Bowl's 86-year-old halftime guest of honor.

When it finally, and mercifully, drew to an end after more than four hours of pain and drama, Louisiana Tech was clinging to a 24-14 lead, and Otis Wilson, the hit man who played linebacker for the Cards was sitting on the bench and bawling his eyes out.

Even accolades from the opposition—"You're a helluva linebacker," said Rod Foppe, Tech's star wide receiver—didn't make Wilson feel any better about what happened before an estimated 18,500 fans.

Bombed out of their minds and almost out of the game by Tech's relentless passing attack in the first half, U of L fought back to where it had a chance to win in the second half—only to blow opportunity after opportunity with a fumble here, a penalty there.

"I felt we should have won the game," said Wilson, the hard-hitting sophomore whose 13 tackles earned him a trophy as the defensive player of the game.

Trailing 24-7 at halftime, the Cards scored on their first possession of the second half and finally looked like a football team. Then, with Wilson and his determined defensive buddies shutting off quarterback Keith Thibodeaux's murderous passing, U of L got a break early in the fourth quarter that could have turned the game all the way around.

Frank Minnifield

With 11:58 remaining, Wilson smacked into Tech's Larry Anderson, causing a fumble that U of L's Mark Besanceny recovered at the Tech one-yard line. Immediately the 1,000 or so U of L supporters went into a frenzy of red-and-white pompon waving. A touchdown here and Louisville surely would have momentum, not to mention a real shot at winning.

So on first down, U of L's Runt Moon lost three yards. And then Calvin Prince, who spent most of the afternoon dropping the ball or losing his footing, fumbled a pitchout that Tech's Johnny Robinson recovered. End of rally.

"That was the key play right there," Gibson said. "We have a chance to win the ball game if we score there."

Even at that, the Cardinals didn't give up. U of L defensive back Zarko Ellis intercepted a pass in the end zone to thwart a Tech drive, and, late in the game, freshman quarterback Terry Mullins had the Cards marching. Mullins even hit tight end Gary Nord with a touchdown pass in the final seconds, but it was nullified by a holding penalty.

"That was the crowning blow," Gibson said. "Understand, I'm not saying the officiating cost us the game. I was just disappointed in the way we reacted to penalties, especially in the first half. We lost our poise."

The next season the Cards seemed on their way to a second consecutive bowl trip after going 7-2. But season-ending losses to Memphis State at home and Southern Miss on the road knocked them out of contention. Then came a 4-6-1 record in 1979, the senior year for Wilson, who went on to a Pro Bowl career with the Chicago Bears. Discouraged by what he perceived as lack of support, Gibson left to take the Tulane job and the Cards replaced him with Bob Weber.

Although Weber had worked on Gibson's staff at both Kansas State and U of L, his main claim to fame in more than 20 years of coaching was a 16-26 record as head coach at the University of Arizona from 1969-72.

"I've got a different way of dressing from Lee Corso and a different accent from Coach Gibson," Weber said, "but I believe 100 percent in promotion. You have to go out and ask people to be involved. I'm going to put my efforts in that direction."

Alas for Weber, however, he was hamstrung

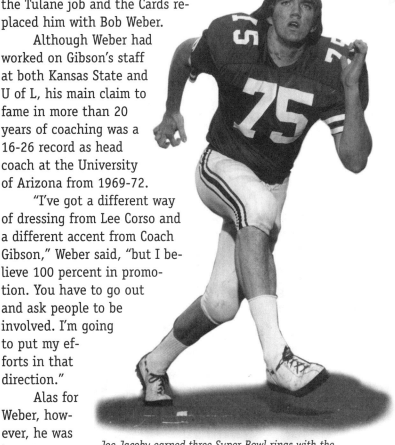

Joe Jacoby earned three Super Bowl rings with the Washington Redskins as one of the NFL's most dominant offensive tackles.

by budget constraints. New U of L president Donald Swain had told Athletics Director Bill Olsen (he succeeded Hart in 1980) that the athletics department must be financially self-sufficient. So Olsen and Weber were faced with the nigh-impossible job of filling the seats and generating wins with resources that were limited in comparison with some of the teams on the Cards' schedule — Miami, Florida State, Florida, Kansas, Missouri, and West Virginia, to name a few of the most prominent.

Under the circumstances, Weber did remarkably well in his first two seasons, which both ended in 5-6 records, mainly because his teams included such individual stars as offensive tackle Joe Jacoby and defensive back Frank Minnifield, who would go on to NFL stardom with the Washington Redskins and Cleveland Browns, respectively.

But when the Cards lost their last seven games after getting off to a 3-1 start in 1983, then followed that with a 2-9 record in 1984 that included a home loss to in-state Division I-AA foe Murray State, Weber was fired.

The new coach would have some nice returning players such as tackle Bruce Armstrong, linebacker Matt Battaglia—who went on to acting fame—receiver Ernest Givins, and quarterback Ed Rubbert. Clearly, however, U of L was at a crossroads. Some critics felt the program would never be competitive in Division I and should drop back to a lesser level. But others felt the time had come for the university to hire a big-time coach and finally make a serious committment to excellence.

On October 31, 1984, with Weber's fate a foregone conclusion, sports editor Billy Reed of *The Courier-Journal* called

After an impressive U of L career, Dwayne Woodruff was a regular in the Pittsburgh Steelers' secondary from 1979-90.

Ernest Givens

Howard Schnellenberger to see if he might possibly be interested in the U of L job. In 1983, Schnellenberger, an All-State player at Louisville Flaget High and an All-American at UK, had coached Miami to the national title. He was one of the hottest properties in coaching, so the idea of him coming to U of L caused snickers to ripple through the football world.

Except none of those snickers belonged to Schnellenberger.

"I'm open to an intial contact," he said. "I don't know how open I would be after that. But I owe that much to the city of Louisville, the people of Kentucky, and my friends up there."

Bob Weber followed Vince Gibson as the Cardinals' head coach from 1980-84.

Chapter 13
Bold Schnellenberger Sets Cards' Course

Traditionally in college football the major stories unfold in such places as South, Bend, Indiana, or Lincoln, Nebraska Or Gainesville, Florida, or Tuscaloosa, Alabama.

But in 1985 a big story took place in Louisville, Kentucky.

It was going on at a university that never had been known as a football factory. Basketball, as practiced by the Doctors of Dunk themselves, is the game that put Louisville on the national collegiate sports map.

But all that began to change in the mid-1980s. The university and the city got excited over the prospect of a big-time college football program under the dynamic leadership of Howard Schnellenberger.

This was the same Howard Schnellenberger who in 1979 took over a University of Miami program that had suffered losing records in eight of its previous 10 seasons. All Schnellenberger did was turn the Hurricanes into a collegiate power that won the national championship in 1983.

In 1985, he was beginning an even more difficult assignment. He inherited a Louisville program that had experienced losing records in 10 of the previous 12 years, including 2-9 in 1984 and 3-8 in 1983, and all Schnellenberger was being asked to do was transform the Cardinals into a football power.

Schnellenberger was facing quite a task in the city in which he grew up. Before the coach joined Miami, the Hurricanes had competed often enough against major college football powers. Louisville, however, never had been able to shake loose from an inferiority complex in football. True, Louisville occasionally had managed an upset (in 1984 it took a 30-28 decision over Cotton Bowl participant Houston), but the Cardinals usually were outclassed against top opposition.

Consider the possibility of a resurgent U of L consistently making the top 20 football rankings. Stranger things had happened in football. As far as many col-

Howard Schnellenberger

lege football observers were concerned, Schnellenberger's acceptance of the Louisville job was strange enough in itself.

What in the name of Knute Rockne was Schnellenberger, one of the most respected coaches in the country, doing at Louisville, of all places?

The opportunity to turn around another program—or "to take Cinderella to the ball a second time," as he phrased it—was appealing. He said he ruled out "going to places that already had established programs where I would just be another coach coming in and taking up where somebody else had left off."

Schnellenberger's goal at Louisville was the same as it was at Miami—football excellence. "We would not take a job here or anyplace without having a goal to be the best," the gray-haired, 51-year-old coach said, rubbing his thick mustache as he sat behind his desk in the U of L football office.

"It's very difficult to be talking in terms of years in this situation, but we're looking for improvement in the first year, we're looking for continued improvement in the second and third years so that we can begin to compete with the best teams on our schedule and somewhere after that to be in that higher echelon of the ranked teams in the country so that if something good's going to happen, we're in a position to take advantage of it."

Through the years, U of L had turned out a number of players who gained fame in the National Football League, including Johnny Unitas, Lenny Lyles, Ernie Green, Joe Jacoby, Tom Jackson, Mark Clayton and Doug Buffone, but the Cardinal teams generally had attracted little national attention. The Cardinals' only final top 20 ranking—16th in The United Press International poll and 18th in The Associated Press—came under head coach Lee Corso in 1972 when they were 9-1.

"It was probably an unrealistic goal to try to be competitive with the top 20 programs in the country," U of L athletic

director Bill Olsen said in 1985. "And to go up against the tradition that they had and that we didn't have was somewhat of a mission impossible."

When Schnellenberger accepted the mission at Louisville in December 1984, interest in the program immediately increased in the city, which rarely had gotten carried away with college football.

The public's attitude was "so much more positive this year than it's ever been before," U of L ticket manager Betty Jackson said in 1985. "People are really excited about going out for the games They're anxious. Instead of football just being something they're going to do between now and basketball, they're looking forward to football season."

Even before Louisville launched a media advertising blitz, more than 16,000 season tickets had been sold for the 1985 season, an increase of 3,000 over 1984. At a U of L kickoff luncheon in the summer of 1985, a turnout of 1,700 was termed as "unbelievable" by New York Yankees owner George Steinbrenner, the guest speaker.

Ernie Green

"Now everybody's interested in football," said Olsen, who was beginning his sixth year as Louisville's athletic director. "In the previous five years, we were selling all of the other things that go with football—the tailgating and the bands—and our whole promotional effort was made to get people to come to the football stadium to have a party on Saturdays with us."

With Schnellenberger in charge, Louisville was selling football, and nobody was making the sales pitch any harder than the coach, who made himself just as visible as the twin spires at Churchill Downs.

Mark Clayton

"There are a lot of great football coaches," Olsen said, "but what sets him apart is he has the ability to market what he's doing and he communicates well with the business leaders and all of the groups that he addresses. He gets involved in so many things in the community. He's involved in charitable organizations. He's giving back to the community, not just taking from it, and that's going to increase his visibility."

Besides numerous speaking engagements ("I've probably made one or two a day for the last five months," Schnellenberger said in his first summer on the job), he had been seen on television and heard on the radio, and his likeness had appeared on billboards around town.

"When it comes to using film and music to underscore his points and build his dreams," wrote sports editor Billy Reed of *The Courier-Journal,* "Schnellenberger is the Steven Spielberg of his profession—light years ahead of his peers in vision and imagination."

Schnellenberger even had a staff member, Roy Hamlin, whose title was director of radio/television development for football and basketball. "We're a big believer in the satellite," said Hamlin, one of 12 full-time U of L staff members—including six assistant coaches—who worked or played for Schnellenberger at Miami. "In 1980, we would put his coach's show out on the satellite. It went out to 440 markets. We were in Hawaii and Alaska. No one heard of Howard Schnellenberger—much less the University of Miami—at the time, but it was picked up. We got some kids from Montana that came in. I think that started the flow of the electronic age for us."

Florida also provided a fertile recruiting ground—19 of Louisville's 30 incoming freshmen in 1985 were from that state.

For Schnellenberger, taking over the Louisville job was a homecoming. Born in southern Indiana, he grew up in Louisville and was a standout football player at the now-defunct Flaget High School, where he was a teammate of Paul Hornung. Schnellenberger was named an All-America end at the University of Kentucky in 1955. As an assistant coach, he learned from men such as Blanton Collier, Paul 'Bear' Bryant, George Allen and Don Shula.

Schnellenberger knew how to build a football power, and in 1985 he already had made major improvements in Louisville's program.

The overall football budget was increased 20 percent, and Olsen said contributions had been made "to do a lot of things that we weren't able to do before."

The size of the strength room in the football complex was doubled, and the amount of equipment there was tripled. As if that weren't enough, a $30,000 unit evaluating and rehabilitating muscles was purchased. Moreover, an irrigated, landscaped football practice area of 10 acres was constructed.

After taking Miami to the 1983 National Championship, Howard Schnellenberger was looked upon by Louisville fans as the man to transform the Cardinals into a football power.

If Schnellenberger was successful in building Louisville into a football power, as some expected him to do, other changes needed to be made. Cardinal Stadium, with a seating capacity of 35,500, was big enough in 1985, but if Louisville hoped to achieve major-power status, a first-class stadium was an absolute must.

Then there was the matter of the schedule. Schnellenberger said six teams on his 1985 schedule—West Virginia, Syracuse, Virginia Tech, Miami (Florida), Houston and probably Southern Mississippi—had programs that were "well ahead" of Louisville's.

"So from that standpoint, this is a tough schedule for us," he said. "However, when you're developing a program, your schedule should always be better than where you are. You should always be elevating your program to meet the schedule. Hopefully, as time goes on, we'll get to that point where a West Virginia won't look like a superpower."

If all went as planned and Louisville developed a top-notch program, the schedule needed to be strengthened to catch the attention of those voting in the polls and those scouting for the major bowls.

But in 1985 that was looking too far down the road. Indeed, many people who insisted from the beginning that Schnellenberger never would accept the Cards' job predicted that he wouldn't remain in Louisville long enough to remember his telephone number. One line of thought had Notre Dame looking for a coach after the 1985 season and Schnellenberger as the man the Fighting Irish would want.

What did Schnellenberger say about such speculation?

Louisville native Howard Schnellenberger and his trademark pipe became a highly visible fixture immediately in the community.

"I don't know where you could find a coach that's had the good fortune to be the coach of a national championship football team, one that has been fortunate enough to have received Coach of the Year honors, that would come to Louisville and use that as a stepping stone to another prestigious university," he said.

He said that a "long-term commitment" was required to accomplish his goal at Louisville. "When that happens, I don't know where there'll be a better place to coach than right here," he said. "So if you look at it logically, it's really hard to think of anyone coming to Louisville and looking to go to a better situation when you just left the national championship situation."

Schnellenberger had a Louisville contract rewarding him $190,000 annually ($70,000 in regular salary, $50,000 in deferred compensation and $70,000 for appearing on a television and radio

Cardinal Football

Howard Schnellenberger was an All-America end at the University of Kentucky in 1955.

show.) "His contract is for five years—that's what he asked for," Olsen said. "I don't think Howard Schnellenberger would have made the decision to come to Louisville—and he wouldn't be working as hard as he's working at building this program—if he was going to use it as a stepping stone. I discount all of that where someone says that we won't have him a year from now.

"I don't know whether it can be done in three years or whether it'll take 13 years, but I think that Howard Schnellenberger is going to make the kind of commitment to us that he will eventually be successful in completing the task that he's started."

Chapter 14
U of L Builds Toward a Dream

On Janaury 1, 1991, the football world was stunned by what happened in the prestigious Fiesta Bowl in Tempe, Arizona. A decided underdog to Alabama, one of the marquee programs in the game, Howard Schnellenberger's sixth U of L team produced the game of its dreams. The Cards not only upset the Crimson Tide, they pounded them. When the final score—Louisville 34, Alabama 7—flashed on TV screens around the country, knowledgeable football people had to recognize that Schnellenberger, the miracle man, had done it again.

It wasn't easy.

In his first three seasons at U of L, the proud Schnellenberger was forced to swallow his pride on numerous occasions. The records were 2-9, 2-8-1, and 3-8. The cynics—those who said NOBODY could build a nationally competitive program at U of L—were locked in an I-told-you-so mode.

But what they didn't realize was that Schnellenberger and his staff had quietly, but steadily, been upgrading the program's talent level. Every year they mined Florida, Schnellenberger's old stomping ground, for good players who were left over when Miami, Florida, and

Florida State had filled their quotas. They also challenged Kentucky for the state's best prospects.

The program's fortunes turned around dramatically in 1988 with an 8-3 record that surprised the pollsters. So the Cards didn't get a bowl invitation despite nice wins over North Carolina, Virginia, and Virginia Tech.

The big breakthrough was supposed to come in 1989, but the Cards went sour after a tough home loss to nationally ranked West Virginia and could do no better than 6-5. But in 1990, Schnellenberger's dreams came true. The final regular-season record of 9-1-1 included wins over West Virginia and Pittsburgh on the road.

The Cards got into the Fiesta Bowl at least partly because of an unfortunate controversy in Arizona that began when that state's voters rejected a proposal to make Dr. Martin Luther King Jr.'s birthday a state holiday.

That became such a political hot potato that the Fiesta Bowl, where Notre Dame and Penn State had clinched national titles in the previous four years, had trouble lining up teams. Some schools declined Fiesta invitations because they were afraid of being accused

of endorsing the vote against the King holiday.

Although the charges lacked merit—King's birthday already was a holiday in Tucson and Phoenix, the state's largest cities—U of L also received some criticism from local civil-rights activists when it accepted a Fiesta bid. But all that was more or less forgotten because of what happened in the game.

Playing in a bowl for the first time in 13 years, the Cards put on a classic display of Schnellenberger football. Senior quarterback Browning Nagle threw for 451 yards, a Fiesta Bowl record, while completing 20 of 33 passes.

The Cards jumped on 'Bama quickly, stunning them with a 25-0 first-quarter outburst. Nagle got it started with a 70-yard TD bomb to Latrell Ware and the Cards never looked back.

"We took this game for everything it was worth," Nagle said. "We wanted to come out here and gain respect, and that's what we did. It's a great tribute to the coaches for getting us focused."

What made U of L's outburst especially impressive was that Alabama had come into the game allowing an average of only 5.4 points in its previous seven games. But this time the Tide defense was outplayed by its U of L counterparts. Against a Cardinal defense led by cornerback Ray Buchanan, who made five tackles, recovered a fumble, and picked up a blocked punt for a TD, Alabama managed only 189 yards in total offense.

"We prepared exceptionally well for this game and Browning had a superhuman performance," said an ecstatic Schnellenberger. "No way in my wildest dreams did I expect us to be in this situation. Just coming here was a quantum leap for us. Winning this was another quantum leap for our program."

Building on the excitement created by the 10-1-1 record and the Fiesta Bowl victory, U of L sold a record 27,000 season tickets for the 1991 season. The schedule included Tennessee, Ohio State, and Florida State, a sure sign the Cards at least were knocking on the door of the college game's penthouse.

The Cards were respectable against

Howard Schnellenberger

Cardinal Football

the premier programs—losing by an average of two touchdowns—but stumbled against the lesser names on their way to a disappointing 2-9 season. But behind quarterback Jeff Brohm, a product of Louisville Trinity High, they rebounded for a 5-6 record in 1992.

In 1993, Brohm's senior year, the Cards got off to a 5-0 start that included home victories over Arizona State and Texas. Then, after a 36-34 loss to West Virginia in Morgantown, U of L ripped off two more wins before collapsing in back-to-back road games against national powers Tennessee and Texas A&M.

But a 28-0 win on the road against Tulsa in the regular-season finale earned the Cards a Liberty Bowl berth against Michigan State.

On the night of December 28 in Memphis, the weather—freezing rain and 20-degree temperatures—hardly seemed ideal for U of L's aerial attack. But Brohm, playing with two steel pins and a steel plate in his throwing hand because of a late-season injury, delivered one of the grittiest performances in U of L his-

tory, completing 19 of 29 passes for 197 yards and a TD.

Entering the final quarter, the Cards trailed, 7-3. But with 12:05 remaining, Brohm connected on a 25-yard dart to Reggie Ferguson to put Schnellenberger's team in front. A few minutes later, the defense had its finest moment when end Joe Johnson and linebacker Tyrus McCloud threw Spartan running back Craig Thomas for a safety.

"It was basically a matter of pride," Johnson said. "We had heard all week about how they were going to run up and down the field."

Instead, the Spartans accumulated only 114 yards rushing.

The 18-7 victory gave U of L its first win over a Big Ten opponent. It also pushed Schnellenberger's head-coaching bowl record to 4-0.

Unfortunately for U of L, Brohm departed for the NFL and wasn't around for the 1993 opener against Kentucky in Lexington's Commonwealth Stadium.

A former UK star end under Paul "Bear" Bryant and Blanton Collier,

Browning Nagle

Ray Buchanan

Schnellenberger early on in his Louisville career side-stepped the issue of a series with the Wildcats. "Let's wait until we get our program to their level," he said.

But after the Fiesta Bowl win over Alabama, Schnellenberger joined Athletics Director Bill Olsen in opening behind-the-scenes negotiations with C.M. Newton, who had become UK's Athletics Director in 1989.

The result was a five-year agreement to play each other in the season opener. All games would be in Commonwealth unless U of L got a new stadium built. Then the series would switch to home-and-home status.

In the weeks before the '93 opener, it was obvious that at least one goal of both schools had been achieved—interest in football, throughout the summer, was running at a record level.

On September 3, before a rabid crowd of 59,162, the Cats upset the Cards, 20-14. With 3:18 remaining in the fourth quarter, UK's Antonio O'Ferral scored from the 4-yard-line to break a 14-14 tie and provide the winning points.

Jeff Brohm

Louisville came closer to Howard Schnellenberger's dream when the Cardinals posted a 10-1-1 season in 1990, winning the Fiesta Bowl and earning a top 15 national ranking.

It was no consolation to Schnellenberger that his team got the better of UK in first downs (23-13), rushing yardage (211 to 197), and passing yardage (215 to 116). But the Cards repeatedly shot themselves in the foot.

Ironically, that would be UK's only victory in a season that marked the beginning of the end for Coach Bill Curry, who eventually was fired during the 1997 season. However, U of L rebounded for a 6-5 record that included wins over Arizona State and North Carolina State.

After the season, unhappy with U of L's plans to join the new Conference USA, Schnellenberger shocked a lot of Cardinal fans by accepting the challenge of rebuilding once-mighty Oklahoma.

Sadly for him, he got caught in an ugly political battle that cost him his job after only one season.

In 10 years at U of L, Schnellenberger's overall record was a seemingly modest 54-56-2. But that's misleading. In a real sense, his building job at Louisville was every bit as impressive as the one he did at Miami. He didn't get to take Cinderella to the ball again—no national championship—but he did elevate the program to its highest level ever.

Take away the first three dismal seasons, and Schnellenberger's record for his last seven years was 46-32-1, with two bowl victories. He also recruited and coached such future pros as Brohm, Nagle, Buchanan, Jamie Asher, Joe Johnson, Roman Oben, Sam Madison, and Ted Washington.

Because of Schnellenberger's success, several "name" coaches expressed an interest in being his successor. But U of L finally settled on a young coach who had been an assistant to Lou Holtz at Notre Dame and done an impressive rebuilding job at Eastern Michigan.

His name was Ron Cooper.

Ted Washington

Chapter 15

From the Locker Room to the Field

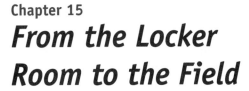

▐▐ Remember what we've talked about. Offense, we gotta do what? Two things. Protect the ball and do what?"

"Run."

"And run the ball. Control the line of scrimmage. On defense, we gotta do what?"

"Stop the run."

"Stop the run, and don't do what? Don't give 'em a big play. The kicking game, we want to do one thing. Make one big play, am I correct? One big play all day in the kicking game. That's it."

Ron Cooper, in his first game as the University of Louisville's head football coach, was standing in front of his team inside the locker room shortly before it was to take the field against the University of Kentucky at Commonwealth Stadium on September 2, 1995.

The stadium was filling up, and soon it would be time to do battle. Before they went onto the field, Cooper wanted his players to be thankful.

"I want everybody to grab a teammate's hand," Cooper said. "First of all, I want everybody in here to be thankful for each other. Be thankful for somebody that you love in your family, somebody that loves you. Be thankful for your teammates who you are about to go

to war with. Keep your head down, I want everybody to listen to me. Grab your teammate's hand. If you feel it enough the way the vibes are going in this room, guys, you can feel each other's heartbeat right through each other's hands. We got to be on the same beat, on the same heartbeat tonight—the same, one heartbeat. We go out there and play within one heartbeat, be on the same wavelength, guys, we're gonna whip 'em. Never let doubt enter your mind. Never let it enter it one time.

"Bob."

"Father," said the Rev. Bob Bailey, "we've prepared, we're ready. Father, I pray You'll keep each young man safe. Father, I pray You'll reward them for their preparedness with victory. We pray this in Jesus' name. Amen."

"Amen."

At halftime, the score was tied 3-3. In the final minute or so before the team left the locker room for the second half, Cooper exhorted: "Defense! Defense! Hasn't been bad at all. Some binds on field position. Other than that, a couple of plays, a couple of reverses. We gotta play ball. The end men on the line check the reverse coming back first, under control, make the play, make them stutter step, we'll be OK. Shut down the reverse.

We got to give it back to our offense more than five times this half. They need eight possessions this half. If we get eight possessions, we'll score on four of 'em, I guarantee.

"Offense, a couple of things. Defense got to get you the ball. We've had the ball five times. We punted the first two. Other than that, we've been inside the 20-yard line, inside the 15 the last three times. We're going to get in the red zone. We're working the red zone, and we're going to put it to 'em. Good job this half of not turning the ball over.

"Let's go out on the field. Grab your teammate's hand, grab your teammate's hand, feel that heartbeat one more time, feel the heartbeat one more time. Close your eyes, meditate, feel it one more time. It'll go right through his hand. Play for each other, play for each other, play for the university, play for the overall team. Guys, we're gonna come back in here, we're gonna celebrate at the end of these 30 minutes. Let's go get after 'em."

The players let out a roar as they left the locker room. It was 8:24 p.m.

At 9:50, the players returned to the locker room, and, yes, indeed, they were celebrating. U of L had scored a touchdown with 1:29 left in the game to win 13-10.

Players and assistant coaches were congratulating each other.

"We got the C-U-U-U-P-P!" yelled

offensive guard Shawn Kries, who had played his heart out on the field and now was proudly kneeling next to the Governor's Cup in the locker room. How sweet it was for this tough lineman from Springfield, Kentucky.

Other players were shouting in jubilation, grabbing each other, shaking hands. It was one big celebration.

Cooper then entered the locker room and delivered a message that his players should long remember. His message didn't deal with X's and O's, or blocking and tackling. It didn't deal with celebrating or gaining revenge on UK. It didn't deal with football at all.

It dealt with love.

"I want everybody up here," said Cooper, standing on a bench in the middle of the room. "Grab your teammate, grab his hand. Meditate and be thankful. Think about somebody you love. Meditate and think about somebody you love. Be thankful for them—somebody who loves you, maybe your parents, aunt, uncle, girl friend, best friend or somebody that loves you and you love back. Be thankful for them. Be thankful for this university and the opportunity to play football here, but more important be thankful for your teammates and this football team. Eyes up."

Cooper smiled and said, "I already got the speech written." The players yelled like hell. "I want you to read it

Ron Cooper guided the Cardinals to their first-ever victory over in-state rival Kentucky in 1995.

Louisville won the second battle for the Governor's Cup with a 38-14 victory at Kentucky.

with me," he said, showing a folder with his prepared post-game speech. "What was I going to say? Great win, we're one and oh, and I love you all."

The players roared.

Cooper proceeded to present 13 game balls—to U of L athletic director Bill Olsen, to the 10 seniors who suited up for this game, head strength coach Ray Ganong, Robert Jones and head trainer Dwayne Treolo.

Looking around the room, Cooper said: "Great job. Great win."

He had one final reminder for his players. "When we go back, make sure you take care of business," he said. "Don't do anything to embarrass yourselves, don't do anything to embarrass the university or your family. You make sure you do the right thing. Any other questions?"

"What do we got to wear back?"

"What did we wear here?" Cooper replied. "Put on your tie. Let's go."

The players erupted with yells, laughter and applause.

• • •

Outside the locker room, Cooper appeared at a press conference and was asked if he was worried with five minutes to go after UK had gone ahead 10-6.

"No, I wasn't," he said. "I felt like we were going to do some good things. We didn't flinch. I think that's what brought us through in the end."

Don't flinch. Back on August 11 at a team meeting inside the locker room at the U of L football complex, Cooper had told his players, "We're gonna be a football team and a coaching staff that won't flinch. Since I took over, this football team has not been a team that flinches."

An observer standing inside the U of L locker room on August 11 and outside the locker room on September 2 at Cooper's post-game press conference couldn't help but remember those words. Don't flinch.

• • •

On September 16, 1995, as Cooper stood inside the Cardinal Stadium to address his players before they took the field against Michigan State in their home opener, it was raining outside.

"Guys, it's a little wet," Cooper said. "When it's a little wet, the No. 1 objective is to protect the football. The No. 1 objective is to protect the football.

They're going to come in here, and they'll be a little sloppy. And there are going to be several balls that they're going to have on the ground. Defense has got to be pursuing like hell to get on 'em.

"Receivers, concentrate, catch the ball, hold onto it. Running backs, same thing—protect the football. Quarterback, protect the football. When it's a little wet, protect the football. Protect the football.

"Defense, let's tackle.

"Offense, let's do what? No turnovers—and what else? Run the damn ball. We're going to run the damn ball."

As Cooper concluded his comments, The Star-Spangled Banner was being played out on the field.

It was time to do battle with Michigan State. "Hey, let's go get 'em!" Cooper shouted to his players as they headed onto the field in the drizzling rain. "Let's go!"

At the intermission, Michigan State held a 13-7 lead, and after the coaches gathered together to discuss the first half, the assistants talked with the players in individual groups. The offensive team was sitting in front of one white diagram board, the defensive team in front of another.

The time neared for the team to leave the locker room, and Cooper had this to say to his players: "We were a little bit sloppy the first half, but so were they. Guys, we're in control of this game right now. Don't think we're not for one damn minute! We're in control.

"Defense, shut 'em down.

"Offense, protect the ball no matter what. Keep running hard. Keep controlling it up front.

"The difference in this game, guys," added Cooper, then lowering his voice, "is they had foolish penalties, we laid it on the ground. That's the difference in the game. "

In the first half, U of L had fumbled six times, losing one. Michigan State had been penalized 55 yards, compared with 17 yards in penalties for U of L.

"No more damn penalties," Cooper went on, speaking more loudly, "Hold onto the ball. Control the line up front."

Then yelling louder than ever, he exclaimed: "DEFENSE, SHUT THE DAMN RUN DOWN THIS HALF. SET THE TEMPO!

"Kickoff team, I want 11 crazy men running down the field to knock somebody's tail off! YOU BETTER SET THE DAMN TEMPO! You set the tempo to start the half!

"Let's go whip 'em!!"

The players let out a yell as they left the locker room. When they returned after the game, they were quiet. Things didn't work out for the Cardinals in the second half, and the final score was Michigan State 30, U of L 7. Louisville had fumbled eight times, losing three, and had been guilty of two interceptions. It had been a long, long afternoon.

Standing in the middle of the locker room, Cooper told his players: "Grab a teammate's hand. Close your eyes."

The players bowed their head, and with his eyes closed, Cooper said, "Be thankful. Think about somebody you love and who loves you, and be thankful for them. Think about somebody who loves you and who you love and be thankful for them. Be thankful for each other, the university and this football team.

"Eyes up.

"All right, we got our butts whipped. We said last night the team that doesn't turn it over and stops the run is gonna win the game. I hope everybody in here is hurting as much as I am because I never ever want to have this feeling again.

"We got our butts whipped as a team—offense, defense and kicking game.

"After tomorrow, we're going to put this one behind us. Then we're moving on to North Carolina.

"We're two and one. We're not losing another football game—not another damn football game. You better put it in your mind.

"We got our butts whipped. It better ache, and it better hurt."

Cooper had dismissed two players and suspended two others during the week for disciplinary reasons, and now that this game was over, he reminded those gathered in front of him: "Don't do anything to embarrass this football team, don't do anything to embarrass your family. More importantly, don't do anything tonight to embarrass yourself. When you come in tomorrow, better come with a clear head. Better come in ready to be corrected on film."

Turning his attention back to the game, Cooper concluded: "Can't turn the ball over, guys. Defense, you can only go in so many times and stop 'em. Can't turn it over. Special teams, you got to continue to get better.

"I will never, ever be embarrassed like I was today."

Cooper's defense was the Cardinals' [stren]gth during the 1995 season.

• • •

"A lot of people are here tonight, a lot of people are looking around the nation," Cooper told his team in the locker room before it took the field on September 21, 1995, for the North Carolina game, which was televised nationally by ESPN.

"Everybody's looking," Cooper said, pacing back and forth in the middle of the locker room. "Let me just say this: Nobody respects us right now. Half the nation doesn't respect us. Sometimes you gotta earn respect. Nobody's gonna give you respect. You gotta earn it.

"Never let the thought of failure enter your mind tonight—nobody," he added, raising his right index finger.

Cooper asked the players to grab a teammate's hand and get down on a knee. "Please meditate and be thankful for somebody," he said. "We got to be on the same beat, the same heartbeat. Play together, play hard for 60 minutes."

The players seemed more fired up than they had been five days earlier for the Michigan State game. They appeared to be in a bad mood. They seemed to mean business on this night.

"Keep your cool," Cooper told the players before they left the locker room. "Don't lose your head. We're gonna be fine."

U of L led 10-7 at halftime. While the coaches were off together in a meeting, the players talked among themselves.

"Time to come together."

"Good job, D."

"Defense, keep it up."

"Offense, drive it down their throat."

At 9:38 p.m., just before it was time to leave the locker room for the second half, the animated Cooper stood on a chair, pointed a finger and yelled: "I want to go out, and I want to pound 'em this half! I don't give a damn if you're tired, defense! I don't give a damn if you're tired, offense! We gotta dig down! We gotta fight! We're ahead! We're in charge! We're at home!

"The game is won with turnovers," he continued. "They turned it over three times—we're ahead," Cooper held up three fingers.

"Offense, helluva job holding on to it. Keep doing it—something's gonna pop soon. Let's be together this half! Let's go out! Let's go whip 'em!"

The players let out a roar. Cooper had a snarl on his face as he left the locker room with his team at 9:40. About an hour and a half later, he stood near the middle of the room, waiting for all of his players to return from the field.

North Carolina had scored a touchdown with 14 seconds left and won the game 17-10.

After the players arrived, Cooper asked them to kneel down. "Close your eyes. Be thankful. Think about somebody you love and who loves you. Be thankful for your teammates and this football team."

When the players raised their heads, they heard Cooper tell them: "You did exactly what I asked. I asked you to go out there and compete. You don't have anything to be ashamed about—nobody in here, nobody. Keep your head up. My head's up, yours oughta be. I thought we played a hard football game. It's a shame it had to end this way. I know this group right here. This group isn't gonna lay down. This group is gonna fight like hell.

"Keep your heads up. Be positive. You played with class—you played hard.

"We're two and two," he said, looking around the room at the players, "and I'm gonna make a statement—and it will hold true: We will finish this season nine and two. We got to keep fighting. We got to keep pushing on."

• • •

"Don't let up. Gonna play hard for 30 minutes, then we're gonna come in here at halftime. I don't care what phase of the game we're in, we're gonna strike 'em. Offensive linemen, you're gonna do what? We're gonna run the damn ball. Defense, I'm gonna tell you something right now. They're gonna try to run the ball straight at us, and I want to shut it out completely."

It was 4 p.m. on November 4, 1995. U of L was preparing to leave the locker room for its home game against Tulane, and Cooper was giving the Cardinals their pep talk.

At 4:05 p.m., it was time to go for combat. "Everybody up to the door," Cooper said.

At the intermission, Tulane held a 14-10 lead, but U of L seemed optimistic about coming back in the second half. As Cooper told the team, "Hey, guys, we have kept them in the game! They made a couple of plays, a couple of runs, an interception for a touchdown. Other than that, we've been in damn control.

"Defense, you better go out—we gotta shut it down! We gotta fight, scratch, do everything we can to shut it down!

"Offense, we haven't been stopped by them. We stopped ourselves. Let's go out and let's cut out the foolish penalties! Defense, you better be damn perfect! Damn perfect!

"Let's go out there," Cooper said, pointing with his right forefinger, "let's play together these 30 minutes!"

The players cheered.

"It's our half right here," Cooper said.

The second half did belong to U of L, which returned to the locker room with a 34-14 victory.

"Grab your teammate's hand," Cooper told his players as they knelt on a knee and formed a circle around their coach, who was standing on a chair, his head bowed. "Think about somebody you love and who loves you. Be thankful for them. Be thankful for each other, be thankful for this football team and this university. Be thankful for the opportunity to play the great game of football."

Those words—"Be thankful for the opportunity to play the great game of football"—had special meaning this week. Just a week ago, sophomore flanker John Bell had been a valuable member of the U of L team. But he suffered a career-ending neck injury in a 31-0 victory over Maryland, and the day before the Tulane game, he underwent surgery in Georgia.

U of L had dedicated this game to him, and after the Rev. Bob Bailey led the team in the Lord's Prayer, a smiling Cooper said: "First of all, guys, give yourselves a hand."

The players broke out into applause.

• • •

"That's the way to go out and put their lights out and play a complete second half—offense, defense and the kicking game," Cooper said. "Guys, there are a lot of guys who deserve game balls. But I'm going to only give one game ball. He couldn't be here. He played his last game last week."

The players cheered and clapped.

"I talked to him right before kick-off," Cooper continued. "He said to deliver a couple of words. He said, 'Go get after their butt and good luck to you guys.' I told him we were gonna win the game for him. We're giving him the only game ball."

Traditionally, after their games, the U of L players gather together in the center of the locker room, reach a hand out and, after a count of "one, two, three," yell in unison, "Cards!"

This time they added a twist to their post-game ritual.

"J.B. on three, baby," one of them said. "One, two three—J.B.!"

Many of the players had remembered Bell by wearing either his number 12 on a wristband or sleeve, on a sock or towel, on the back of a hand or helmet. Some wore his initials, J.B.

He was in a hospital many miles away, but if ever a player was with a team in spirit, it was John Bell for this particular game.

John Bell

Traditions.

Besides its "Cards" cheer, the U of L football team has certain other locker-room traditions.

In 1994, new carpeting was laid in the locker room, with a brown football—about five yards long—in the middle. Smack in the center of the football was the head of a Cardinal bird. A tradition was born with this football and redbird. Nobody is supposed to step on the ball or the bird. The tradition was founded out of respect to the Cardinal bird and to the university.

"We're trying to get a little tradition going," explained offensive guard Shawn Kries.

"I've been known to step on that football a couple times," Kries added, "but you don't step on the red."

Cooper, in his first year as U of L's head man, has been known to step on the football himself, but when he drew up a punt-return coverage before the Northeast Louisiana game in the Cardinal Stadium locker room on November 11, 1995, those players who gathered around to look at the diagram and listen to their coach all made sure not to step on the

nearby football.

With the time for kickoff drawing near, Cooper then delivered his pre-game talk: "Let's outhit 'em from the start. Execute the game plan on offense and defense, outhit 'em and make sure, offense, we win the time of possession. Control the clock. Defense, STOP THE DAMN RUN! Don't let 'em run the ball at all. Cut it out completely, no big plays and force some turnovers. Play as hard as you can play. Got a couple minutes. Get yourselves ready in your own individual way."

The offensive linemen met together in the shower, and someone was heard to say of Northeast Louisiana: "They'll roll over and die."

Leaving the locker room for the Northeast Louisiana game, the U of L players went out and followed Cooper's instructions from the outset, gaining their opponent 126 to three yards rushing and controlling the clock (9 minutes and 42 seconds, compared with the opponent's 5:18) in the first quarter. U of L led 12-0 at the end of that period and 25-0 at the half. A touchdown late in the half came when the hustling Kries recovered a fumble in the end zone. In celebrating his first collegiate touchdown, Kries spiked the football, which drew a 15-yard penalty.

Cooper would remind him of that penalty.

Soon after the team returned to the locker room at halftime, the 5-foot-11 Kries stood on a chair and told his teammates: "Hey, I want to apologize for getting us a 15-yard penalty on my touchdown—but (bleep) it."

So much for a formal apology.

When freshman punter Jeremy Borseth walked across the middle of the locker room and stepped on the bird, somebody noticed and said, "Get off that Cardinal, man." Borseth quickly hopped off the Cardinal.

After the coaches met as a group at halftime, the assistants came into the locker room and talked to the players. Cooper later entered and, while walking across the middle of the locker room, he unknowingly stepped on the football in the middle of the carpet. After realizing what he had done, he stepped back off the ball quickly, shaking his head with a smile.

With U of L in charge of the game, Cooper stressed to his players not to let up in the second half. "First of all," he stressed, "let me just say this: The damn game isn't over. I've been ahead before 31-7 and got beat. The second thing is I refuse to let it get sloppy. I'm talking about penalties, I'm talking about turnovers, I'm talking about pushing and shoving, I'm talking about us looking dis-

Shawn Kries

organized. We will NOT look sloppy! We will go finish this damn game. I don't care who's in the game, you gotta play hard and you better know what the hell to do and it will not look sloppy.

"Defense, I want to keep that on the damn board," Cooper said, forming a zero with his right hand. "I want to keep a damn zero on the board. Defensive backs, don't give 'em a damn big play. Whatever happens, offense, protect the damn ball. We're gonna control the line of scrimmage up front."

Before the team left the locker room, Cooper spotted Kries and, with a smile, said: "Hey, Spike Man, you owe me one. Get a couple pancakes (referring to a block that flattens a defensive player)."

After U of L returned to the locker room following a rousing 39-0 victory, after Cooper told the players to grab a teammate's hand and think about somebody they loved, after the Lord's Prayer was said in unison, the coach told his team: "All right, first of all, give your-

selves a hand."

Players applauded and whistled.

"Now that's the way to go finish a game off," Cooper said. "Hell of a win. Hell of a win. I'm only going to give a couple of game balls tonight. This young man should have definitely had one last week. I'm going to give him one this week—Miguel Montano."

Cheers rang out.

Cooper also awarded a game ball to safety Rico Clark, who had two interceptions.

Former U of L star tight end Jamie Asher, a rookie with the Washington Redskins, was a visitor in the locker room, and Cooper made it a point to single him out. "Give him a hand," Cooper said. "If I understand correctly, he caught his first pass last week in the NFL," Cooper said. The players cheered.

Afterward, Kries was sitting in front of his locker, having an outside layer of tape removed from his shoes.

How did it feel to score a touch-

Jamie Asher

Miguel Montano

down?

"It felt like I was about 10 feet tall," Kries said. "I've been waiting to do that for five years."

Assistant coach Greg Nord walked by and told Kries: "Spike, good job."

Spike Kries. A nickname may have been born on this evening at Cardinal Stadium.

• • •

It was halftime of the season's final game for Ron Cooper's first U of L team. U of L was leading North Texas 30-7 at Cardinal Stadium on November 18, 1995, and while the coaches were meeting to review the first half and discuss strategy, the players were a talkative bunch in the locker room. They were a happy group, especially a smiling Miguel Montano, who had caught his first career touchdown pass at U of L in the first quarter and made another scoring reception in the second period. (He would catch still another TD pass in the second half.)

The coaches came into the locker room, diagrammed plays and alignments and then it was time for Cooper to give his final halftime talk of the season. "Everybody listen up," he said. "It was a helluva first half. Helluva first half. I want to clean the damn thing up now. I don't want to look sloppy. This team's moving the ball a little bit, defense. I don't want any damn more points. Offense, control the line of scrimmage. Play as hard as you can play, offense. No more turnovers. Whip their ass up front. Defense, no more points. Guys, we got the ball to start it off. Let's put them under. To start off, offense, let's shove it right down their throat."

U of L went out and finished the job off in the second half, winning 57-14.

Afterward, Cooper stood on a chair in the locker room and said: "Everybody over to that side. Give me just the seniors right up here. All the seniors up here."

The 12 seniors on the team flanked him. "First of all, grab your teammate's

hand," Cooper said, standing with one arm around Roman Oben and the other around Shawn Kries, two of the U of L seniors.

When the team left the locker room on September 2 for the season opener at Kentucky, Cooper asked the players to grab a teammate's hand and be thankful, a recurring theme throughout the season, and now, with the last game having been played, he said: "First of all, grab your teammate's hand, close your eyes, meditate, be thankful, think about somebody you love and who loves you. Be thankful for your teammates and this football team and this university. Be thankful for these seniors, who played as hard as they could play and helped lead this team this year."

After the Lord's Prayer, Cooper said: "Guys, what a way to end the season. I came in December 29th, took over, met with this group (the seniors) early January. You're talking about a coaching change, a change of philosophy, a successful program, and I want to say that this group up here has been the best group that any head football coach could come in and be in charge of. What a way to help me with the attitude of this football team, to help with the change, to help us keep pushing on when things were a little down this year. I think everybody in here needs to give this group a hand."

The rest of the team applauded the seniors.

"One heck of a win," Cooper said. "Only good can happen from here."

Cooper reminded the team that some high-school and junior-college recruits were in the locker room. "Make sure you meet 'em," he told his team.

Cooper shook hands with several recruits, telling them: "Guys, you need to be here next year."

With a 7-4 record under his belt in his first season at U of L, Ron Cooper was looking to the future at the University of Louisville.

• • •

Alas for Cardinal fans, however, Cooper wasn't able to build on the promise of the 1995 season. The Cards beat Kentucky again, 38-14, to open the 1996 season and whipped Michigan State in East Lansing, 30-20, in the fourth game. But the final record was 5-6, disappointing for a team that had a defense ranked 13th in the nation.

The bottom fell out in 1997. Despite a potent offense built around quarterback Chris Redman and receivers Ibn Green and Miguel Montano, the Cards struggled in at 1-10, the most losses in the program's history.

With attendance and support dwindling the year before the move to the new stadium, Tom Jurich, U of L's new Athletics Director, reluctantly fired Cooper after the season. Within a week, however, Jurich had the new coach in place—a plain-talking, pass-happy veteran who wore cowboy boots and had never coached east of the Rocky Mountains: John L. Smith.

Louisville's defensive unit was 13th in the nation in 1996 under Ron Cooper.

Chapter 16
The Dawning of a New Day

On September 5, 1998, a crowd of 42,643, largest ever to see a football game in Louisville, showed up for the dedication game of Papa John's Cardinal Stadium and the first game of the John L. Smith era. The opponent, fittingly, was a University of Kentucky team led by ballyhooed junior quarterback Tim Couch, one of the preseason front-runners to win the Heisman Trophy. Before the game, Smith told Ashley McGeachy of *The Courier-Journal* that, realistically, it would take three years before the Cards could "start putting (bowl) rings on these kids' fingers." However, Smith added a tantalizing bit of speculation.

"I don't put it out of the (realm of) possibility that we could go to a bowl this year," he said. "We're going to have to have some luck and some things go right and stay healthy."

That sort of optimism is one of the reasons U of L Athletics Director Tom Jurich hired Smith to replace Ron Cooper. It was a breathtaking process. The only name on Jurich's short list was Smith, who had impressed him for years with his work at Idaho and Utah State. So there was no search committee, no long interviewing process. Jurich simply went after "The Cowboy," as he affectionately calls Smith, and won him over in a whirlwind

recruiting process that included a private plane trip to Louisville for a day at Churchill Downs.

Smith, who was born on November 15, 1948, was a native of Idaho who played quarterback at Weber State from 1969-71. After beginning his coaching career as a graduate assistant at his alma mater, Smith eventually hooked up with Dennis Erickson, who later coached Miami to a national championship. After serving on Erickson's staff at Idaho, Wyoming and Washington State, Smith got the head job at Idaho in 1989. In six seasons there, Smith coached the Vandals to five NCAA I-AA playoff appearances and developed 12 All-Americans (including future NFL quarterbacks John Friesz and Doug Nussmier).

In 1995, he moved into Division I at Utah State. In three seasons under Smith, the perennially downtrodden Aggies went 4-7, 6-5 and 6-6. His 1997 team won the Big West Conference and played in the Humanitarian Bowl.

"John L. Smith is a man of high integrity and a real blue-collar guy with a tremendous work ethic," Jurich said.

During spring practice, Smith quickly discovered that U of L needed a lot of help on defense and in its offensive line. But he also was impressed with a

solid core of offensive "skill" players that included record-setting quarterback Chris Redman and tight end Ibn Green, who had been friends and teammates at Louisville Male High before signing with U of L. In addition, Smith liked speedy wideout Arnold Jackson, who was dangerous as both a big-play receiver and a punt returner, and running back Leroy Collins, a junior college transfer who challenged Frank Moreau for the starting job.

In Redman, the Cards had a potential future NFL quarterback who also had deep roots in the community. His grandfather, Lloyd, and his dad, Bob, both played at U of L. As a senior at Male in 1994, Redman set all kinds of passing records and was picked as the High School Player of the Year by Parade Magazine.

He was set to go to U of L to play for Howard Schnellenberger. However, when Schnellenberger took the Oklahoma job, Redman went to Illinois to play for quarterback coach Greg Landry. When Landry was fired the day after Redman signed, Redman petitioned to the NCAA to let him out of his letter-of-intent. His request was granted and he considered joining Schnellenberger at Oklahoma. However, when Schnellenberger was fired after one season, Redman chose to stay home at U of L.

That turned out to be a lucky break for the Cards. In 1996 he put together the most prolific freshman season of any quarterback in U of L history, and a year later, he shattered the school single-season passing marks for attempts, completions and yardage. As he headed into his junior season, Redman was considered to be one of the nation's top passers.

Still, only the most rabid Card partisans figured the team had a serious chance to upset Kentucky and its "Air Raid II" passing attack. The previous year, new Coach Hal Mumme had turned the offense over to Couch, who had proceeded to set all sorts of school conference and national records. That team had

a 5-6 record that easily could have been 7-4, leading to much talk of a possible bowl season in 1998. When the players reported for fall practice, Mumme had given them T-shirts imprinted with the date 1-1-99, and never mind that UK hadn't been to a New Year's Day bowl since 1952.

It was a memorable grand opening for the new stadium, rife with hot-air

New coach John L. Smith directed the Cardinals to the nation's best turnaround in 1998, rising from a 1-10 mark before his arrival to a 7-4 record and a Motor City Bowl berth in his initial year.

balloons, world-class tailgating and appropriate pre-game ceremonies. One of the dignitaries was Johnny Unitas, who seemed thrilled that the office complex at the north end of the stadium would include the BellSouth Johnny Unitas Football Museum and a statue of the U of L great who came to be known as "Mr.

Ibn Green

Chris Redman

Quarterback" in his career with the Baltimore Colts.

"They haven't done anything like this for me in Baltimore," Unitas said. "I don't know why. But it's an honor for U of L to do it for me here. Usually they wait until you're dead. Hey, do you think they're telling me something?"

Speaking of dead, the heat was killing. It was so hot—more than 90 degrees at kickoff—that some fans left in the first quarter, not so much because of UK's early domination but because there was air-conditioning to be found in their vehicles. Otherwise, however, the opening was a hit. The traffic and parking problems weren't nearly as horrific as anticipated, and even UK fans seemed impressed with the new stadium and its amenities.

The only disappointment, from U of L's standpoint, was the game.

With Couch living up to his hype, the Cats jumped all over the Cards and rolled up 801 yards on the way to a 68-34 victory. So much for Smith's declaration that U of L needed to "rip off the rearview mirror" and forget the previous season. The Cards who opened the new stadium looked depressingly like the ones who had closed the old one. "I was mad and a little frustrated," Smith said, "because I felt like we were better than we showed."

The next week the Cards traveled to Utah, a program that Smith had butted heads with during his years at Utah State. Opening a new stadium for the second consecutive week, the Cards allowed the Utes to jump to a 14-0 lead in the first two minutes. Redman got off to a tough start, with two dropped passes and three interceptions in his first seven attempts. Although U of L rallied for a 14-14 tie, the Utes dedicated their new Rice Stadium with a 45-22 win.

"At that point," Jurich later admitted, "I was wondering if we would win a game."

The following Thursday, September 17, Smith gathered the players and deliv-

ered a blistering speech. He said that anybody who wasn't willing to give 100 percent on every play should get out of the program. The next day, after the team had arrived in Champaign, Illinois, for its game against Illinois, Collins was the catalyst of a players-only meeting. He read his teammates an inspirational poem that he had written and distributed pieces of chains, asking everybody to attach them to their shoelaces in a display of unity.

The result: U of L 35, Illinois 9.

After a game in which Redman drilled the Big Ten team for 275 yards and Collins rushed for 159 yards and three TDs, Smith affectionately slapped each of his players' faces. "We had to get one win," Smith said. "We had to start the belief that there could be more."

And there were.

The Cards came home to play an unbeaten Boston College team that owned a win over Georgia Tech. In one of the Cards best all-around performances in years, the offense racked up 465 yards (with Redman passing for 362), the defense held BC running star Mike Cloud to only 124 yards, and the special teams sprung loose Zek Parker for an average of 46.5 yards per kick return in U of L's win.

Moving into Conference USA play, the Cards moved to 3-2 by drilling hapless Cincinnati, 62-19 at home. They

Mike Watkins

went on the road with high hopes of upsetting Southern Mississippi in Hattiesburg, only to be thrashed, 56-21, by a team that was physically superior on both sides of the ball.

But the setback was only temporary.

Going against unbeaten Tulane on October 17 in the Louisiana Superdome, the Cards fell barely short of upsetting the Green Wave, then ranked No. 23 in the country. With only seconds remaining and U of L inside the Green Wave 10-yard line, a heavy Tulane rush forced Redman to hurry his throw to Lavell Boyd. The ball barely fell short, a sad ending for Redman on a day when he broke his C-USA records for completions (41) and passing yards (477).

After that, the Cards ran the table.

In a 35-32 win over Memphis on October 24, Redman threw for 506 yards, breaking Jay Gruden's career records for TD passes and pass attempts in the process. Next came a 63-34 victory over Division I-AA Western Kentucky in which Collins (five TDs, 154 yards) and Jackson (11 catches for 126 yards and a touchdown) had big games.

After an off week that allowed the horse-racing fans among their supporters to watch the Breeders Cup at Churchill Downs, the Cards traveled to East Carolina on No-

Coach John L. Smith brought a potent offensive scheme to U of L and orchestrated the nation's biggest turnaround in his initial year in 1998.

vember 14 and came away with a 63-45 win that guaranteed a winning season. However, U of L's euphoria was tempered by an injury to Redman, who had riddled the Pirates for 44 completions and 592 yards (yes, new C-USA records in those categories). Hit by an East Carolina defender, Redman suffered a sprained left knee.

All week before the season finale against Army in U of L's new stadium, the newspapers and airwaves were filled with speculation about whether Redman would play. It wasn't announced officially that he would be out until just before kickoff. However, with Redman watching from the sidelines, backup Mike Watkins did a masterful job, completing 20 of 30 passes to lead the Cards to a 35-21 victory.

At midfield immediately after the game, Smith, Jurich and U of L president Dr. John Shumaker accepted an invitation to play in the Motor City Bowl on December 23 in the Pontiac Silverdome, home of the NFL's Detroit Lions.

"It just shows you we got a bunch of not-so-very-smart kids because they

believe everything we tell 'em and try to do it," Smith said. "It was a miraculous year."

The bowl game against Marshall turned out to be anti-climactic.

Like U of L, the Thunderin' Herd had high-octane attack built around 6-foot-3 Chad Pennington, a potential future NFL quarterback. After reviewing videotapes of Marshall, Smith cracked that "the first one to 49 wins."

At halftime, the teams were tied at 21. But then U of L's injury-riddled defense reverted to the sloppy play it had exhibited in the opening game against Kentucky and allowed the Herd to break the game open with 17 unanswered points. Although Redman played admirably, completing 35 of 54 passes for 336 yards, he wasn't protected as well as Pennington, who riddled the Cards for 411 yards and four TDs on sensational 18-of-24 passing.

"Our players are to be congratulated and commended on the season," Smith said, "but we have got to get a lot better. And we will. This made us realize how much better we have to get."

The positives of the bowl trip included extra practice and, more importantly for the long term, an impressive turnout of fans. Although the weather in Detroit was frightfully cold and the game was only two days before Christmas, an estimated 18,000 Cardinal fans showed up in the Silverdome—a fact that will be duly noted the next time the team is eligible for a bowl.

But perhaps the biggest payoff came in recruiting. The combination of the new stadium and the bowl season resulted in the signing of 24 recruits who have the potential to speed up Smith's steady drive toward the Top 25.

"Our staff did a great job of going out and finding the best talent," a pleased Smith said. "From the very beginning of the recruiting process, we said we weren't going to take a backseat to bigger programs—and we didn't."

When U of L Director of Athletics Tom Jurich (from left) introduced new coach John L. Smith and his wife Diana on November 24, 1997, few could have imagined that the Cardinals would have the nation's top offense and a 7-4 record in his first season.

Chapter 17
Appendices

UNIVERSITY OF LOUISVILLE
ALL-TIME YEAR-BY-YEAR RESULTS

Year	Overall				Home				Away			
	W	L	T	Pct	W	L	T	Pct.	W	L	T	Pct.
1912	3	1	0	.750	2	0	0	1.000	1	1	0	.500
1913	5	1	0	.833	4	1	0	.800	1	0	0	1.000
1914	1	4	0	.200	1	2	0	.333	0	2	0	.000
1915	1	5	1	.214	1	4	1	.250	0	1	0	.000
1916	2	3	1	.417	2	2	1	.500	0	1	0	.000
1917-1920			No Formal Teams									
1921	2	2	1	.500	2	0	0	1.000	0	2	1	.125
1922	2	7	0	.222	1	4	0	.200	1	3	0	.250
1923	5	3	0	.625	4	1	0	.800	1	2	0	.333
1924	3	5	1	.389	2	2	0	.500	1	3	1	.300
1925	8	0	0	1.000	4	0	0	1.000	4	0	0	1.000
1926	6	2	0	.750	2	1	0	.667	4	1	0	.800
1927	4	4	0	.500	3	1	0	.750	1	3	0	.250
1928	1	7	0	.125	1	3	0	.250	0	4	0	.000
1929	3	5	0	.375	2	3	0	.400	1	2	0	.333
1930	5	3	0	.625	4	1	0	.800	1	2	0	.333
1931	0	8	0	.000	0	5	0	.000	0	3	0	.000
1932	0	9	0	.000	0	4	0	.000	0	5	0	.000
1933	1	7	0	.125	1	3	0	.250	0	4	0	.000
1934	2	5	0	.286	1	2	0	.333	1	3	0	.250
1935	1	6	1	.188	1	3	0	.250	0	3	1	.125
1936	4	4	0	.500	3	1	0	.750	1	3	0	.250
1937	2	5	1	.313	2	2	1	.500	0	3	0	.000
1938	2	6	0	.333	1	3	0	.250	1	3	0	.250
1939	5	2	1	.688	4	0	0	1.000	1	2	1	.375
1940	3	5	1	.437	1	2	1	.375	2	3	0	.400
1941	4	4	0	.500	2	2	0	.500	2	2	0	.500
1942	2	3	0	.400	1	2	0	.333	1	1	0	.500
1943-45			No Formal Teams									
1946	6	2	0	.750	4	0	0	1.000	2	2	0	.500
1947	7	0	1	.938	5	0	0	1.000	2	0	1	.833
1948	5	5	0	.500	4	1	0	.800	1	4	0	.200
1949	8	3	0	.727	5	2	0	.714	3	1	0	.750

UNIVERSITY OF LOUISVILLE
ALL-TIME YEAR-BY-YEAR RESULTS (Continued)

Year	Overall W	L	T	Pct	Home W	L	T	Pct.	Away W	L	T	Pct.
1950	3	6	1	.350	2	2	0	.500	1	4	1	.250
1951	5	4	0	.556	4	2	0	.667	1	2	0	.333
1952	3	5	0	.375	2	1	0	.667	1	4	0	.200
1953	1	7	0	.125	0	3	0	.000	1	4	0	.200
1954	3	6	0	.333	3	2	0	.600	0	4	0	.000
1955	7	2	0	.778	5	0	0	1.000	2	2	0	.500
1956	6	3	0	.667	3	3	0	.500	3	0	0	1.000
1957	9	1	0	.900	5	0	0	1.000	3	1	0	.750
1958	4	4	0	.500	3	1	0	.750	1	3	0	.250
1959	6	4	0	.600	3	1	0	.750	3	3	0	.500
1960	7	2	0	.778	5	1	0	.833	2	1	0	.667
1961	6	3	0	.667	3	2	0	.600	3	1	0	.750
1962	6	4	0	.600	3	2	0	.600	3	2	0	.600
1963	3	7	0	.300	2	3	0	.400	1	4	0	.200
1964	1	9	0	.100	0	5	0	.000	1	4	0	.200
1965	6	4	0	.600	4	1	0	.800	2	3	0	.400
1966	6	4	0	.600	4	1	0	.800	2	3	0	.400
1967	5	5	0	.500	4	1	0	.800	1	4	0	.200
1968	5	5	0	.500	2	3	0	.400	3	2	0	.600
1969	5	4	1	.550	4	1	0	.800	1	3	1	.300
1970	8	3	1	.700	5	0	0	1.000	3	3	0	.500
1971	6	3	1	.650	4	1	0	.800	2	2	1	.500
1972	9	1	0	.900	4	1	0	.800	5	0	0	1.000
1973	5	6	0	.454	3	2	0	.600	2	3	0	.333
1974	4	7	0	.363	2	4	0	.333	2	3	0	.400
1975	2	9	0	.189	2	3	0	.400	0	6	0	.000
1976	5	6	0	.455	4	2	0	.667	1	4	0	.200
1977	7	4	1	.625	5	1	1	.800	2	2	0	.500
1978	7	4	0	.636	5	2	0	.714	2	2	0	.500
1979	4	6	1	.409	2	3	1	.416	2	3	0	.400
1980	5	6	0	.455	3	3	0	.500	2	3	0	.400
1981	5	6	0	.455	4	2	0	.667	1	4	0	.200
1982	5	6	0	.455	4	2	0	.667	1	4	0	.200
1983	3	8	0	.273	3	3	0	.500	0	5	0	.000
1984	2	9	0	.182	1	5	0	.167	1	4	0	.200
1985	2	9	0	.182	2	4	0	.333	0	5	0	.000
1986	3	8	0	.273	2	3	0	.400	1	5	0	.200
1987	3	7	1	.428	3	3	0	.500	0	4	1	.000
1988	8	3	0	.727	5	1	0	.833	3	2	0	.600
1989	6	5	0	.545	2	2	0	.500	4	2	0	.667
1990	10	1	1	.875	6	0	0	1.000	3	1	1	.700
1991	2	9	0	.182	2	4	0	.333	0	5	0	.000
1992	5	6	0	.454	3	2	0	.600	2	4	0	.333
1993	9	3	0	.750	5	0	0	1.000	3	3	0	.500
1994	6	5	0	.545	4	2	0	.667	2	3	0	.400
1995	7	4	0	.636	4	2	0	.667	3	2	0	.600
1996	5	6	0	.454	2	3	0	.400	3	3	0	.500
1997	1	10	0	.091	1	5	0	.167	0	5	0	.000
1998	7	5	0	.583	5	1	0	.833	2	4	0	.333
Totals	**351**	**380**	**17**	**.481**	**228**	**158**	**6**	**.589**	**120**	**220**	**19**	**.361**

Note: Louisville holds a 3-2-1 record in games played at neutral sites.

UNIVERSITY OF LOUISVILLE
ALL-TIME COACHING RECORDS

Coach	Seasons	Yrs	W	L	T	Pct.
Lester Larson	1912-13	2	8	2	0	.800
Dr. Bruce Baker	1914	1	1	4	0	.200
Will Duffy	1915-16	2	3	8	2	.308
Bill Duncan	1921-22	2	4	9	1	.321
Fred Enke	1923-24	2	8	8	1	.500
Tom King	1925-30	6	27	21	0	.563
Jack McGrath	1931	1	0	8	0	.000
C.V. Money	1932	1	0	9	0	.000
Ben Cregor	1933-35	3	4	18	1	.196
Laurie Apitz	1936-42	7	22	29	3	.435
Frank Camp	1946-68	23	118	95	2	.556
Lee Corso	1969-72	4	28	11	3	.690
T.W. Alley	1973-74	2	9	13	0	.409
Vince Gibson	1975-79	5	25	29	2	.464
Bob Weber	1980-84	5	20	35	0	.364
H. Schnellenberger	1985-94	10	54	56	2	.491
Ron Cooper	1995-97	3	13	20	0	.394
John L. Smith	1998-	1	7	5	0	.583
Totals		**79**	**351**	**380**	**17**	**.481**

Note: Louisville suspended its football program from 1917 to 1920 due to World War I and from 1943 to 1945 due to World War II.

Schnellenberger (left) returned to U of L as an honorary coach in the Cards' 1998 spring game as new Cardinal head coach John L. Smith prepared for his first campaign.

UNIVERSITY OF LOUISVILLE
ALL-TIME GAME-BY-GAME RESULTS

1912 (Won 3, Lost 1)
COACH: Lester Larson
CAPTAIN: Stanley Walker

Date	Site	Dec.	Score
Oct. 11	Transylvania (A)	W	32-0
Oct. 17	Centre (H)	W	23-6
Oct. 28	Kentucky (A)	L	0-41
Nov. 15	Hanover (H)	W	73-0
			128-47

1913 (Won 5, Lost 1)
COACH: Lester Larson
CAPTAIN: Stanley Walker

Date	Site	Dec.	Score
Oct. 4	Bethel (Ky.) (H)	W	48-0
Oct. 11	Moore's Hill (A)	W	77-0
Oct. 18	Wash. (Tenn.) (H)	W	100-0
Oct. 25	Cumberland (H)	W	6-0
Nov. 1	Butler (H)	W	20-0
Nov. 22	Kentucky (H)	L	0-20
			251-20

1914 (Won 1, Lost 4)
COACH: Bruce Baker
CAPTAIN: Roy Daniel

Date	Site	Dec.	Score
Oct. 17	Tennessee (H)	L	0-66
Oct. 31	Wabash (H)	L	3-7
Nov. 7	Cumberland (A)	L	0-20
Nov. 14	Kentucky (A)	L	0-42
Nov. 21	Rose Poly (A)	W	23-0
			26-135

1915 (Won 1, Lost 5, Tied 1)
COACH: Will Duffy
CAPTAIN: Owen Foster

Date	Site	Dec.	Score
Oct. 2	Centre (H)	T	0-0
Oct. 9	Wabash (A)	L	0-38
Oct. 16	Chattanooga (H)	L	6-21
Oct. 30	Rose Poly (H)	W	22-6
Nov. 6	Kentucky (H)	L	0-15
Nov. 13	Franklin (H)	L	7-13
Nov. 25	Transylvania (H)	L	0-26
			35-119

1916 (Won 2, Lost 3, Tied 1)
COACH: Will Duffy
CAPTAIN: Maurice Daniel

Date	Site	Dec.	Score
Oct. 14	Centre (H)	T	0-0
Oct. 21	Chattanooga (H)	W	6-0
Oct. 28	Butler (H)	W	19-7
Nov. 4	Georgetown Coll. (H)	L	0-41
Nov. 18	Franklin (H)	L	12-16
Nov. 30	Transylvania (H)	L	0-13
			37-77

1917-1920
No Formal Teams

1921 (Won 2, Lost 2, Tied 1)
COACH: Bill Duncan
CAPTAIN: E.B. Kirk

Date	Site	Dec.	Score
Oct. 22	Hanover* (H)	W	19-8
Oct. 29	Bethel (Ky.) (A)	T	0-0
Nov. 5	Transylvania (A)	L	0-7
Nov. 18	Ky. Wesleyan (H)	W	30-0
Nov. 26	Marshall (A)	L	0-14
			49-29

*Louisville won by forfeit when the
Hanover coach disagreed with an official's
call and took his team off the field.

1922 (Won 2, Lost 7)
COACH: Bill Duncan
CAPTAIN: Tommy Kienzie

Date	Site	Dec.	Score
Sept. 30	Western Kentucky (H)	L	0-6
Oct. 7	Bethel (Ky.) (H)	L	12-14
Oct. 14	Kentucky (A)	L	0-63
Oct. 21	Franklin (H)	L	6-27
Oct. 28	Centre (A)	L	7-32
Nov. 4	Cincinnati (H)	W	28-0
Nov. 11	Rose Poly (A)	W	6-0
Nov. 18	Centenary (H)	L	13-39
Nov. 30	Marshall (A)	L	7-21
			79-202

1923 (Won 5, Lost 3)
COACH: Fred Enke
CAPTAIN: Art Vandervert

Date	Site	Dec.	Score
Sept. 29	Western Kentucky (A)	L	7-19
Oct. 6	Union University (A)	L	6-13
Oct. 13	Morris Harvey (H)	W	27-0
Oct. 20	Franklin (H)	L	0-35
Oct. 27	Rose Poly (H)	W	13-0
Nov. 3	Transylvania (H)	W	12-0
Nov. 10	Ky. Wesleyan (H)	W	7-0
Nov. 17	Georgetown Coll. (A)	W	12-6
			84-73

1924 (Won 3, Lost 5, Tied 1)
COACH: Fred Enke
CAPTAIN: Paul Osborne

Date	Site	Dec.	Score
Oct. 4	Kentucky (A)	L	0-29
Oct. 11	Western Kentucky (H)	W	12-7
Oct. 18	Georgetown Coll. (A)	W	9-6
Oct. 25	Transylvania (H)	L	0-3
Nov. 1	Rose Poly (A)	L	6-18
Nov. 8	Ky. Wesleyan (A)	T	0-0
Nov. 15	King (H)	L	0-16
Nov. 22	Chattanooga (H)	W	10-0
Nov. 27	Marshall (A)	L	6-16
			43-95

1925 (Won 8, Lost 0)
COACH: Tom King
CAPTAIN: Armand Fischer

Date	Site	Dec.	Score
Oct. 3	Evansville (H)	W	20-0
Oct. 10	Western Kentucky (A)	W	6-0
Oct. 17	Hanover (A)	W	24-0
Oct. 24	Ky. Wesleyan (H)	W	6-0
Oct. 30	Transylvania (A)	W	7-0
Nov. 7	Rose Poly (H)	W	30-0
Nov. 21	Toledo (H)	W	33-0
Nov. 26	Marshall (A)	W	7-2
			133-2

1926 (Won 6, Lost 2)
COACH: Tom King
CAPTAIN: Jack Dougherty

Date	Site	Dec.	Score
Oct. 2	Ogden (A)	W	79-0
Oct. 9	Rose Poly (A)	W	49-0
Oct. 16	Xavier (A)	L	7-20
Oct. 30	Centre (H)	L	0-6
Nov. 6	Western Kentucky (H)	W	26-10
Nov. 13	Ky. Wesleyan (A)	W	25-12
Nov. 20	Marshall (H)	W	27-3
Nov. 25	Florida Southern (A)	W	13-0
			226-51

1927 (Won 4, Lost 4)
COACH: Tom King
CAPTAIN: Harvey Mayhall

Date	Site	Dec.	Score
Oct. 8	Transylvania (H)	W	25-6
Oct. 15	Murray State (H)	W	14-0
Oct. 22	Marshall (A)	L	6-37
Oct. 29	Centre (H)	W	40-7
Nov. 5	Western Kentucky (A)	L	6-7
Nov. 12	Eastern Kentucky (A)	W	21-13
Nov. 19	Davids & Elkins (H)	L	0-32
Nov. 24	Centenary (A)	L	2-59
			114-161

1928 (Won 1, Lost 7)
COACH: Tom King
CAPTAIN: Jim Tom Robertson

Date	Site	Dec.	Score
Oct. 6	Eastern Kentucky (H)	W	72-0
Oct. 13	Detroit (A)	L	0-46
Oct. 20	Chattanooga (A)	L	0-70
Oct. 27	Transylvania (H)	L	0-18
Nov. 3	Western Kentucky (A)	L	0-20
Nov. 10	Centre (H)	L	0-7
Nov. 17	St. Louis (A)	L	0-12
Nov. 24	Marshall (H)	L	0-13
			72-186

118

Cardinal Football

1929 (Won 3, Lost 5)
COACH: Tom King
CAPTAIN: Game Captains

Date	Site	Dec.	Score
Oct. 2	Cincinnati (H)	L	0-7
Oct. 11	Transylvania (A)	L	0-9
Oct. 19	Western Kentucky (H)	L	0-13
Oct. 26	Marshall (A)	L	6-25
Nov. 2	Eastern Kentucky (A)	W	19-6
Nov. 9	Centre (H)	L	0-41
Nov. 16	Earlham (H)	W	6-0
Nov. 23	Georgetown Coll. (H)	W	6-0
			37-101

1930 (Won 5, Lost 3)
COACH: Tom King
CAPTAIN: Tommy Thompson

Date	Site	Dec.	Score
Oct. 4	Hanover (H)	W	32-12
Oct. 11	Transylvania (H)	W	18-0
Oct. 17	Eastern Kentucky (H)	W	52-0
Oct. 25	Western Kentucky (A)	L	6-7
Nov. 1	Centre (H)	L	0-28
Nov. 8	DePaul (A)	L	0-14
Nov. 15	Marshall (A)	W	13-12
Nov. 22	Earlham (H)	W	13-0
			134-73

1931 (Won 0, Lost 8)
COACH: Jack McGrath
CO-CAPTAINS: Ben Reid and Guy Schearer

Date	Site	Dec.	Score
Oct. 2	Hanover (H)	L	0-3
Oct. 9	Transylvania* (H)	L	0-1
Oct. 16	Butler (A)	L	6-61
Oct. 24	Eastern Kentucky* (H)	L	0-1
Oct. 31	Western Kentucky (A)	L	6-20
Nov. 7	DePaul (H)	L	0-46
Nov. 14	Georgetown College (A)	L	6-20
Nov. 21	Centre (H)	L	0-75
			18-227

*Although Louisville originally beat both Transylvania (13-12) and Eastern Kentucky (19-14), the games were forfeited on Nov. 13, 1931, when it was discovered that Louisville had used two ineligible players.

1932 (Won 0, Lost 9)
COACH: C.V. (Red) Money
CAPTAIN: Tom Giannini

Date	Site	Dec.	Score
Sept. 24	Marshall (A)	L	0-66
Oct. 1	Union (Ky.) (H)	L	6-32
Oct. 8	Murray State (A)	L	0-105
Oct. 15	Eastern Kentucky (A)	L	0-38
Oct. 22	Transylvania (H)	L	12-34
Oct. 28	Morehead St. (H)	L	0-20
Nov. 4	Oakland City (A)	L	0-19
Nov. 12	Georgetown Coll. (H)	L	0-20
Nov. 19	Western Kentucky (A)	L	0-58
			18-392

1933 (Won 1, Lost 7)
COACH: Ben Cregor
CAPTAIN: Bill Threlkeld

Date	Site	Dec.	Score
Sept. 30	Centre (H)	L	0-30
Oct. 6	Georgetown College (A)	L	0-13
Oct. 13	Union (Ky.) (A)	L	0-19
Oct. 21	Western Kentucky (H)	L	0-45
Oct. 28	Morehead State (A)	L	0-13
Nov. 4	Murray State (H)	L	6-54
Nov. 11	Miami (Fla.) (A)	L	7-33
Nov. 18	Eastern Kentucky (H)	W	13-7
			26-214

1934 (Won 2, Lost 5)
COACH: Ben Cregor
CAPTAIN: Bill Threlkeld

Date	Site	Dec.	Score
Oct. 6	Georgetown Coll. (H)	W	14-6
Oct. 13	Toledo (A)	L	7-19
Oct. 27	Hanover (A)	L	6-7
Nov. 3	Centre (H)	L	0-46
Nov. 10	Transylvania (A)	L	0-13
Nov. 17	Eastern Kentucky (A)	W	13-6
Nov. 24	Union (Ky.) (H)	L	0-7
			40-104

1935 (Won 1, Lost 6, Tied 1)
COACH: Ben Cregor
CO-CAPTAINS: Kenny Doll and Walt Kirkendahl

Date	Site	Dec.	Score
Sept. 28	Butler (A)	L	0-29
Oct. 5	Transylvania (H)	L	7-14
Oct. 11	Union (Ky.) (A)	L	7-13
Oct. 19	Hanover (A)	T	6-6
Oct. 26	Eastern Kentucky (H)	L	0-9
Nov. 2	Georgetown College (A)	L	0-21
Nov. 9	Toledo (H)	L	7-41
Nov. 16	Morehead State (H)	W	20-0
			47-133

1936 (Won 4, Lost 4)
COACH: Laurie Apitz
CAPTAIN: Melzar Lowe

Date	Site	Dec.	Score
Oct. 3	Union (Ky.) (H)	W	13-0
Oct. 10	Hanover (A)	W	12-2
Oct. 17	Eastern Kentucky (A)	L	6-9
Oct. 24	Union (Univ.) (A)	L	7-27
Oct. 30	Georgetown Coll. (H)	W	12-8
Nov. 7	Alfred Holbrook (H)	W	31-7
Nov. 14	Morehead State (A)	L	7-14
Nov. 21	Baldwin-Wallace (H)	L	0-67
			88-134

1937 (Won 2, Lost 5, Tied 1)
COACH: Laurie Apitz
CAPTAIN: Ralph Emerson

Date	Site	Dec.	Score
Sept. 25	Hanover (H)	L	7-13
Oct. 2	Transylvania (A)	L	6-19
Oct. 9	Wayne State (A)	L	0-32
Oct. 15	Union (Univ.) (H)	W	14-6
Oct. 23	St. Joseph's (H)	W	13-6
Oct. 30	Georgetown Coll. (A)	L	7-12
Nov. 11	Centre (H)	L	7-20
Nov. 20	Eastern Kentucky (H)	T	6-6
			60-114

1938 (Won 2, Lost 6)
COACH: Laurie Apitz
CAPTAIN: Alex Davidson

Date	Site	Dec.	Score
Sept. 24	Cincinnati (A)	L	0-19
Oct. 7	Wayne State (H)	W	14-12
Oct. 15	St. Joseph's (A)	L	0-2
Oct. 22	Georgetown Coll. (H)	L	0-6
Oct. 29	Transylvania (H)	L	7-13
Nov. 4	Evansville (A)	W	6-0
Nov. 11	Hanover (A)	L	13-14
Nov. 19	Centre (A)	L	0-14
			40-80

1939 (Won 5, Lost 2, Tied 1)
COACH: Laurie Apitz
CO-CAPTAINS: Fred Schloemer and Lou Zimlich

Date	Site	Dec.	Score
Sept. 22	Transylvania (A)	W	25-0
Sept. 30	Indiana State (A)	L	0-7
Oct. 6	Evansville (H)	W	7-6
Oct. 13	Alfred Holbrook (H)	W	20-3
Oct. 19	St. Joseph's (H)	W	13-0
Oct. 28	Centre (A)	T	0-0
Nov. 4	Georgetown Coll. (A)	L	7-14
Nov. 18	Hanover (H)	W	20-0
			92-30

1940 (Won 3, Lost 5, Tied 1)
COACH: Laurie Apitz
CAPTAIN: Jimmy Caufield

Date	Site	Dec.	Score
Sept. 21	Indiana St. (H)	T	0-0
Sept. 28	Cincinnati (A)	L	0-7
Oct. 5	Evansville (A)	W	13-7
Oct. 12	St. Joseph's (A)	L	6-24
Oct. 18	Centre (A)	L	0-28
Oct. 25	Alfred Holbrook (H)	W	38-7
Nov. 2	Georgetown Coll. (H)	L	14-19
Nov. 9	Hanover (A)	W	14-13
Nov. 16	Long Island (A)	L	6-29
			91-134

1941 (Won 4, Lost 4)
COACH: Laurie Apitz
CO-CAPTAINS: Clure Moser and Jimmy Rosenfield

Date	Site	Dec.	Score
Sept. 22	Rio Grande (H)	W	58-0
Sept. 27	Cincinnati (A)	L	7-28
Oct. 4	Evansville (H)	W	31-6
Oct. 17	Transylvania (H)	L	7-19
Oct. 23	Georgetown Coll. (A)	L	6-13
Nov. 1	DePauw (A)	L	6-13
Nov. 8	Hanover (A)	W	21-6
Nov. 15	Vanderbilt (H)	L	0-68
			143-140

1942 (Won 2, Lost 3)
COACH: Laurie Apitz
CO-CAPTAINS: Jim Brady and Bud Bruning

Date	Site	Dec.	Score
Sept. 17	Rio Grande (H)	W	25-0
Sept. 26	Cincinnati (A)	L	0-51
Oct. 10	Evansville (A)	W	20-0
Oct. 17	DePauw (H)	L	6-19
Oct. 24	Indiana State (H)	L	7-25
			58-95

Cardinal Football

1943-1945
No Formal Teams

1946 (Won 6, Lost 2)
COACH: Frank Camp
CAPTAIN: Vince Lococo

Date	Site	Dec.	Score
Sept. 26	Evansville (A)	W	13-7
Oct. 4	Wittenberg (H)	W	19-0
Oct. 11	Georgetown Coll. (A)	W	20-0
Oct. 19	Western Kentucky (A)	L	19-20
Oct. 25	Georgetown Coll. (H)	W	20-0
Nov. 2	St. Joseph's (H)	W	13-7
Nov. 9	Eastern Kentucky (A)	L	7-28
Nov. 16	Union (Univ.) (H)	W	25-0
			136-62

1947 (Won 7, Lost 0, Tied 1)
COACH: Frank Camp
CAPTAIN: Art Heitlauf

Date	Site	Dec.	Score
Sept. 26	Wittenberg (H)	W	40-3
Oct. 4	DePauw (A)	W	37-0
Oct. 10	Evansville (H)	W	20-7
Oct. 24	Western Kentucky (H)	W	19-13
Nov. 1	St. Joseph's (A)	T	7-7
Nov. 7	Eastern Kentucky (H)	W	14-13
Nov. 14	Southeastern La. (A)	W	23-0
Nov. 22	Washington (Mo.) (H)	W	33-20
			193-63

1948 (Won 5, Lost 5)
COACH: Frank Camp
CAPTAIN: George Bertram

Date	Site	Dec.	Score
Sept. 25	Memphis State (A)	L	7-13
Oct. 2	St. Joseph's (H)	W	20-0
Oct. 8	Xavier (A)	L	26-47
Oct. 16	Akron (A)	W	13-0
Oct. 23	Western Kentucky (H)	W	19-6
Oct. 30	Buffalo (H)	L	19-48
Nov. 6	Catawba (H)	W	33-21
Nov. 13	Evansville (A)	L	6-18
Nov. 20	Bradley (H)	W	31-14
Nov. 27	Washington (Mo.) (A)	L	12-27
			186-194

1949 (Won 8, Lost 3)
COACH: Frank Camp
CAPTAIN: George Bertram

Date	Site	Dec.	Score
Sept. 17	St. Joseph's (H)	W	33-7
Sept. 24	Western Kentucky (A)	W	47-7
Sept. 30	Murray State (H)	W	34-14
Oct. 8	Miami (Fla.) (H)	L	0-26
Oct. 15	Akron (H)	W	62-6
Oct. 21	Xavier (H)	L	7-19
Oct. 29	Bradley (A)	W	35-12
Nov. 3	Catawba (A)	W	41-7
Nov. 12	Washington (Mo.) (H)	W	35-12
Nov. 19	Evansville (H)	W	28-7
Nov. 24	Southern Miss (A)	L	21-26
			343-143

1950 (Won 3, Lost 6, Tied 1)
COACH: Frank Camp
CAPTAIN: Tom Lucia

Date	Site	Dec.	Score
Sept. 23	St. Francis, Pa. (H)	W	34-14
Sept. 30	Buffalo (H)	W	48-19
Oct. 7	Cincinnati (A)	L	20-28
Oct. 14	Houston (A)	L	7-27
Oct. 21	Xavier (A)	L	13-36
Oct. 28	Duquesne (H)	L	20-27
Nov. 4	Washington (Mo.) (A)	W	28-7
Nov. 10	Miami (Fla.) (A)	T	13-13
Nov. 18	Washington & Lee (H)	L	28-33
Nov. 25	Southern Miss. (A)	L	28-34
			239-238

1951 (Won 5, Lost 4)
COACH: Frank Camp
CAPTAIN: Charles Asher

Date	Site	Dec.	Score
Sept. 29	Wayne State (A)	W	28-12
Oct. 5	Boston Univ. (H)	L	7-39
Oct. 13	Cincinnati (A)	L	0-38
Oct. 19	Xavier (H)	L	6-47
Oct. 27	St. Bonaventure (A)	L	21-22
Nov. 2	North Carolina St. (H)	W	26-2
Nov. 10	Houston (H)	W	35-28
Nov. 17	Washington & Lee (H)	W	14-7
Nov. 23	Southern Miss (H)	W	14-13
			151-208

1952 (Won 3, Lost 5)
COACH: Frank Camp
CAPTAIN: Otto Knop

Date	Site	Dec.	Score
Sept. 27	Wayne State (H)	W	19-12
Oct. 4	Florida State (A)	W	41-14
Oct. 11	Dayton (H)	L	0-20
Oct. 18	Xavier (H)	L	13-27
Oct. 31	Chattanooga (A)	L	14-47
Nov. 8	Memphis State (A)	L	25-29
Nov. 15	Eastern Kentucky (H)	W	34-20
Nov. 22	Southern Miss (A)	L	26-55
			172-224

1953 (Won 1, Lost 7)
COACH: Frank Camp
CAPTAIN: Jim Hollowell

Date	Site	Dec.	Score
Sept. 19	Murray State (A)	W	19-14
Sept. 26	Camp Atterbury* (H)	L	7-15
Oct. 3	Florida State (A)	L	0-59
Oct. 10	Xavier (H)	L	13-19
Oct. 17	Dayton (A)	L	13-20
Oct. 24	Tennessee (A)	L	6-59
Oct. 30	Chattanooga (A)	L	6-44
Nov. 7	Cincinnati (A)	L	0-41
Nov. 14	Eastern Ky. (H)	L	13-20
			70-276

*Exhibition Game

1954 (Won 3, Lost 6)
COACH: Frank Camp
CAPTAIN: Johnny Unitas

Date	Site	Dec.	Score
Sept. 18	Murray State (H)	L	13-33
Sept. 24	Wayne State (A)	L	0-13
Oct. 2	Florida State (H)	L	6-47
Oct. 9	Dayton (A)	L	7-27
Oct. 16	Evansville (H)	W	26-6
Oct. 23	Centre (H)	W	27-6
Oct. 30	Western Kentucky (A)	L	7-25
Nov. 6	Morehead State (H)	W	24-0
Nov. 13	Eastern Kentucky (A)	L	6-20
			116-177

1955 (Won 7, Lost 2)
COACH: Frank Camp
CAPTAIN: Jim Wolf

Date	Site	Dec.	Score
Sept. 17	Murray State (A)	L	14-33
Sept. 24	Xavier (A)	L	20-49
Oct. 1	Wayne State (H)	W	72-0
Oct. 8	Dayton (H)	W	19-7
Oct. 15	Evansville (A)	W	29-7
Oct. 29	Western Kentucky (H)	W	20-0
Nov. 5	Morehead State (H)	W	37-12
Nov. 12	Eastern Kentucky (A)	W	45-13
Nov. 19	Toledo (H)	W	33-13
			289-134

1956 (Won 6, Lost 3)
COACH: Frank Camp
CAPTAIN: John Noon

Date	Site	Dec.	Score
Sept. 22	Toledo (A)	W	27-12
Sept. 29	Kent State (H)	L	0-7
Oct. 6	Evansville (H)	W	41-13
Oct. 13	Murray State (H)	W	7-6
Oct. 20	Morehead State (A)	W	19-7
Oct. 27	Ohio (A)	W	25-19
Nov. 3	Dayton (H)	L	6-7
Nov. 10	Xavier (H)	L	14-34
Nov. 17	Eastern Kentucky (H)	W	14-6
			153-111

1957 (Won 9, Lost 1)
COACH: Frank Camp
CAPTAIN: Gil Sturtzel

Date	Site	Dec.	Score
Sept. 21	Evansville (A)	W	33-7
Sept. 27	Eastern Kentucky (A)	W	40-14
Oct. 5	Toledo (H)	W	48-20
Oct. 12	Murray State (A)	W	35-0
Oct. 19	Dayton (H)	W	33-19
Oct. 26	Central Michigan (H)	W	40-0
Nov. 9	Kent State (A)	L	7-13
Nov. 16	Ohio (H)	W	40-7
Nov. 22	Morehead State (H)	W	40-6
Sun Bowl (El Paso, Texas)			
Jan. 1	Drake (N)	W	34-20
			350-106

120

Cardinal Football

Stories About the University of Louisville's Football Past

1958 (Won 4, Lost 4)
COACH: Frank Camp
CAPTAIN: Ed Young

Date	Site	Dec.	Score
Sept. 27	Eastern Kentucky (H)	W	20-7
Oct. 4	Toledo (A)	L	7-13
Oct. 11	Murray State (H)	W	27-0
Oct. 18	Dayton (A)	L	13-26
Oct. 25	Central Michigan (A)	W	40-7
Nov. 8	Kent State (H)	W	21-0
Nov. 15	Ohio (A)	L	6-23
Nov. 22	North Texas State (H)	L	10-21
			144-97

1959 (Won 6, Lost 4)
COACH: Frank Camp
CO-CAPTAINS: Ken Porco and Howard Turley

Date	Site	Dec.	Score
Sept. 15	Western Kentucky (H)	W	19-0
Sept. 19	Xavier (A)	L	13-28
Sept. 25	Eastern Kentucky (A)	W	14-7
Oct. 3	Bradley (A)	W	28-8
Oct. 10	Murray State (A)	W	28-0
Oct. 17	Dayton (H)	W	32-6
Oct. 31	Marshall (H)	W	48-6
Nov. 7	North Texas State (A)	L	7-39
Nov. 14	Ohio (H)	L	15-22
Nov. 21	Kent State (A)	L	14-16
			218-132

1960 (Won 7, Lost 2)
COACH: Frank Camp
CAPTAIN: Ron Petty

Date	Site	Dec.	Score
Sept. 17	Tennessee Tech (A)	L	7-21
Sept. 23	Eastern Kentucky (H)	W	28-7
Sept. 30	Bradley (H)	W	40-6
Oct. 7	Murray State (H)	W	12-6
Oct. 15	Dayton (A)	W	36-0
Oct. 21	Western Kentucky (H)	W	44-0
Oct. 29	Marshall (A)	W	7-0
Nov. 5	Xavier (H)	L	0-29
Nov. 11	Kent State (H)	W	22-8
			196-77

1961 (Won 6, Lost 3)
COACH: Frank Camp
CAPTAIN: John Finn

Date	Site	Dec.	Score
Sept. 16	Tennessee Tech (H)	W	29-13
Sept. 22	Eastern Kentucky (A)	W	33-6
Sept. 30	Marshall (H)	W	32-6
Oct. 7	Memphis State (H)	L	13-28
Oct. 14	Dayton (A)	L	6-7
Oct. 21	Western Kentucky (H)	W	20-0
Nov. 4	Xavier (A)	L	8-16
Nov. 11	Kent State (A)	W	19-15
Nov. 18	North Texas State (A)	W	20-0
			180-91

1962 (Won 6, Lost 4)
COACH: Frank Camp
CAPTAIN: John Giles

Date	Site	Dec.	Score
Sept. 15	Wichita State (A)	W	21-20
Sept. 22	Western Michigan (H)	W	27-21
Sept. 29	Marshall (A)	W	18-0
Oct. 6	Memphis State (A)	L	0-49
Oct. 13	Dayton (A)	W	21-0
Oct. 20	Tulsa (A)	L	7-25
Nov. 3	Xavier (H)	L	12-13
Nov. 10	Kent State (H)	W	29-8
Nov. 17	North Texas State (H)	W	14-10
Nov. 24	Houston (H)	L	25-27
			174-173

1963 (Won 3, Lost 7)
COACH: Frank Camp
CAPTAIN: Ken Kortas

Date	Site	Dec.	Score
Sept. 28	+North Texas State (A)	L	6-26
Oct. 5	Southern Illinois (H)	L	7-13
Oct. 12	+Dayton (H)	W	13-12
Oct. 19	+Wichita State (H)	L	14-47
Oct. 26	Marshall (H)	W	27-14
Nov. 2	Memphis State (H)	L	0-25
Nov. 9	Kent State (A)	L	7-26
Nov. 16	Western Michigan (A)	W	21-7
Dec. 7	+Tulsa (A)	L	16-22
Dec. 14	Houston (A)	L	7-21
			118-213

+MVC Game

1964 (Won 1, Lost 9)
COACH: Frank Camp
CAPTAIN: Tom LaFramboise

Date	Site	Dec.	Score
Sept. 19	Western Michigan (H)	L	7-10
Sept. 26	Southern Illinois (A)	L	6-7
Oct. 3	+North Texas State (H)	L	0-22
Oct. 10	+Dayton (A)	W	21-7
Oct. 17	+Tulsa (H)	L	0-58
Oct. 24	Marshall (A)	L	6-28
Oct. 31	Kent St. (A)	L	7-14
Nov. 7	+Wichita State (A)	L	15-23
Nov. 14	Memphis State (A)	L	0-34
Nov. 21	Drake (H)	L	8-14
			70-217

+MVC Game

1965 (Won 6, Lost 4)
COACH: Frank Camp
CAPTAIN: Doug Buffone

Date	Site	Dec.	Score
Sept. 18	Western Michigan (A)	L	13-17
Sept. 25	Southern Illinois (H)	W	13-0
Oct. 2	+North Texas State (A)	W	29-21
Oct. 9	+Dayton* (H)	W	34-0
Oct. 16	East Carolina (H)	L	20-34
Oct. 23	Marshall (H)	W	23-7
Oct. 30	+Wichita State (H)	W	30-10
Nov. 6	+Tulsa (A)	L	18-51
Nov. 13	Drake (A)	W	32-17
Nov. 20	Kent St. (A)	L	6-7
			218-164

+MVC Game

1966 (Won 6, Lost 4)
COACH: Frank Camp
CAPTAIN: Benny Russell

Date	Site	Dec.	Score
Sept. 24	Southern Illinois (A)	W	16-7
Oct. 1	+North Texas State (H)	L	19-20
Oct. 8	Dayton (A)	L	17-20
Oct. 15	Drake (H)	W	66-26
Oct. 22	Marshall (A)	W	35-15
Oct. 29	+Wichita State (A)	L	2-9
Nov. 5	Kent State (H)	W	23-20
Nov. 12	+Cincinnati (A)	L	3-17
Nov. 19	+Tulsa (H)	W	29-18
Nov. 26	East Carolina (H)	W	21-7
			231-159

+MVC Game

1967 (Won 5, Lost 5)
COACH: Frank Camp
CAPTAIN: Ed Harmon

Date	Site	Dec.	Score
Sept. 16	Drake (A)	W	46-7
Sept. 23	Southern Illinois (H)	W	26-0
Sept. 30	+North Texas State (A)	L	28-30
Oct. 7	Dayton (H)	W	29-7
Oct. 14	East Carolina (A)	L	13-18
Oct. 21	Marshall (H)	W	43-7
Oct. 28	+Wichita State (H)	W	24-17
Nov. 4	Kent State (A)	L	21-28
Nov. 11	+Cincinnati (H)	L	7-13
Dec. 2	+Tulsa (A)	L	23-35
			260-162

+MVC Game

1968 (Won 5, Lost 5)
COACH: Frank Camp
CO-CAPTAINS: Pete Compise and Medford Lee

Date	Site	Dec.	Score
Sept. 21	Southern Illinois (A)	W	33-10
Oct. 5	Dayton (A)	L	14-28
Oct. 12	+Tulsa (H)	W	16-7
Oct. 19	Marshall (A)	W	13-10
Oct. 26	+Wichita State (A)	W	21-14
Nov. 2	Kent State (H)	W	23-9
Nov. 9	+Cincinnati (A)	L	7-37
Nov. 16	+North Texas State (H)	L	14-36
Nov. 23	Drake (H)	L	37-38
Nov. 30	+Memphis State (H)	L	14-44
			192-233

+MVC Game

1969 (Won 5, Lost 4, Tied 1)
COACH: Lee Corso
CO-CAPTAINS: Mike Detenber, Greg Karem

Date	Site	Dec.	Score
Sept. 13	Drake (A)	T	24-24
Sept. 20	Southern Illinois (H)	W	17-13
Oct. 4	Dayton (H)	W	24-17
Oct. 18	Marshall (H)	W	34-17
Oct. 25	+North Texas State (A)	L	13-31
Nov. 1	Kent State (A)	L	6-35
Nov. 8	+Cincinnati (H)	L	21-31
Nov. 15	+Wichita State (H)	W	13-7
Nov. 22	+Memphis State (A)	L	19-69
Nov. 27	*Tulsa (A)	W	35-29
			206-273

* MVC Game

1970 (Won 8, Lost 3, Tied 1)
Missouri Valley Conference Champions
COACH: Lee Corso
CAPTAIN: Cookie Brinkman

Date	Site	Dec.	Score
Sept. 12	Florida State (A)	L	7-9
Sept. 19	Southern Illinois (A)	L	28-31
Sept. 26	+North Texas State (H)	W	13-2
Oct. 3	Dayton (A)	L	11-28
Oct. 10	+Tulsa (H)	W	14-8
Oct. 17	Marshall (A)	W	16-14
Oct. 31	Kent State (H)	W	14-13
Nov. 7	+Memphis State (H)	W	40-27
Nov. 14	Cincinnati (A)	W	28-14
Nov. 21	Drake (H)	W	23-14
Nov. 28	+Wichita State (A)	W	34-24
Pasadena Bowl (Pasadena, Calif.)			
Dec. 19	Long Beach St. (N)	T	24-24
			252-208

+MVC Game

1971 (Won 6, Lost 3, Tied 1)
COACH: Lee Corso
CAPTAIN: Amos Martin

Date	Site	Dec.	Score
Sept. 18	Vanderbilt (A)	T	0-0
Sept. 25	Drake (A)	L	7-10
Oct. 2	Dayton (H)	W	41-13
Oct. 9	+Memphis State (A)	W	26-20
Oct. 16	+North Texas State (A)	L	17-20
Oct. 23	+Wichita State (H)	W	21-5
Oct. 30	Tampa (H)	W	21-10
Nov. 6	+Tulsa (A)	W	17-0
Nov. 13	Southern Illinois (H)	W	24-14
Nov. 27	Cincinnati (H)	L	16-19
			190-111

+MVC Game

1972 (Won 9, Lost 1)
Missouri Valley Conference
Tri-Champions
COACH: Lee Corso
CAPTAIN: Tom Martin

Date	Site	Dec.	Score
Sept. 16	Kent State (H)	W	34-0
Sept. 30	Dayton (A)	W	28-11
Oct. 7	Tampa (A)	W	17-14
Oct. 14	+North Texas State (H)	W	56-6
Oct. 21	+Wichita State (A)	W	46-3
Oct. 28	Cincinnati (A)	W	38-13
Nov. 4	+Tulsa (H)	L	26-28
Nov. 11	Southern Illinois (A)	W	20-16
Nov. 18	+Memphis State (H)	W	17-0
Nov. 25	+Drake (H)	W	27-0
			309-91

+MVC Game

1973 (Won 5, Lost 6)
COACH: T.W. Alley
CAPTAIN: Joe Lee Phillips

Date	Site	Dec.	Score
Sept. 8	+Memphis State (A)	L	21-28
Sept. 15	Kent State (A)	L	3-10
Sept. 22	+Drake (A)	W	27-17
Oct. 6	+Wichita State (H)	W	24-10
Oct. 13	+North Texas State (A)	L	6-7
Oct. 20	Mississippi State (H)	L	7-18
Oct. 27	Cincinnati (H)	W	10-8
Nov. 3	+Tulsa (A)	L	9-17
Nov. 10	Dayton (H)	L	9-10
Nov. 17	Furman (H)	W	35-14
Nov. 24	+West Texas State (A)	W	21-9
			172-148

+MVC Game

1974 (Won 4, Lost 7)
COACH: T.W. Alley
CO-CAPTAINS: Steve Jewell and
Cardell Parker

Date	Site	Dec.	Score
Sept. 7	Memphis State (H)	L	10-16
Sept. 14	Auburn (A)	L	3-16
Sept. 28	Cincinnati (A)	L	6-7
Oct. 5	+Wichita State (A)	W	14-7
Oct. 12	+North Texas State (A)	W	24-10
Oct. 19	+Drake (H)	L	35-38
Oct. 26	Mississippi State (A)	L	7-56
Nov. 2	+Tulsa (H)	L	7-37
Nov. 9	Dayton (H)	W	20-15
Nov. 23	Vanderbilt (H)	L	0-44
Nov. 30	+West Texas State (H)	W	10-8
			136-254

+MVC Game

1975 (Won 2, Lost 9)
COACH: Vince Gibson
CAPTAIN: Bob Riser

Date	Site	Dec.	Score
Sept. 13	Western Kentucky (H)	L	17-21
Sept. 20	Drake (A)	L	7-31
Sept. 27	Cincinnati (H)	L	27-46
Oct. 4	Wichita State (A)	L	10-13
Oct. 11	Chattanooga (H)	W	6-3
Oct. 18	Memphis State (A)	L	7-41
Oct. 25	Mississippi State* (H)	W	14-28
Nov. 1	Tulsa (A)	L	14-38
Nov. 8	Dayton (H)	L	13-32
Nov. 15	N.E. Louisiana (A)	L	10-14
Nov. 22	West Texas State (A)	L	23-49
			108-316

*Won by Forfeit

1976 (Won 5, Lost 6)
COACH: Vince Gibson
CAPTAIN: Norman Heard

Date	Site	Dec.	Score
Sept. 18	Mississippi State* (A)	W	21-30
Sept. 25	Drake (H)	W	37-24
Oct. 2	Wichita State (H)	W	28-14
Oct. 9	Pittsburgh (A)	L	6-27
Oct. 16	N.E. Louisiana (H)	W	36-8
Oct. 23	Alabama (A)	L	3-24
Oct. 30	Tulsa (H)	L	10-20
Nov. 6	Rutgers (A)	L	0-34
Nov. 13	Memphis State (A)	L	14-26
Nov. 20	Boston University (H)	W	16-7
Nov. 27	Cincinnati (A)	L	6-20
			177-234

*Won by Forfeit

1977 (Won 7, Lost 4, Tied 1)
COACH: Vince Gibson
CAPTAIN: Tom Abood

Date	Site	Dec.	Score
Sept. 10	Northern Illinois (H)	W	38-0
Sept. 17	Cincinnati (H)	T	17-17
Sept. 24	William & Mary (H)	L	7-21
Oct. 1	Memphis State (A)	W	14-13
Oct. 8	Tulsa (H)	W	33-0
Oct. 15	Dayton (A)	L	10-14
Oct. 22	Alabama (A)	L	6-55
Oct. 29	Marshall (A)	W	56-0
Nov. 5	Wichita State (H)	W	51-21
Nov. 12	Drake (H)	W	18-13
Nov. 20	Indiana State (H)	W	27-16
Independence Bowl (Shreveport, La.)			
Dec. 17	Louisiana Tech (N)	L	14-24
			291-194

1978 (Won 7, Lost 4)
COACH: Vince Gibson
CO-CAPTAINS: Ron Heinrich, Billy Perrin,
Nathan Poole and Ricky Skiles

Date	Site	Dec.	Score
Sept. 9	South Dakota State (H)	W	54-7
Sept. 16	Maryland (H)	L	17-24
Sept. 23	Cincinnati (A)	W	28-14
Sept. 30	Indiana State (H)	W	31-12
Oct. 7	Tulsa (A)	L	7-24
Oct. 14	N'west Louisiana (H)	W	51-7
Oct. 21	Boston University (H)	W	35-7
Oct. 28	William & Mary (H)	W	33-21
Nov. 4	Wichita State (A)	W	38-20
Nov. 11	Memphis State (H)	L	22-29
Nov. 18	Southern Miss (A)	L	3-37
			319-202

1979 (Won 4, Lost 6, Tied 1)
COACH: Vince Gibson
CO-CAPTAINS: Stu Stram, Otis Wilson,
Randy Butler, and Zarko Ellis

Date	Site	Dec.	Score
Sept. 8	Virginia Tech (H)	L	14-15
Sept. 15	Miami (Fla.) (A)	L	12-24
Sept. 22	Cincinnati (H)	W	22-19
Sept. 29	Drake (A)	W	31-21
Oct. 6	Florida State (H)	L	0-27
Oct. 13	Tulsa (H)	W	24-7
Oct. 20	Indiana State (A)	W	34-10
Nov. 3	Southern Miss (H)	T	10-10
Nov. 10	Memphis State (A)	L	6-10
Nov. 17	Maryland (A)	L	7-28
Nov. 25	Rutgers (H)	L	7-31
			167-202

122

Cardinal Football

1980 (Won 5, Lost 6)
COACH: Bob Weber
CO-CAPTAINS: Eddie Johnson, Dan Dihtzeruk, Joe Jacoby and Jamie Perrin

Date	Site	Dec.	Score
Sept. 6	Miami (Fla.) (H)	L	10-24
Sept. 13	Florida State (A)	L	0-52
Sept. 20	Murray State (H)	L	9-13
Sept. 27	Kansas (A)	W	17-9
Oct. 11	Memphis State (H)	W	38-14
Oct. 18	Indiana State (H)	W	27-17
Oct. 25	Florida (A)	L	0-13
Nov. 1	Temple (H)	L	12-17
Nov. 8	Pittsburgh (A)	L	23-41
Nov. 15	Cincinnati (H)	W	20-0
Nov. 22	Southern Miss (A)	W	6-3
			162-203

1981 (Won 5, Lost 6)
COACH: Bob Weber
CAPTAIN: Game Captains

Date	Site	Dec.	Score
Sept. 5	Florida State (A)	L	0-17
Sept. 12	Toledo (H)	W	31-6
Sept. 19	Long Beach State (H)	W	35-13
Sept. 26	Missouri (A)	L	3-34
Oct. 3	Marshall (H)	W	36-0
Oct. 10	Memphis State (A)	W	14-7
Oct. 17	Tennessee State (H)	L	30-42
Oct. 24	Oklahoma State (A)	L	11-19
Nov. 7	N.E. Louisiana (H)	L	7-40
Nov. 14	Cincinnati (A)	L	0-24
Nov. 21	Southern Miss (H)	W	13-10
			180-212

1982 (Won 5, Lost 6)
COACH: Bob Weber
CO-CAPTAINS: Mike Nuzzolese, Frank Minnifield, Anthony Williams

Date	Site	Dec.	Score
Sept. 4	Western Kentucky (H)	W	20-10
Sept. 11	Cincinnati (A)	L	16-38
Sept. 25	Oklahoma State (H)	W	28-22
Oct. 2	Miami (Fla.) (H)	L	6-28
Oct. 9	Temple (H)	L	14-55
Oct. 16	Richmond (H)	W	35-0
Oct. 23	Southern Miss (A)	L	0-48
Oct. 30	Pittsburgh (A)	L	14-63
Nov. 6	Indiana State (H)	W	35-23
Nov. 13	Florida State (A)	L	14-49
Nov. 20	Memphis State (A)	W	38-19
			220-355

1983 (Won 3, Lost 8)
COACH: Bob Weber
CO-CAPTAINS: Dean May, Tom Andrews, Mike Trainor

Date	Site	Dec.	Score
Sept. 3	Southern Methodist (A)	L	6-24
Sept. 10	Western Kentucky (H)	W	41-22
Sept. 17	Army (H)	W	31-7
Sept. 24	Cincinnati (H)	W	31-23
Oct. 1	Virginia Tech (A)	L	0-31
Oct. 8	Miami (Fla.) (A)	L	14-42
Oct. 15	Pittsburgh (H)	L	10-55
Oct. 20	Florida State (A)	L	7-51
Nov. 5	Southern Miss (H)	L	3-27
Nov. 12	Temple (A)	L	3-24
Nov. 24	Memphis State (H)	L	7-45
			157-351

1984 (Won 2, Lost 9)
COACH: Bob Weber
CAPTAIN: Game Captains

Date	Site	Dec.	Score
Sept. 1	Murray State (H)	L	23-26
Sept. 8	West Virginia (A)	L	6-30
Sept. 15	Southern Methodist (H)	L	7-41
Sept. 29	Houston (A)	W	30-28
Oct. 6	Western Kentucky (H)	W	45-17
Oct. 13	Indiana State (H)	L	21-44
Oct. 20	Rutgers (A)	L	21-38
Oct. 27	Cincinnati (A)	L	21-40
Nov. 3	Miami (Fla.) (H)	L	23-38
Nov. 10	Tennessee State (H)	L	15-24
Nov. 17	Southern Miss (A)	L	25-34
			237-369

1985 (Won 2, Lost 9)
COACH: Howard Schnellenberger
CAPTAIN: Game Captains

Date	Site	Dec.	Score
Sept. 7	West Virginia (A)	L	13-52
Sept. 14	Indiana (A)	L	28-41
Sept. 21	Western Kentucky (H)	W	23-14
Sept. 28	Houston (A)	L	27-49
Oct. 5	Syracuse (A)	L	0-48
Oct. 12	Southern Miss (H)	L	12-42
Oct. 19	Cincinnati (H)	L	9-31
Oct. 26	Miami (Fla.) (A)	L	7-45
Nov. 2	Central Florida (H)	W	42-21
Nov. 9	Virginia Tech (A)	L	17-41
Nov. 23	Eastern Kentucky (H)	L	21-45
			199-429

1986 (Won 3, Lost 8)
COACH: Howard Schnellenberger
CAPTAIN: Game Captains

Date	Site	Dec.	Score
Sept. 6	Illinois (A)	L	0-23
Sept. 13	Indiana (A)	L	0-21
Sept. 20	Western Kentucky (H)	W	45-6
Sept. 27	Memphis State (H)	W	34-8
Oct. 4	Cincinnati (A)	L	17-24
Oct. 18	Boston College (A)	L	7-41
Oct. 25	Florida State (H)	L	18-54
Nov. 1	Rutgers (H)	L	0-41
Nov. 8	Tulane (A)	W	23-12
Nov. 15	West Virginia (A)	L	19-42
Nov. 22	Southern Miss (H)	L	16-31
			179-276

1987 (Won 3, Lost 7, Tied 1)
COACH: Howard Schnellenberger
CAPTAIN: Game Captains

Date	Site	Dec.	Score
Sept. 5	Tulane (H)	W	42-40
Sept. 12	Cincinnati (H)	L	0-25
Sept. 19	Purdue (A)	T	22-22
Sept. 26	Murray State (H)	W	34-10
Oct. 3	Southern Miss (H)	L	6-65
Oct. 10	Marshall (H)	L	31-34
Oct. 17	Florida State (A)	L	9-32
Oct. 24	Akron (H)	W	31-10
Oct. 31	Tulsa (A)	L	22-26
Nov. 7	Tennessee (A)	L	10-41
Nov. 14	Memphis State (A)	L	8-43
			215-348

1988 (Won 8, Lost 3)
COACH: Howard Schnellenberger
CAPTAIN: Game Captains

Date	Site	Dec.	Score
Sept. 3	Maryland (A)	L	16-27
Sept. 10	Wyoming (H)	L	9-44
Sept. 17	Memphis State (H)	W	29-18
Sept. 24	North Carolina (A)	W	38-34
Oct. 1	Southern Miss (A)	L	23-30
Oct. 8	Tulsa (H)	W	9-3
Oct. 15	Virginia (H)	W	30-28
Oct. 22	Tulane (A)	W	38-35
Oct. 29	Cincinnati (H)	W	21-6
Nov. 5	Virginia Tech (H)	W	13-3
Nov. 12	Western Kentucky (H)	W	35-17
			261-245

1989 (Won 6, Lost 5)
COACH: Howard Schnellenberger
CAPTAIN: Game Captains

Date	Site	Dec.	Score
Sept. 2	Wyoming (A)	W	28-21
Sept. 9	Kansas (A)	W	33-28
Sept. 23	West Virginia (H)	L	21-30
Sept. 30	Cincinnati (H)	W	37-17
Oct. 14	Southern Miss (H)	L	10-16
Oct. 21	Tulsa (H)	L	24-31
Oct. 28	Virginia (A)	L	15-16
Nov. 4	Western Kentucky (H)	W	55-7
Nov. 11	Memphis State (A)	W	40-10
Nov. 18	Boston College (A)	W	36-22
Dec. 2	Syracuse (Tokyo)	L	13-24
			312-222

1990 (Won 10, Lost 1, Tied 1)
COACH: Howard Schnellenberger
CAPTAIN: Game Captains

Date	Site	Dec.	Score
Sept. 1	San Jose State (A)	T	10-10
Sept. 8	Murray State (H)	W	68-0
Sept. 15	Kansas (H)	W	28-16
Sept. 22	West Virginia (A)	W	9-7
Sept. 29	Southern Miss (A)	L	13-25
Oct. 6	Tulsa (H)	W	38-14
Oct. 13	Memphis State (H)	W	19-17
Oct. 20	Pittsburgh (A)	W	27-20
Oct. 27	Western Kentucky (H)	W	41-7
Nov. 3	Cincinnati (A)	W	41-6
Nov. 10	Boston College (H)	W	17-10
Fiesta Bowl (Phoenix, Ariz.)			
Jan. 1	Alabama (N)	W	34-7
			345-149

1991 (Won 2, Lost 9)
COACH: Howard Schnellenberger
CAPTAIN: Game Captains

Date	Site	Dec.	Score
Aug. 8	Eastern Kentucky (H)	W	24-14
Sept. 5	Tennessee (H)	L	11-28
Sept. 14	Ohio State (A)	L	15-23
Sept. 28	Southern Miss (H)	W	28-14
Oct. 5	Cincinnati (H)	L	7-30
Oct. 12	Boston College (A)	L	3-33
Oct. 19	Army (H)	L	12-37
Oct. 26	Virginia Tech (A)	L	13-41
Nov. 2	Florida State (H)	L	15-40
Nov. 9	Memphis State (A)	L	7-35
Nov. 16	Tulsa (A)	L	0-40
			135-335

1992 (Won 5, Lost 6)
COACH: Howard Schnellenberger
CAPTAINS: Jeff Brohm, Andy Culley

Date	Site	Dec.	Score
Sept. 5	Ohio State (A)	L	19-20
Sept. 12	Memphis State (H)	W	16-15
Sept. 19	Arizona State (A)	L	0-19
Sept. 26	Wyoming (H)	L	24-26
Oct. 3	Syracuse (H)	L	9-15
Oct. 10	Virginia Tech (H)	W	21-17
Oct. 17	Tulsa (H)	W	32-27
Oct. 24	Florida (A)	L	17-31
Oct. 31	Cincinnati (A)	W	27-17
Nov. 7	Texas A&M (A)	L	18-40
Nov. 14	Pittsburgh (A)	W	31-16
			214-243

1993 (Won 9, Lost 3)
COACH: Howard Schnellenberger
CAPTAINS: Jeff Brohm, Tom Cavallo, Aaron Bailey

Date	Site	Dec.	Score
Sept. 4	San Jose State (H)	W	31-24
Sept. 11	Memphis State (A)	W	54-28
Sept. 18	Arizona State (H)	W	35-17
Sept. 25	Texas (H)	W	41-10
Oct. 2	Pittsburgh (A)	W	29-7
Oct. 9	West Virginia (A)	L	34-36
Oct. 16	Southern Miss (H)	W	35-27
Oct. 23	Navy (H)	W	28-0
Nov. 6	Tennessee (A)	L	10-45
Nov. 13	Texas A&M (A)	L	7-42
Nov. 25	Tulsa (A)	W	28-0
Liberty Bowl (Memphis, Tenn.)			
Dec. 28	Michigan State	W	18-7
			350-243

1994 (Won 6, Lost 5)
COACH: Howard Schnellenberger
CAPTAINS: Marty Lowe, Terry Quinn, Brandon Brookfield

Date	Site	Dec.	Score
Sept. 3	Kentucky (A)	L	14-20
Sept. 10	Texas (A)	L	16-30
Sept. 17	Arizona State (A)	W	25-22
Oct. 1	Pittsburgh (H)	W	33-29
Oct. 8	North Carolina St. (H)	W	35-14
Oct. 15	Army (A)	L	29-30
Oct. 22	Navy (A)	W	35-14
Oct. 29	Memphis (H)	W	10-6
Nov. 3	Boston Coll. (H)	L	14-35
Nov. 12	Texas A&M (H)	L	10-26
Nov. 26	Tulsa (H)	W	34-27
			255-253

1995 (Won 7, Lost 4)
COACH: Ron Cooper
CAPTAINS: Alan Campos, Marty Lowe, Tyrus McCloud, Roman Oben

Date	Site	Dec.	Score
Sept. 2	Kentucky (A)	W	13-10
Sept. 9	Northern Illinois (A)	W	34-21
Sept. 16	Michigan State (H)	L	7-30
Sept. 21	North Carolina (H)	L	10-17
Sept. 30	Memphis (A)	W	17-7
Oct. 7	Southern Miss (A)	L	21-25
Oct. 14	Wyoming (A)	L	20-27
Oct. 28	Maryland (H)	W	31-0
Nov. 4	Tulane (H)	W	34-14
Nov. 11	N.E. Louisiana (H)	W	39-0
Nov. 18	North Texas (H)	W	57-14
			283-165

1996 (Won 5, Lost 6)
COACH: Ron Cooper
CAPTAINS: Jason Payne, Tyrus McCloud, Sam Madison, Rico Clark

Date	Site	Dec.	Score
Aug. 31	Kentucky (A)	W	38-14
Sept. 7	Penn State (A)	L	7-24
Sept. 14	Baylor (H)	L	13-14
Sept. 21	Michigan State (A)	W	30-20
Sept. 28	Southern Miss(H) +	L	7-24
Oct. 12	Tulane (A)+	W	23-20
Oct. 19	Northern Illinois (H)	W	27-3
Oct. 26	Cincinnati (H)+	L	7-10
Nov. 2	Memphis (H)+	W	13-10
Nov. 9	North Carolina (A)	L	10-28
Nov. 16	Houston (A)+	L	7-38
			182-205

+Conference USA Game

1997 (Won 1, Lost 10)
COACH: Ron Cooper
CAPTAINS: Terry Rice-Locket, Miguel Montano, Kendrick Gholston, Graig Hoffman, Ryan Wade

Date	Site	Dec.	Score
Aug. 30	Kentucky (A)	L	24-28
Sept. 6	Utah (H)	L	21-27
Sept. 13	Illinois (H)	W	26-14
Sept. 20	Penn State (H)	L	21-57
Sept. 27	Oklahoma (A)	L	14-35
Oct. 4	Southern Miss(A) +	L	24-42
Oct. 11	Tulane (H)+	L	33-64
Oct. 25	Houston (H)+	L	22-36
Nov. 1	East Carolina (H)+	L	31-45
Nov. 8	Cincinnati (A)+	L	9-28
Nov. 15	Memphis (A)+	L	20-21
			245-407

+ Conference USA Game

1998 (Won 7, Lost 5)
COACH: John L. Smith
CAPTAINS: Rick Nord, Chris Redman, Courtney Dinkins, Mike Gantous

Date	Site	Dec.	Score
Sept. 5	KENTUCKY	L	34-68
Sept. 12	at Utah	L	22-45
Sept. 19	at Illinois	W	35-9
Sept. 26	BOSTON COLLEGE	W	52-28
Oct. 3	CINCINNATI+	W	62-19
Oct. 10	at Southern Miss+	L	21-56
Oct. 17	at Tulane+	L	22-28
Oct. 24	MEMPHIS+	W	35-32
Oct. 31	WESTERN KENTUCKY	W	63-34
Nov. 14	at East Carolina+	W	63-45
Nov. 21	ARMY+	W	35-23
+ Conference USA Game			444-387
Motor City Bowl (Pontiac, Mich.)			
Dec. 23	vs. Marshall	L	29-48

Sam Madison

UNIVERSITY OF LOUISVILLE
ALL-TIME FOOTBALL LETTERMEN

A

Abbey, Jack (1946)
Abood, Tom (1974-77)
Adams, John (1983-86)
Ahmay, Rick (1977)
Akers, David (1993-96)
Alexander, Arthur (1986-89)
Allan, Tim (1975)
Alverez, Ron (1993)
Anderson, Brad (1987-91)
Anderson, Braxton (1997-98)
Anderson, Ken (1951-52)
Anderson, Mike (1973, 75-76)
Anderson, Richard (1957-58)
Andrews, Tom (1981-83)
Annear, W. (1938)
Apke, Bill (1960-63)
Archer, Ira (1934-35)
Arden, David (1932)
Armstrong, Bruce (1983-86)
Arnett, Hall (1948)
Arnold, Andrew (1972)
Arnold, Clarence (1925-28)
Arsenault, Jim (1972)
Arrington, Calvin (1992-95)
Arthur, Dave (1980-82)
Ascher, Charles (1948-51)
Asher, Jamie (1991-94)
Aspy, David (1950)
Atcher, Kim (1993)
Atkins, Xzavia (1992)
Atkinson, John (1926-28)
Austin, G.T. (1913)
Autry, Keith (1976)
Axline, Matt (1991)
Ayandele, Francis (1969)
Ayers, John (1981)

B

Bach, Arthur (1914)
Bacik, Joe (1973-74)
Backauskas, Chip (1983)
Baden, Harry (1921-23)
Bagley, Bob (1962)
Bailey, Aaron (1992-93)
Bailey, Ray (1984)
Bain, Charles (1927-30)
Baisch, Keith (1993)
Baker, Ben (1968-69)
Baker, Bruce (1912-13)
Barker, Paul (1992)
Ball, Larry (1969-71)
Ballard, Tom (1966-67)
Banta, Frank (1937)
Barbato, Pat (1957-59)
Bare, Bob (1987-88)
Barker, Paul (1990-91, '93)
Barlock, James (1950)

Barnes, Bruce (1973-74)
Barnes, Gary (1970-72)
Barney, Zoe (1991)
Barnett, George (1925-26)
Bass, Sonny (1940-42)
Bates, Robert (1994-96)
Battaglia, Matt (1983-86)
Bauer, Bob (1948-50)
Beach, Chad (1995-97)
Beard, R.E. (1941)
Beard, Todd (1989-92)
Bearden, Bob (1959)
Beatty, Brian (1994)
Beauchamp, J. (1940)
Becker, John (1953-55)
Bednarski, Dan (1966-67)
Bell, Anwar (1991, '93-94)
Bell, Brian (1977)
Bell, James (1985)
Bell, John (1994-95)
Bell, Ron (1987-90)
Bender, Bob (1951-53)
Bennette, Ivan (1995-97)
Bernahl, Dave (1965-67)
Berry, Phil (1973-76)
Bertleson, Dick (1933)
Bertram, George (1946-49)
Besanceney, Mark (1976-77)
Besong, Jeff (1983)
Beswick, Steve (1987-90)
Bethea, Hal (1949-51)
Bethea, Herman (1952)
Bethel, Tony (1993-96)
Betz, Dave (1979-80)
Bibb, Don (1996-)
Billings, Edward (1913-14)
Birden, Anthony (1994)
Bishop, Richard (1972-73)
Black, Amos (1947-50)
Black, Roger (1913)
Black, W.W. (1935)
Blackerby, Jim (1924-27)
Blackford, William (1989-91)
Blackman, R.H. (1916)
Blackmon, Fred (1980-81)
Blair, Cordell (1994-96)
Blair, Scott (1994)
Blair, Tom (1980-81)
Blair, Tony (1981)
Blakey, Mike (1968)
Blalock, C.M. (1948-49)
Bland, Lou (1941)
Blasinsky, Mark (1980-81)
Blessinger, E. (1929)
Blessinger, Ed (1942)
Blumeier, Kevin (1990-92)
Blunk, Steve (1913-15)
Boardman, Jerome (1930)

Boarman, Dick (1963)
Bock, John (1990-92)
Bogan, Mike (1994-97)
Boggs, Wilbur (1975-76)
Boling, Dave (1970-71)
Bond, A.H. (1932)
Bonner, Anthony (1998)
Bonokofsky, C. (1939)
Borseth, Jeremy (1995-98)
Booher, Bill (1969-70)
Booker, Dave (1949-50)
Booker, Deon (1985-88)
Borgman, Ted (1926-28)
Bosler, Jim (1980)
Bosworth, Bill (1988-91)
Bott, Kenny (1928-31)
Bottom, Alan (1971)
Botts, Mike (1981-83)
Bouchee, Chris (1973-75)
Bouggess, Lee (1967-69)
Boughen, Mal (1942)
Bowen, Greg (1973)
Bowen, Pete (1980-81)
Bowman, Ed (1916)
Bowman, Roger (1963)
Boyd, Lavell (1997-)
Boykin, Deral (1991-92)
Boyle, Walter (1940-42)
Bradshaw, David (1975-77)
Brady, Jim (1940-42)
Bradwell, Antonio (1994)
Brand, Fred (1937-38)
Brasher, Ralph (1931)
Braxton, Joe (1975-76)
Brayan, Ramon (1994-95, '97)
Breuleux, Pete (1975)
Brewer, John (1948-51)
Bridges, Anthony (1991-93)
Brinkman, Cookie (1968-70)
Brinley, Don (1963-65)
Broaden, Larry (1959-62)
Brohm, Bill (1921-22)
Brohm, Greg (1989-92)
Brohm, Jeff (1990, '92-93)
Brohm, Oscar (1968-69)
Brookfield, Brandon (1991-94)
Broomfield, Eric (1987-90)
Brown, Connor (1927)
Brown, D.J. (1996)
Brown, H.H. (1926-29)
Brown, James (1975-78)
Brown, Keith (1982-84)
Brown, Kendall (1991-94)
Brown, Mark (1983)
Brown, Reggie (1971-72)
Brown, Sherman (1975)
Browne, Kenneth (1927-28)
Browning, Jack (1950)

Bruenig, Ray (1946-47)
Brumback, Bill (1969)
Brundula, Dennis (1972-73)
Bruner, Steve (1989-90)
Bruning, Bud (1940-42)
Bryant, Pete (1957-60)
Bryon, Louis (1961-63)
Buchanan, Ray (1989-92)
Buehler, Don (1974)
Buffone, Doug (1962-65)
Buffone, Jerry (1963-65)
Bullard, William (1934)
Burdock, Tony (1970-72)
Burkey, Pete (1987-90)
Burlington, Anson (1928)
Burrell, Xavier (1997-)
Burroughs, Tim (1973-75)
Burton, Ralph (1921)
Buster, Curtis (1983-84)
Butler, Liggett (1991-92)
Butler, Randy (1976-79)
Butler, Robbie (1974)
Butler, Zach (1996-)
Bynm, Pete (1987-90)
Bynoe, Rawle (1989-92)
Byrd, Anthony (1996-)

C

Cade, Jon (1982-83)
Cadwell, Larry (1957-59)
Cain, Dan (1973-74, 76)
Cain, George (1954-57)
Caldwell, C.N. (1912-13, '15)
Calland, Lee (1959-62)
Calvin, Ralph (1969-71)
Campbell, Greg (1970-71)
Campbell, Mike (1971)
Campbell, Tony (1980-82)
Campos, Alan (1992-95)
Canady, Bob (1968)
Caras, Tom (1955)
Carpenter, Ken (1939-40)
Carrick, Brian (1974-76)
Carroll, Allen (1998-)
Carroll, Tom (1992-93)
Carroll, Tom (1974)
Carroll, Tom (1941-42, '46)
Carswell, Ivan (1934-35)
Casey, Bob (1965, '67)
Caswell, Jason (1996-)
Caudill, Fred (1923-24)
Caufield, Jimmy (1937-40)
Cavallo, Tom (1990-93)
Cavitt, Volney (1922)
Cerione, Danny (1983-86)
Chance, Jerry (1957)
Chapman, Tim (1984)
Charasika, Tendia (1996)

Cheppo, Mario (1954-57)
Chinn, Kevin (1989-93)
Clark, Colburn (1987)
Clark, S.S. (1934)
Clark, Rico (1993-96)
Clay, Roger (1979-82)
Clayton, B. (1950)
Clayton, Mark (1979-82)
Cleveland, Bob (1959-62)
Click, Steve (1946-48)
Clower, Bill (1941-42)
Coldiron, George (1946)
Coldiron, Greg (1973)
Cole, Calvert (1984-86)
Coleman, Jack (1946-47)
Coleman, Tom (1938-41)
Collage, Dick (1981-82)
Collina, Elmer (1955-59)
Collins, Andre (1998)
Collins, Charles (1968)
Collins, Chris (1989, '91)
Compise, Pete (1966-68)
Compton, Larry (1961, 63)
Conner, L.E. (1962-64)
Conner, Prentiss (1921)
Conrad, Bernie (1974-76)
Contento, Mike (1974-76)
Conway, Doug (1982-84)
Conway, Matt (1995-96)
Coode, Dave (1975-77)
Cook, Kevin (1991-93)
Copeland, Anthony (1984)
Copeland, John (1969-70)
Corley, Martise (1997-)
Corso, Marty (1922-25)
Cosby, Don (1983-86)
Cosby, Rene (1990)
Craft, Donnie (1978-81)
Crafts, Jerry (1989-90)
Crago, Lester (1931)
Crawford, Wilbur (1932)
Crecelics, Tom (1941-42)
Crivello, Jason (1994)
Crocetti, Dominic (1946)
Croley, Gary (1994-96)
Crowder, M.O. (1928-30)
Crowe, John (1930-31)
Cruz, Mike (1980-82)
Cruz, Rick (1976-78)
Cuby, John (1977-79)
Cully, Jeff (1974-78)
Culley, Andy (1989-92)
Cumberworth, Matt (1976-77)
Cumings, Lamar (1982-83)
Cummings, Anthony (1987-90)
Cunningham, Don (1966-68)
Cupito, Steve (1979)
Curella, L. (1965)
Curry, Ron (1969)
Curry, Sebastian (1980-82)

D

Daffron, Jeff (1982)
Daniel, John (1912-14)
Daniel, Maurice (1914-16)
Daniel, Roy (1913-14)
Daniels, Anthony (1985)
Daniels, Jim (1953)
Dardzinski, Aaron (1998-)
Darling, John (1975)
Daugherty, Harry (1922-24)

Daugherty, Jack (1924-26)
Davenport, Ron (1981-84)
Davidson, Alex (1937-38)
Davis, Antonio (1985-86)
Davis, Harry (1935)
Davis, Jack (1946)
Davis, Mark (1974)
Dawkins, Bernie (1974, '77)
Dawkins, Ralph (1990-93)
Day, Ken (1948-51)
Debold, Dave (1990-93)
Delozier, Roscoe (1916)
Deluca, Pete (1971)
DeMarco, John (1981-83)
Dennis, James (1995, '97-98)
Dennis, Mike (1964-66)
DePauola, Len (1972-74)
Depree, Julian (1928-29)
Derricoatte, Bernard (1974)
Desenberg, Bill (1952)
Detenber, Gene (1948-50)
Detenber, Mike (1967-69)
Deward, Mike (1951)
Dezelan, Dave (1967)
Dickens, Torrence (1983-84)
Dickerson, Mike (1975-77)
Dickerson, Rolland (1983)
Didier, Jim (1975)
Dihtzeruk, Dan (1978-80)
Dillion, Samuel (1987)
Dimoff, Greg (1978-80)
Dinkins, Courtney (1996-)
Dixson, Calvin (1985-86, '88)
Dobbs, Bill (1962-64)
Dobbs, Steve (1968-69)
Dobina, Don (1974)
Dolack, Bob (1957)
Dole, Jim (1952)
Doll, Kenny (1933-35)
Doll, Paul (1934-35)
Donahue, Steve (1977)
Donnelly, Bob (1957-58)
Dorsch, Bill (1968-69)
Dotson, Don (1927-30)
Doty, Jeff (1983)
Douglas, Allen (1986-89)
Downs, Bill (1965-67)
Dozier, Nate (1980, 82)
Drachman, David (1977-79)
Dressler, Bill (1932)
Drewery, Austin (1926-29)
Dudderar, Ed (1946)
Dudley, Kim (1974)
Dueberry, Vince (1992-93)
Duenweg, Rudy (1912-13)
Duganich, Joe (1971-72)
Duke, J.W. (1947-49)
Dunbar, Don (1957-58)
Durand (1916)
Dwyer, George (1913-14)

E

Earl, Dave (1928)
Eberenz, Josh (1996-98)
Eble, Rob (1998-)
Edelen, Marshall (1933-34)
Edelen, Tom (1969-72)
Edelen, Tony (1991)
Edelhauser, Ed (1936-38)
Edwards, Roger (1974)
Edwards, Welby (1968)

Egan, Nick (1974)
Eggleston, Ken (1965-67)
Elbert, Norbert (1939-40)
Ellington, Ron (1973-76)
Ellis, Phil (1981-84)
Ellis, Zarko (1977-79)
Elsler, Dick (1925-28)
Embry, Jim (1976-78)
Embry, Bob (1984-85)
Emerson, Ralph (1934-37)
Ennis, Ed (1987-88)
Ernie, C. Pralle (1915)
Ernst, Charles (1926-28)
Espie, Marshall (1925-26)
Esters, Tony (1995-96)
Evans, Brad (1967)
Evans, Lamar (1978-81)
Ewald, George (1912)
Ewers, E.M. (1913)

F

Falleri, Joe (1983-84)
Farmer, Albert (1984-85)
Farmer, Ray (1952-53, 55)
Fanning, Jay (1992-93)
Feagan, Gene (1948-50)
Ferguson, Reggie (1992-93)
Fields, Mike (1976-77)
Figg, Carey (1989-91)
Fike, Ed (1946)
Finger, Ernie (1946)
Finger, Fred (1931-34)
Finley, Glenn (1915)
Finn, John (1957-61)
Firkins, Curtis (1954-56)
Fishback, Ford (1926-28)
Fishback, Olen (1946)
Fisher, Armand (1922-26)
Fisher, Steve (1992-93)
Fitzgerald, Pat (1987-90)
Fitzpatrick, Chris (1992-94)
Florence, Bill (1972-73)
Flores, Mike (1987-90)
Floyd, Otis (1996-)
Fluellen, Larry (1973-75)
Ford, Salem (1914-15)
Ford, Tom (1925-27)
Forrest, Bill (1947)
Forsee, Tyre (1933-34)
Fortune, Chad (1986-89)
Fountain, Frank (1994-95)
Frame, Jim (1966-68)
Francis, William (1941)
Frazier, Russell (1916)
Freeman, Jakale (1997)
French, Jim (1974)
Frost, Johnny (1992-95)
Fuizotte, Joe (1924-26)
Fults, Jim (1952)
Fultz, George (1942)
Fuqua, John (1994-97)
Furman, Larrame (1992)

G

Gagel, Nick (1976-78)
Gaines, Brian (1998-)
Gaines, Kevin (1990-93)
Gainey, John (1987-90)
Galcik, Larry (1984-86)
Gall, Mark (1974)

Gallagher, Jack (1977)
Galloway, Wayne (1967)
Gangwer, Dan (1987-90)
Gannon, Scott (1979-82)
Gantous, Mike (1996-)
Gardis, Curt (1974)
Gardner, Carwell (1989)
Gardner, Merle (1990)
Gatewood, Jim (1955-56)
Gatschler, Frank (1949)
Gatti, Bill (1968-70)
Gentile, John (1924-25)
George, Harry (1986-87, '89)
Gergosky, Mike (1988)
German, Ron (1988-90)
Gernert, E.R. (1916)
Getch, Rich (1966-68)
Getch, Val (1962)
Gholston, Kendrick (1994-97)
Giannini, Tom (1930-33)
Gibson, Greg (1976-78)
Gibson, Robert (1986-89)
Gibson, Stu (1946-47)
Gilbert, Lonny (1966-68)
Giles, John (1959-62)
Gillam, Jack (1948, '50-51)
Gipe, Marty (1976-77)
Gitschier, Frank (1946-49)
Gitschier, Frank, III (1971-73)
Givens, Eric (1983-84)
Givens, Kelvin (1994)
Givins, Ernest (1984-85)
Glasper, Chris (1987-88)
Glass, Ira (1967-69)
Glenn, Earl (1912-14)
Godbolt, Johnnie (1968-70)
Golden, Lynn (1935)
Gonzalez, Gerry (1982)
Gonzalez, Jose (1990-92)
Goodman, Arvell (1946)
Goodman, Casswell (1995-98)
Gordon, Donnell (1996-97)
Gorman, John (1971-73)
Gossman, W. (1937-38)
Gotcher, Craig (1998-)
Graham, Jack (1937-38)
Graham, Steve (1982)
Grandy, Mark (1984)
Grant, J.D. (1914)
Gray, Bill (1985-89)
Gray, Leon (1921)
Gray, Preston (1984)
Grednic, Frank (1948-51)
Green, Bobby (1975)
Green, Ernie (1958-61)
Green, Ibn (1996-)
Green, Ken (1946)
Green, Paul (1952)
Green, Phillip (1985-87)
Griffin, Jeff (1984-85)
Griffin, Larry (1970-72)
Griffin, Sam (1991-93)
Griggs, Derric (1993)
Grivna, Mark (1997-)
Groves, F.C. (1930-31)
Groves, Fergus (1933)
Grubb, Troy (1992-94)
Gruden, Jay (1985-88)
Gruneisen, Roger (1968, '70)
Guertin, Gary (1961-64)
Gumm, Gary (1998)

Stories About the University of Louisville's Football Past

Gutridge, Steve (1967-69)
Gwinner, Dwayne (1996)

H
Haas, Danny (1983-84)
Haberlin, Clarence (1941)
Haberline, Charles (1940-41)
Hackett, Fred (1973-76)
Haden, Bo (1978-80)
Hagan, Gene (1978-81)
Hale, Floyd (1913)
Hall, Bob (1988-89)
Hall, R.L. (1928-30)
Hall, Ron (1963-65)
Hallal, Eli (1968)
Haller, Jim (1948)
Hallmark, Bill (1948-49)
Hamilton, Joey (1985-88)
Hamm, Dave (1960-61)
Hampton, Chris (1993)
Hampton, Tom (1936-39)
Handley, Marcus (1980)
Hanna, Jim (1990-93)
Hannah, Jim (1964)
Hardaway, Richard (1916)
Hardin, John (1928)
Hargrove, Reggie (1998-)
Harmon, Ed (1965-67)
Harmon, Harold (1934)
Harnden, Ken (1992)
Harold, Don (1974-77)
Harper, Robert (1975-76)
Harris, Rashad (1997-)
Hart, Larry (1968, 70)
Hartman, Toby (1963)
Harvey, Kevin (1986-87)
Hatcher, Kevin (1984)
Hatfield, David (1981-84)
Hawley, Roger (1962)
Haws, Watson (1922-24)
Hawthorne, Derek (1988-90)
Hayden, William (1916)
Haydock, Robert (1972-73)
Hayes, Brian (1988-91)
Haynes, Da-Woyne (1988-89)
Headrick, R. (1940)
Heard, Norman (1973-74, '76)
Heinichen, Al (1946)
Heinrich, Ron (1976-79)
Heironymous, Russ (1928)
Heitlauf, Art (1946-47)
Henchey, Matt (1932)
Henchy, Stephen (1992-94)
Henderson, Ivey (1990,'92-93)
Henry, Herb (1991)
Henry, Jeff (1976-79)
Henry, O.P. (1913)
Hermes, W.B. (1942)
Herring, Bud (1997-)
Hesselgrave, Mike (1959)
Hessler, Mike (1977)
Hickey, Tom (1972-74)
Hickman, Greg (1979-82)
Hicks, Ralph (1973-76)
Hicks, Richard (1966-67)
Higgs, Andy (1985-86, '88-89)
Hilbert, Jon (1997-)
Hill, Don (1951)
Hill, Ken (1994)
Hill, Kevin (1978-79)
Hill, Marcus (1991-93)

Hladio, Steve (1957-60)
Hobbs, Stan (1946-47)
Hockaden, Dave (1962-63)
Hockensmith, Don (1959-62)
Hocker, Al (1923-24)
Hocker, Charles (1921-22)
Hodge, Steve (1965, 68)
Hoerter, Jr., Kenny (1993-98)
Hoffman, Graig (1994-97)
Holben, LeRoy (1950-52)
Hollowell, Jim (1946-47,'52-53)
Holman, Rashad (1997-)
Holzer, Tom (1964-66)
Hood, Howard (1984)
Hornsby, Rick (1972-73)
Hortert, Jeff (1980-83)
Houser, J. (1934-35)
Houser, Jim (1953-54)
Houston, Les (1956-58)
Howard, Bob (1950-52)
Howard, Charles (1946)
Howard, James (1986)
Howard, Rick (1971-72)
Howard, Ted (1951, '56-58)
Hrovat, Larry (1972-73)
Hudson, Bob (1959)
Huff, Howard (1929-31)
Huffman, Gary (1984-87)
Hughes, Fred (1951, '53, '56)
Hulette, Virgil (1939)
Humphries, Keith (1981-83)
Hunt, Johnny (1959-60)
Huser, Jay (1969)
Hutt, J.D. (1940)

I
Inman, Gary (1969-71)
Isenberg, Charles (1938-41)

J
Jackson, Arnold (1997-)
Jackson, Calvin (1983-85)
Jackson, Joe (1985)
Jackson, Mike (1992)
Jackson, Shawn (1991-94)
Jackson, Tom (1970-72)
Jacobs, A.J. (1973-74)
Jacobs, Stan (1941-42)
Jacobs, Ted (1992-93)
Jacoby, Joe (1978-80)
Jaegers, Dick (1963)
Jaggers, Gene (1954-55)
Janelsins, Gunars (1965, '67)
Janiak, Bill (1963-65)
Jefferies, Owen (1928)
Jefferson, Bobby (1983-86)
Jelinek, Steve (1971-73)
Jenkins, Chris (1991-94)
Jenkins, J.E. (1913)
Jenne, E.E. (1940)
Jesukaitis, Tom (1969-71)
Jeter, Courtney (1980-82)
Jewell, Steve (1972-74)
Johnican, Larry (1977)
Johnson, Grant (1998-)
Johns, G.F. (1913)
Johnson, Alvin (1988)
Johnson, Charlie (1963-65)
Johnson, Don (1984-86)
Johnson, Dwayne (1981)
Johnson, Eddie (1977-80)

Johnson, Joe (1991-93)
Johnson, Matt (1994-96)
Johnson, Reggie (1987-90)
Johnson, Robbie (1989)
Johnson, Steve (1980)
Johnson, Wayne (1958)
Jones, Alton (1992-95)
Jones, Clyde (1925-26)
Jones, Fred (1988-91)
Jones, F.C. (1938)
Jones, Greg (1980-81)
Jones, Horace (1968-70)
Jones, James (1984-85)
Jones, Jason (1998-)
Jones, Junior (1983-85)
Jones, Mel (1971-72)
Jones, Pete (1984)
Jones, Walt (1965-66)

K
Kachler, Edmund (1916)
Kacvinsky, Bob (1974)
Kaczmarek, Jim (1969-70)
Kader, Joe (1980-82)
Kaminski, Dale (1971-73)
Karaglanis, Frank (1959-60)
Karem, Greg (1967-69)
Karibo, Jim (1946)
Karns, Bill (1948-51)
Karrh, Bill (1949)
Katchen, Tony (1980)
Katope, Chris (1941)
Kavanaugh, Charles (1913)
Keeling, Crawford (1935)
Keisel, John (1928)
Keller, Billy (1931)
Keller, Ken (1940-41)
Kemp, C.W. (1929-31)
Kennedy, Derrick (1996-)
Kennedy, J.L. (1929)
Kennedy, Kirk (1984-87)
Kennedy, Orville (1922)
Kibbey, Rick (1975-76)
Kidd, Don (1946-49)
Kielkopf, Bill (1925-26)
Kienzle, Tommy (1921-24)
Kimbel, Dewey (1923)
Kincaid, Addison (1931)
King, Jim (1969)
Kingston, Joe (1938)
Kirbus, Rich (1973)
Kirk, E.B. (1921)
Kirkendahl, Walt (1935)
Kirsch, John (1958)
Klein, Nellis (1949-51)
Kloehs, David (1992-94)
Knighton, Rodney (1984-87)
Knop, Brian (1978)
Knop, Kurt (1980-81)
Knop, Otto (1949-52)
Knop, Otto, Jr. (1977-79)
Knuutila, Robert (1990-92)
Kolb, Bruce (1982-83)
Kolter, John (1965-67)
Kordic, Brad (1973-74)
Kortas, Ken (1960-63)
Kosman, Bill (1971)
Koster, Fred (1924-27)
Koubratoff, H. (1984-85)
Kovanda, Dick (1952-54)
Kozuhik, Miles (1953-54)

Kraft, Ted (1930)
Kratsas, John (1970-71)
Krebs, David (1982-84)
Kreutzjans, Gerald (1974)
Kries, Shawn (1993-95)
Kriever, Hugh (1953)
Kron, Max (1930)
Kunzman, Bill (1968-69)
Kurk, Henry (1938-39)

L
LaDuke, Joe (1946)
LaFramboise, Tom (1962-64)
Lake, R.C. (1928-29)
Lakeman, Gil (1946)
Lamar, Harmon (1933-36)
Langan, Ed (1926-29)
Langan, Gene (1936-39)
Langan, M. (1939)
Lannan, Joe (1994)
Lantz, Terry (1987-89)
Larkins, Ellsworth (1980-82)
Laurin, Jack (1986)
Law, Bill (1957)
Lawson, Steward (1931)
Lawton, Eric (1987-88)
Layne, Bill (1954-55)
Leahy, Tom (1936-39)
Lee, Medford (1966-68)
Lee, Wink (1946)
Leggett, V.M. (1912)
Lettie, Bill (1964-66)
Levinstin, Louis (1928)
Levy, Stuart (1914)
Lewis, Eric (1986)
Lichtenberg, Tom (1959-61)
Lichvar, Bob (1951-53)
Lillard, Derrick (1992-95)
Lindsey, Wilbur (1935)
Lipsey, Curtis (1989-90)
Lipsitz, Bernard (1931)
Lively, Bill (1951-53)
Lobitz, James (1992)
Lococo, Vince (1941-42, '46)
Lohrke, Brett (1982)
Long, Ed (1970-72)
Long, Harry (1933-34)
Long, Tom (1983-85)
Lotspeich, Bob (1935-37)
Lowe, Marty (1991, '93-95)
Lowe, Melzar (1933-36)
Lucas, Doug (1984)
Lucas, John (1963-64)
Lucia, Tom (1947-50)
Lyles, Lenny (1954-57)
Lyons, George (1912)

M
MacFarlane, Al (1963-65)
Mack, Lawrence (1978-80)
Maddox, Sidney (1937)
Madeya, John (1970-72)
Madison, Sam (1993-96)
Madrick, Ron (1985-87)
Maduaka-Cain, Ikem (1995)
Mager, Matt (1977-79)
Mahoney, Tom (1965-66)
Mahoney, Tony (1966-67)
Majeed, Kaaba (1994-95)
Mallory, I.J. (1955-56)
Mancini, Rick (1975)

Mannheimer, Milton (1941)
Mantchen, Ralph (1947)
Marcus, Scott (1970-72)
Marion, Mike (1968)
Marks, Poachy (1925-26)
Marney, Ron (1983-84)
Marsh, Rondel (1994-97)
Marshall, Avery (1982-85)
Marshall, John (1985-88)
Marshall, Steve (1978)
Martin, Amos (1968, '70-71)
Martin, Raymond (1983)
Martin, Tom (1970-72)
Mascenik, Paul (1973-74)
Massaro, Gene (1951-52)
Masterson, Ches (1934-37)
Mathews, Marc (1983)
Mattingly, Chip (1998-)
Mattingly, Paul (1969-71)
Mauzy, Mike (1986-88)
Maxwell, Tim (1986)
May, Dean (1980-83)
Mayer, John (1933)
Mayhall, Harvey (1924-27)
McAllister, Scott (1987-90)
McBarnette, Geoff (1998-)
McBirth, Willie (1976)
McCaleb, Harin (1913-15)
McCartney, Pete (1983-84)
McClain, John (1938-41)
McClanahan, C.W. (1912)
McCloud, Tyrus (1993-96)
McConnell, Bob (1958)
McCray, Quincy (1983)
McCullough, Lewis (1973)
McDevitt, Coleman (1930)
McDonald, Bennie (1926-28)
McDonald, Brian (1998-)
McDonald, Mike (1953)
McDonald, Richard (1935)
McDowell, K. (1935-36)
McDowell, Kenny (1932)
McDowell, Paul (1989-90)
McFadden, Ricky (1989-91)
McGinnis, Henry (1941)
McKay, Don (1936-39)
McKay, Ken (1987-90)
McKay, Paul (1936-38)
McKinney, Mike (1987-89)
McKinney, Ray (1928-31)
McMahon, Bill (1964-66)
McMahon, Mike (1961-62)
McMahon, Todd (1980)
McVey, R. (1950)
Meade, Jack (1953-55)
Meadows, Brenon (1993-94)
Meeks (1916)
Merriweather, B.M. (1913-14)
Mershon, Oliver (1932)
Mihaljevic, Tom (1983)
Mihm, Tom (1969-71)
Miles, Steve (1994)
Mills, Mel (1988-91)
Miller, Brian (1983-84)
Miller, Brook (1983)
Miller, Charles (1935)
Miller, David (1985-87)
Miller, Greg (1981)
Miller, Jim (1978-81)
Miller, Kevin (1974-77)
Miller, Uncas (1925-27)

Miller, V. (1926-28)
Mingus, Marvin (1951)
Minnifield, Frank (1979-82)
Minogue, Mike (1983-86)
Misetic, Steve (1996)
Mitchell, C. (1939-40)
Mitchell, Lamonte (1980)
Mitchell, Marc (1975-77)
Mitchell, Robert (1979-81)
Mitchem, Bill (1949-50)
Moll, Ken (1974-76)
Montano, Miguel (1994-97)
Montgomery, Bob (1931-32)
Montgomery, David (1974)
Montgomery, Tom (1961-62)
Moody, Mike (1979)
Moon, Ron (1976-78)
Mooney, Jim (1955-56)
Moore, Frank (1966)
Moore, Herbert (1938-41)
Moore, Tom (1981-83)
Moorhatch, John (1942)
Moran, J.R. (1928, 31)
Moreau, Frank (1995, '97-)
Morey, Tom (1959-60)
Mosby, Danny (1996-98)
Mosher, Clure (1938-41)
Moss, Anthony (1984-85)
Moss, Scedric (1980-82)
Moyler, David (1988-90)
Mudd, Charlie (1962-63)
Muir, P.B. (1921)
Muldoon, Phil (1942-46)
Mulhall, R.E. (1931)
Mullins, Terry (1978)
Mumma, John (1974)
Mumphrey, Kevin (1994)
Murphree, Mallory (1915)
Murrer, David (1982)
Musgrave, Mark (1980-82)
Myers, Keith (1951)

N

Nabor, Chuck (1957)
Nachand, Clarence (1926)
Nagle, Browning (1989-90)
Naimaister, Dave (1982-84)
Najjar, Larry (1974)
Nauert, Jim (1984, '86-87)
Navarro, Todd (1983-84)
Neafus, Stan (1946)
Neat, L.R. (1931)
Neely, Mike (1991)
Neidert, John (1965-67)
Newman, Bud (1929-31)
Nichols, Les (1983-84)
Nickerson, Bruce (1972-74)
Nicoletti, Joe (1951-53)
Niece, Robert (1980-82)
Noafus, Roy (1946)
Noon, John (1953-56)
Nord, Gary (1977-79)
Nord, Rick (1995-98)
Norman, E.J. (1937)
Norris, Bobby (1978)
Norris, Dave (1968-70)
Norris, Jim (1983)
Nugent, R.C. (1912)
Nunn, Bob (1948-50)
Nuss, Dave (1963-64)
Nuss, Kevin (1981-84)

Nuzzolese, Mike (1979-82)

O

Oben, Roman (1992-95)
O'Connor, John (1974)
Ogden, J.D. (1936)
Oldham, Richard (1936, '38-39)
Olejack, Greg (1975-76)
Olinger, Ashley (1937)
Olmstead, Jim (1951-53)
O'Neal, Bob (1960-62)
O'Neal, Pete (1985)
Orem, Dale (1957-59)
Osborne, Paul (1921-24)
O'Shaughnessy, Joe (1997-)
Osorio, Vasco (1912-13)
Otte, Frank (1953-56)
Owen, Bill (1957-59)
Oyler, Wally (1966-68)

P

Painter, Benny (1983-84)
Painter, Jed (1983)
Papania, Joe (1947-50)
Pardieu, Ben (1973)
Pardieu, Chris (1982-83)
Parker, Cardell (1972-74)
Parker, Zek (1998-)
Parrott, Herb (1983)
Patrick, Garrin (1991-93)
Patrick, Wayne (1965-67)
Patterson, Danny (1993)
Patterson, Pat (1979-81)
Payne, James (1992-93)
Payne, Jason (1994-96)
Payton, Ray (1977-79)
Peacock, Walter (1972-75)
Peak, Andy (1996)
Pearson, E.C. (1931)
Pence, Bill (1950-51)
Pennella, Rick (1976-77)
Perrin, Billy (1976-79)
Perrin, Jamie (1978-80)
Perry, Kirk (1983-84)
Perry, Pat (1939, '41-42)
Perry, W. (1950)
Pesavento, James (1995-97)
Peterson, Rick (1972)
Petry, Charlie (1967)
Petty, Ron (1957-60)
Phelps, Herbie (1967-68)
Phelps, Tanny (1961-63)
Phillips, Art (1941)
Phillips, Charlie (1953-54)
Phillips, Joe Lee (1972-74)
Pianko, Greg (1983-85)
Pierce, G.S. (1939)
Pierre-Louis, Frank (1986)
Pierson, Glenn (1935)
Pillitary, Ben (1947)
Pinski, Dave (1966)
Pirkey, E.L. (1933)
Pitchford, Jack (1926)
Pitters, Lenny (1978)
Poelking, T.J. (1988-89)
Pointer, Chris (1994)
Pointer, Jeff (1987-88)
Pok, Jack (1979-80)
Pollock, Ed (1993)
Pomeroy, Don (1973-75)
Pongonis, Mark (1975-78)

Pontius, Bill (1913)
Poole, Nathan (1975-78)
Porco, Ken (1957-59)
Posadas, Pedro (1976-77)
Powell, Carl (1995-96)
Price, Keith (1983-84)
Prince, Calvin (1976-77)
Pritchett, Doug (1982-84)
Pryor, Bill (1923)
Pugh, Roy (1951-52, '57)
Pullem, David (1974)
Purcell, Chris (1974-75, '77)
Purcell, Don (1952-53)
Purry, Dar-Shay (1996-98)
Putnam, Rufus (1933)

.

Q

Quick, Rhonyia (1991)
Quinn, Terry (1991-94)

R

Racel, David (1984)
Radmacher, Frank (1966-68)
Rager, Dick (1947)
Ramey, Roy (1947)
Ramsey, Frank (1946-49)
Rasmussen, Roy (1929)
Raush, Russ (1946)
Ray, Babe (1950-51)
Ray, Bill (1948-50)
Ray, Gerald (1949-51)
Ray, Leonard (1990-93)
Raymond, Warren (1940-42)
Recherman, James (1930, 32)
Rechtin, Les (1950-52)
Redman, Bob (1968-69)
Redman, Chris (1996-)
Redman, Lloyd (1946)
Reese, John (1921)
Reese, Steve (1971-73)
Reid, Ben (1927, '30-31)
Reid, Jack (1958-61)
Reiling, George (1938-40)
Renner, Rich (1995-96)
Reynolds, Ed (1987-90)
Rhodes, Walter (1987, '89-91)
Rice, Quinn (1995-96)
Rice-Locket, Terry (1994-97)
Richart, Phil (1962-63)
Richardson, Josh (1997-98)
Richey, Harper (1921-22)
Rideout, Dave (1947)
Riser, Bob (1974-75)
Ritchie, Norm (1965)
Rivenbark, Dave (1949-52)
Roberts, Eugene (1946)
Robertson, Jim Tom (1925-28)
Robinson, Kenny (1977-80)
Robinson, Rex (1957)
Rodgers, Clarence (1912-13)
Rodriguez, Sean (1991)
Roe, Jeff (1982)
Rollins, Eric (1979, '82)
Roman, Israel (1971, '74)
Romey, J.H. (1937)
Rommell, Bill (1946)
Rooney, George (1939)
Roper, Ricky (1994)
Roscoe, Terrence (1991-94)
Rose, Harold (1937-38)

Rosenfield, Jimmy (1938-41)
Rossoll, Don (1957-59)
Roth, Horace (1927-29)
Rothfield, D. (1940)
Roundtree, Antonio (1997-)
Rowan, Watson (1912-13)
Rowe, Lionel (1916)
Rubbert, Ed (1983-86)
Rusley, Bobby (1984)
Russell, Benny (1964-66)
Russell, Ron (1971-73)
Ryan, Bill (1933-34)
Ryan, D. (1938)
Ryan, George (1932-34)

S

Sales, Larry (1975)
Sammons, Bill (1959-60, '62)
Sander, Mark (1987-90)
Sanders, Raynard (1986)
Sanks, David (1967-69)
Santho, Rick (1974)
Sartini, Gene (1950, '54-55)
Saunders, Gerald (1977)
Schad, Bill (1961-63)
Schaeffer, Jim (1963)
Schaller, Paul (1983-86)
Scharre, Stan (1937-38)
Scheper, Guy (1977-79)
Scherma, Joe (1963)
Schiengold, Pat (1921-23)
Schloemer, Fred (1936-39)
Schloemer, Louis (1938-40)
Schmitt, Paul (1956)
Schneider, B. (1928)
Schonsiegel, (1912)
Schrader, (1912)
Schuhmann, George (1932)
Schuler, Dave (1975-77)
Schuler, Lonnie (1972-73)
Schultz, Tim (1976)
Schuppert, Ray (1941, '46)
Scott, Chris (1997)
Scott, Leslie (1933)
Scott, Mike (1995)
Scroggins, Tyrann (1994)
Searcy, Ed (1937)
Searcy, Greg (1978-79)
Sehlinger, George (1933-34)
Sekeres, Duke (1957, 60)
Seldon, Joe (1931)
Sellers, Chris (1985-87)
Semak, Tony (1990)
Senkevich, John (1968-69)
Settle, Mickey (1964-66)
Sexton, Matt (1998-)
Sgroi, Anthony (1938-40)
Shaw, Rick (1985-86)
Shearer, Guy (1928-31)
Sheehy, Mike (1974-76)
Sheeley, J.J. (1937)
Sheffield, Charles (1996-)
Shelby, Willie (1982-85)
Shelman, Anthony (1992-94)
Shell, H.E. (1931)
Shelton, Don (1946-49)
Shelton, John (49-52)
Shepherd, Mark (1990-93)
Sherman, Jack (1937-38)
Shields, Harry (1928-29)
Shively, Brett (1996-98)

Sholly, Jeff (1996-98)
Short, Bill (1966-67)
Silliman, Harlan (1952)
Silverstein, Phillip (1921)
Simon, John (1970-71)
Simpson, Reneau (1972)
Sims, Coswell (1994-95)
Sims, T. (1925)
Singleton, Neil (1986-87)
Sipe, Ken (1939-41)
Six, Bob (1974)
Skaaland, Ed (1971)
Skarja, Joe (1977-78)
Skiles, Ricky (1975-79)
Skinner, Roy (1946)
Slater, W.L. (1935)
Slechter, Rex (1955-56)
Slider, Bill (1936, 38)
Smith, Bernard (1938-40)
Smith, Brevin (1989, '91-92)
Smith, Bryon (1951-52)
Smith, Clarence (1948-50, '53)
Smith, Dwight (1989)
Smith, E.R. (1932)
Smith, Jeff (1986-88)
Smith, Jerry (1959-62)
Smith, Joe (1965-66)
Smith, Joey (1987-90)
Smith, Marty (1972-74)
Smith, Tony (1974-77)
Smith, Walter (1946)
Smyrichinsky, Tod (1986)
Snow, John (1929)
Solberg, Cliff (1960)
Sonye, Anthony (1992-94)
Sonye, Eric (1992-94)
Sosnin, Hershell (1931-34)
Sowa, John (1954-55)
Sparkman, Alan (1946)
Speedy, Jeff (1981-82)
Spencer, Charles (1927-28)
Spencer, Clarence (1964-65)
Spillman, Ben (1971)
Spratt, Greg (1983-85)
Stahl, Scott (1982)
Stallings, Jim (1966-68)
Stallings, Tony (1998-)
Starks, Price (1925-26)
Starnes, Bob (1960-62)
Steger, Roy (1976)
Steiger, Joe (1932)
Stephens, Gerald (1987-89)
Stephens, Keith (1986-88)
Stern, Walter (1931-32)
Stevens, Howard (1971-72)
Stickrod, Kelly (1980-83)
Stiers, Bill (1946)
Stinson, Jason (1992-95)
Stitch, Charles (1960-62)
Stone, Joe (1938-41)
Stram, Stu (1976-79)
Street, Al (1974)
Strickland, Rod (1992-93)
Stricklin, Larry (1985-86, '88)
Striegel, Harold (1949-50)
Strull, Asher (1931-33)
Struss, Ed (1928)
Struve, Dudley (1915-16)
Sturgeon, John (1977)
Sturtzel, Gil (1955-57)
Sullivan, Leonard (1983-84)

Summers, Wilbur (1972-75)
Sumpter, Ben (1990-93)
Suski, Jon (1996-98)
Sutherland, Lou (1959-60)
Swabek, Craig (1986-89)
Swafford, Darryl (1987-88, '90)
Swanson, Gunard (1982)
Swope, Kurt (1971)

T

Tarleton, Eric (1982-84)
Taylor, Al (1931-33)
Taylor, Bill (1942)
Taylor, Dewayne (1997-)
Taylor, Leland (1996)
Taylor, Wayne (1980)
Teague, G. (1949)
Terry, Elmer (1921)
Terry, Prentiss (1915-16)
Tharpe, Richard (1979-82)
Theiss, Jim (1971)
Thieneman, Chris (1983-84, '86-87)
Thiry, Bob (1978-80)
Thomas, Ben (1916)
Thomas, Danny (1983-86)
Thomas, DeForest (1978)
Thompson, Glenn (1990-93)
Thompson, Sam (1922-23)
Thompson, Tommy (1927-30)
Thomas, Justin (1998-)
Thomas, Troy (1992)
Thomas, Tyrone (1988)
Thompson, Willard (1928)
Thrasher, Robert (1976-77)
Threlkeld, (1932-35)
Tibbals, Luther (1931)
Tillery, John (1978)
Tipton, Roy (1946)
Tisci, Nunzio (1953-55)
Todd, Bob (1946)
Todd, Bryan (1979-80)
Todd, Grover (1913)
Touche' (1995-96)
Townsel, Wyman (1951-52)
Townsell, Ray (1951-52)
Trabue, Joe (1946-49)
Trainor, Mike (1980-81, '83)
Trautwein, Jay (1980-82)
Trautwein, Jerry (1982)
Trawick, J.D. (1930)
Trimble, Harry (1972-73)
Triplett, Tom (1990)
Tucker, Eric (1986)
Tucker, James (1929)
Turley, Howard (1956-59)
Turner, Harold (1936-39)
Turner, Ken (1946-47, '49-50)
Tuyo, John (1987)
Tyson, Jeryl (1994-95)

U

Uhrig, Phil (1941)
Underwood, George (1980)
Underwood, James (1994)
Unitas, Joe (1954-56)
Unitas, Johnny (1951-54)
Urton, F.W. (1916)
Utley, Shedrick (1992)

V

Valvo, Jack (1951-52)
Vandervert, Art (1922-23)
Varajohn, Milan (1958)
Vari, Bob (1969)
Vaughn, Eric (1984, '86)
Velesig, Dave (1966-67)
Veto, Mike (1983-86)

W

Wade, Ryan (1995-97)
Waggoner, Dave (1971)
Wagner, Mike (1965)
Wagoner, Jim (1972-75)
Walker, Andy (1954-57)
Walker, Cleo (1967-69)
Walker, Dan (1959-61)
Walker, Sanford (1973)
Walker, Stanley (1912-13)
Wall, John (1980-82)
Waller, John (1968)
Waltman, Earl (1941-42)
Ward, Jerry (1974-77)
Ware, Kevin (1998-)
Ware, Latrell (1987-90)
Ware, Yeasive (1996-98)
Wareing, W.A. (1939)
Warner, Rex (1950-51)
Warren, Gary (1985-87)
Washington, David (1996)
Washington, Ted (1987-90)
Watkins, Mike (1997-)
Watson, Olante (1993)
Watson, Richard (1967-69)
Watts, Bill (1936, 38)
Watts, Erik (1991)
Watzek, Joe (1968, 71)
Wayland, Bob (1949)
Wayne, Rollo (1915-16)
Webb, Don (1973-74)
Weber, C.J. (1932)
Weber, Pat (1926)
Weedman, William (1985)
Weidner, Garland (1922-23)
Weihe, Cofer (1935-36)
Weining, Harry (1947-50)
Welch, Joe (1970-72)
Welch, Joe (1983)
Wells, Spencer (1984)
Wetherby, L. (1927-28)
Wheat, Donte (1983-84)
White, Dan (1957-59)
White, Marcus (1989)
White, R.G. (1938)
Whitehead, Roger (1961-64)
Whittkamp, Jack (1946)
Wibbels, Jerry (1953)
Wiggins, Anthony (1985-86)
Wiley, Deran (1995-97)
Wiljanen, Roy (1970-71)
Williams, Andy (1965-67)
Williams, Anthony (1981-82)
Williams, Bill (1916)
Williams, Bob (1955-58)
Williams, Carl (1982-84)
Williams, Charles (1925, '27-29)
Williams, Dan (1982)
Williams, David (1986)
Williams, Deron (1988-90)
Williams, Ebb (1976-78)
Williams, George (1985-88)

Williams , Jermaine (1992-94)
Williams, Jim (1950-52)
Williams, Leon (1978-81)
Williams, Rico (1996-98)
Williams, Vic (1978)
Williams, Waymon (1997-98)
Willis, Gerald (1967)
Wilmsmeyer, Klaus (1988-91)
Wills, Don (1978)
Wilshire, Jim (1952)
Wilson, Dilbert (1946)
Wilson, Mark (1978-81)
Wilson, O'Harlan (1929)

Wilson, Otis (1977-79)
Wilson, Richard (1946-47)
Wilson, Robert (1980-82)
Wimberly, Darrell (1980-82)
Winningham, Roy (1985)
Winrich, Dave (1985)
Winters, Jim (1968-70)
Wirpio, Carl (1937-38)
Wise, Walter (1987-88)
Wolf, Jim (1948-50, '55)
Wolford, Maury (1948-51)
Wolke, Joe (1968-70)
Womack, Bill (1946-47)

Woodring, Andy (1984)
Woodruff, Dwayne (1976-78)
Worden, N.A. (1940-41)
Wordlow, Antuan (1994)
Wright, Adolph (1932)
Wright, Hugh (1939-41)
Wright, Les (1932-33)
Wright, Steve (1976)
Wyatt, Jason (1995-98)
Wyatt, Jim (1964-66)

Y
Yamin, Rick (1984-88)
Young, Antonio (1984-85)

Young, Ed (1955-58)
Young, James (1986)
Young, Mike (1970-71)
Young, Steve (1970-72)

Z
Zamberlan, Jim (1965-67)
Zangaro, Fred (1954)
Zariczny, P.J. (1997-98)
Ziggler, Bernard (1985, '87)
Zilko, Randy (1997-98)
Zimlich, Lou (1936-39)

Browning Nagle

Arnold Jackson

YEAR-BY-YEAR LEADERS

RUSHING

Year		Att	Yds	Avg
1947	Tom Lucia	43	407	9.5
1948	Tom Lucia	87	659	7.8
1949	Tom Lucia	115	800	6.9
1950	Jim Williams	126	693	5.5
1951	Jim Williams	138	642	4.6
1952	No record			
1953	Mike McDonald	67	336	5.0
1954	John Sowa	47	259	5.5
1955	Lenny Lyles	101	780	7.7
1956	Lenny Lyles	119	610	5.1
1957	Lenny Lyles	177	1207	6.8
1958	No record			
1959	Ernie Green	114	510	4.5
1960	No record			
1961	Lee Calland	108	600	5.6
1962	Lee Calland	125	650	4.5
1963	Larry Compton	69	199	2.9
1964	Ron Hall	86	301	3.5
1965	Wayne Patrick	99	428	4.3
1966	Benny Russell	117	273	2.3
1967	Wayne Patrick	155	582	3.8
1968	Herbie Phelps	96	468	4.9
1969	Lee Bouggess	267	1064	4.0
1970	Bill Gatti	207	981	4.7
1971	Howard Stevens	250	1429	5.7
1972	Howard Stevens	259	1294	5.0
1973	Wayne Peacock	290	1294	4.4
1974	Wayne Peacock	237	827	3.5
1975	Wayne Peacock	262	1013	3.9
1976	Calvin Prince	213	1028	4.8
1977	Calvin Prince	218	1050	4.8
1978	Nathan Poole	212	1394	6.6
1979	Greg Hickman	150	648	4.3
1980	Don Craft	140	687	4.9
1981	Don Craft	136	475	3.5
1982	Ron Davenport	120	526	4.4
1983	Willie Shelby	107	447	4.2
1984	Ron Davenport	130	501	3.9
1985	John Adams	140	514	3.7
1986	Deon Booker	112	537	4.6
1987	Deon Booker	135	671	4.9
1988	Deon Booker	217	1011	4.6
1989	Carwell Gardner	139	595	4.3
1990	Ralph Dawkins	121	542	4.5
1991	Ralph Dawkins	154	622	4.0
1992	Anthony Shelman	85	418	4.9
1993	Ralph Dawkins	129	579	4.8
1994	Anthony Shelman	241	1084	4.5
1995	Calvin Arrington	255	1016	4.0
1996	Donnell Gordon	115	482	3.8
1997	Frank Moreau	120	573	4.8
1998	Leroy Collins	218	1134	5.2

Cardinal Football

PASSING

Year		Att	Comp	Yds	TD
1947	Frank Gitschier	47	31	422	0
1948	No record				
1949	No record				
1950	Bill Karns	50	27	517	5
1951	Johnny Unitas	99	46	602	9
1952	Johnny Unitas	198	106	1540	12
1953	Johnny Unitas	95	49	470	3
1954	Jim Houser	86	39	560	0
1955	Bob Williams	25	13	361	5
1956	Bob Williams	67	28	699	3
1957	Dale Orem	56	26	483	4
1958	No record				
1959	No record				
1960	No record				
1961	John Giles	172	78	1209	9
1962	John Giles	181	90	1222	8
1963	Tom LaFramboise	204	104	1205	8
1964	Tom LaFramboise	242	122	1380	4
1965	Benny Russell	246	115	1791	11
1966	Benny Russell	310	142	2016	14
1967	Wally Oyler	192	83	1039	5
1968	Wally Oyler	240	112	1410	6
1969	Gary Inman	182	78	843	12
1970	John Madeya	244	121	1750	11
1971	John Madeya	201	97	1045	7
1972	John Madeya	301	146	1709	16
1973	Len DePaola	168	73	808	2
1974	Len DePaola	97	32	428	6
1975	John Darling	137	66	946	3
1976	Stu Stram	93	36	394	1
1977	Stu Stram	78	36	455	5
1978	Stu Stram	149	70	929	8
1979	Stu Stram	118	52	806	3
1980	Pat Patterson	167	69	933	2
1981	Dean May	105	41	589	4
1982	Dean May	311	141	2034	17
1983	Dean May	263	139	1609	6
1984	Ed Rubbert	363	184	2465	18
1985	Ed Rubbert	256	120	1475	5
1986	Ed Rubbert	210	103	1304	4
1987	Jay Gruden	397	209	2481	17
1988	Jay Gruden	382	224	2605	17
1989	Browning Nagle	334	187	2503	16
1990	Browning Nagle	263	146	2150	16
1991	Erik Watts	260	115	1294	6
1992	Jeff Brohm	297	155	2008	9
1993	Jeff Brohm	304	185	2626	20
1994	Marty Lowe	319	186	2091	9
1995	Marty Lowe	350	195	2268	16
1996	Chris Redman	272	144	1773	8
1997	Chris Redman	445	261	3079	18
1998	Chris Redman	473	309	4042	29

132

Cardinal Football

RECEIVING

Year		Rec	Yds	Avg
1952	Dave Riverbank	40	521	13.0
1953	Mike McDonald	9	101	11.2
1954	Gene Sartini	17	235	13.8
1955	Lenny Lyles	6	163	27.2
1956	Ed Young	13	358	27.5
1957	Ed Young	10	263	26.3
1958	No record			
1959	No record			
1960	No record			
1961	Don Hockensmith	20	392	19.6
1962	Don Hockensmith	32	408	12.8
1963	Charlie Mudd	25	367	14.7
1964	Roger Whitehead	33	370	11.2
1965	Al MacFarlane	35	524	15.0
1966	Jim Zamberlan	59	747	12.7
1967	Jim Zamberlan	45	559	12.4
1968	Larry Hart	25	375	15.0
	Rick Getch	25	315	12.6
1969	Cookie Brinkman	25	357	14.3
1970	Cookie Brinkman	48	647	13.5
1971	Tony Burdock	33	361	10.9
1972	Gary Barnes	52	655	12.6
1973	Dale Kaminski	18	262	14.6
1974	Kevin Miller	25	361	14.7
1975	Tony Smith	26	382	14.7
1976	Marc Mitchell	15	147	9.8
1977	Marc Mitchell	24	358	14.9
1978	Ken Robinson	29	534	18.4
1979	Randy Butler	20	347	17.3
1980	Ken Robinson	26	401	15.4
1981	Mark Clayton	27	596	22.17
1982	Mark Clayton	53	1112	21.0
1983	David Hatfield	49	543	11.1
1984	Ernest Givins	33	689	20.9
1985	Ernest Givins	34	577	17.0
1986	Eric Vaughn	34	697	20.5
1987	Rodney Knighton	43	409	9.5
1988	Deon Booker	41	391	9.5
1989	Carwell Gardner	46	614	13.3
1990	Anthony Cummings	28	473	16.8
1991	Ralph Dawkins	44	297	6.8
1992	Ralph Dawkins	43	506	11.8
1993	Jamie Asher	52	658	12.7
1994	Jamie Asher	70	794	11.3
1995	Miguel Montano	50	694	13.9
1996	Miguel Montano	48	602	12.5
1997	Miguel Montano	67	875	13.1
1998	Arnold Jackson	90	1165	12.9

SCORING

Year		TD	PAT	CV	FG	Pts
1947	Stu Gibson	4	12	0	0	36
1948	No Record					
1949	No Record					
1950	Tom Lucia	7	0	0	0	42
	Gene Sartini	7	0	0	0	42
1951	Jim Williams	5	0	0	0	30
1952	No Record					
1953	John Unitas	3	0	0	0	18
1954	Lenny Lyles	7	0	0	0	42
1955	Lenny Lyles	14	0	0	0	84
1956	Lenny Lyles	7	0	0	0	42
1957	Lenny Lyles	21	6	0	0	132
1958	Ken Porco	7	0	0	0	42
1959	No Record					
1960	No Record					
1961	Lee Calland	6	0	0	0	36
1962	Lee Calland	8	0	0	0	48
1963	Charlie Mudd	5	0	0	0	30
1964	Al MacFarlane	4	2	0	1	29
1965	Al MacFarlane	8	15	0	3	72
1966	Pete Compise	0	27	0	6	45
1967	Wayne Patrick	10	0	0	0	60
1968	Herbie Phelps	6	0	0	0	36
1969	Lee Bougess	6	0	0	0	36
	David Shanks	0	21	0	5	36
1970	Larry Hart	8	0	0	0	48
1971	Howard Stevens	13	0	0	0	78
1972	Howard Stevens	17	0	0	0	102
1973	Walter Peacock	12	0	0	0	72
1974	Wilbur Summers	0	14	0	6	32
1975	Walter Peacock	6	0	0	0	36
1976	Calvin Prince	10	2	0	0	62
1977	Calvin Prince	13	0	0	0	78
1978	Nathan Poole	16	0	0	0	96
1979	Greg Hickman	4	0	0	0	24
1980	Dave Betz	0	15	0	13	54
1981	Tony Blair	0	18	0	8	42
	Don Craft	7	0	0	0	42
1982	Mark Clayton	6	4	0	0	40
1983	Phil Ellis	0	16	0	8	40
1984	Phil Ellis	0	25	0	6	43
1985	Dan Cerione	0	18	0	9	45
1986	Deon Booker	8	0	0	0	48
1987	Rodney Knighton	10	0	2	0	64
1988	Deon Booker	12	0	0	0	72
1989	Ron Bell0	3	0	0	15	75
1990	Anthony Cummings	10	0	0	0	60
1991	Klaus Wilmsmeyer	0	9	0	10	39
1992	Ralph Dawkins	10	0	0	0	60
1993	David Akers	0	36	0	8	60
1994	Anthony Shelman	15	0	0	0	90
1995	David Akers	0	31	0	12	67
1996	David Akers	0	18	0	7	39
1997	Arnold Jackson	8	0	0	0	48
	Ibn Green	8	0	0	0	48
1998	Leroy Collins	19	0	1	0	116

TACKLES

Year		No	Year		No
1962	Ken Kortas	52	1980	Eddie Johnson	144
1963	Doug Buffone	101	1981	Mike Trainor	119
1964	Doug Buffone	177	1982	Anthony Williams	159
1965	Doug Buffone	201	1983	Brian Miller	133
1966	No Record		1984	Brian Miller	132
1967	No Record		1985	Matt Battaglia	153
1968	No Record		1986	Matt Battaglia	166
1969	Mike Detenber	122	1987	Chris Sellars	134
1970	Tom Jackson	131	1988	Mark Sander	167
1971	Tom Jackson	122	1989	Mark Sander	134
1972	Tom Jackson	120	1990	Mark Sander	116
1973	Joe Lee Phillips	131	1991	Andy Culley	121
1974	Marty Smith	107	1992	Ben Sumpter	103
1975	Larry Fluellen	106	1993	Tom Cavallo	93
1976	Ricky Skiles	129	1994	Tyrus McCloud	133
1977	Otis Wilson	175	1995	Tyrus McCloud	126
1978	Otis Wilson	157	1996	Tyrus McCloud	144
1979	Ricky Skiles	167	1997	Terry Rice-Locket	155
			1998	Bud Herring	135

Matt Battaglia

Mark Sander

Cardinal Football

PUNT RETURN AVERAGE

Year		No	Yds	Avg	Year		No	Yds	Avg
1965	Bill McMahon	10	200	20.0	1983	Keith Humphries	9	61	6.8
1966	Bill McMahon	17	197	11.6	1984	Eric Vaughn	20	158	7.9
1967	Herbie Phelps	40	363	9.1	1985	Ernest Givens	18	154	8.6
1968	Herbie Phelps	16	231	14.4	1986	Keith Stephens	28	261	9.3
1969	Richard Watson	12	80	6.7	1987	Joey Hamilton	17	209	12.3
1970	Greg Campbell	16	267	16.7	1988	Keith Stephens	14	122	8.7
1971	Greg Campbell	26	164	6.2	1989	Dee Smith	14	207	14.8
1972	Howard Stevens	31	378	12.2	1990	Joey Smith	29	382	13.1
1973	Jim Wagoner	8	153	19.1	1991	Derek Hawthorne	13	48	3.7
1974	Jim Wagoner	15	160	10.6	1992	Aaron Bailey	14	145	10.4
1975	Kevin Miller	10	50	5.0	1993	Aaron Bailey	10	130	13.0
1976	Kevin Miller	12	64	5.3	1994	Tony Bethel	21	105	5.0
1977	Kevin Miller	32	290	9.1	1995	Rico Clark	6	51	8.5
1978	Greg Searcy	9	64	7.1	1996	Rico Clark	32	238	8.1
1979	Jamie Perrin	21	115	5.5		Danny Mosby	10	81	8.1
1980	Jamie Perrin	8	105	13.1	1997	Arnold Jackson	15	215	14.3
1981	Keith Humphries	16	239	14.9	1998	Arnold Jackson	31	216	7.0
1982	Frank Minnifield	11	165	15.0					

Kevin Miller

Cardinal Football

KICKOFF RETURN AVERAGE

Year		No	Yds	Avg
1965	Andy Williams	15	338	22.5
1966	Frank Moore	15	419	27.9
1967	Herbie Phelps	9	216	24.0
1968	Mike Blakey	13	407	31.3
1969	Ira Glass	19	311	16.4
1970	Greg Campbell	19	311	16.4
1971	Greg Campbell	10	146	14.6
1972	Howard Stephens	12	240	20.0
1973	Walter Peacock	14	401	28.6
1974	Walter Peacock	23	457	19.8
1975	Walter Peacock	28	633	22.9
1976	Kevin Miller	18	286	15.9
1977	Kevin Miller	16	387	24.2
1978	Ken Robinson	29	534	18.4
1979	Ken Robinson	13	262	20.2
1980	Mike Bell	12	225	18.7
1981	Frank Minnifield	11	334	30.4
1982	Keith Humphries	12	345	28.7
1983	Keith Humphries	24	434	18.1
1984	Eric Vaughn	34	630	18.5
1985	Ernest Givins	29	801	27.6
1986	Keith Stephens	42	901	21.5
1987	Keith Stephens	25	589	23.6
1988	Keith Stephens	33	737	22.3
1989	Dee Smith	14	351	25.2
1990	Joey Smith	19	372	19.6
1991	Tony Edelen	20	349	17.5
1992	Aaron Bailey	25	559	22.4
1993	Aaron Bailey	26	622	23.9
1994	Calvin Arrington	19	291	15.3
1995	Coswell Sims	8	140	17.5
1996	Rico Clark	11	227	20.6
1997	Antonio Roundtree	32	693	21.7
1998	Zek Parker	21	463	22.0

Aaron Bailey

INTERCEPTIONS

Year	Name	Int	Year	Name	Int
1965	Clarence Spencer	4	1979	Leon Williams	3
1966	Wally Oyler	7	1980	Leon Williams	4
1967	Dan Bednarski	5	1981	Sebastian Curry	5
1968	Charles Collins	4	1982	Sebastian Curry	3
1969	Mike Detenber	4	1983	Kirk Perry	7
1970	Paul Mattingly	5	1984	Doug Pritchett	5
1971	Ralph Calvin	3	1985	James Bell	1
	Gary Inman	3		Don Cosby	1
	Tom Jackson	3	1986	Antonio Davis	2
	Ed Long	3	1987	Terry Lantz	2
	Paul Mattingly	3	1988	John Gainey	4
	Joe Welch	3	1989	John Gainey	4
1972	Tom Martin	2	1990	William Blackford	5
	Lonnie Schuler	2	1991	Ray Buchanan	8
	Steve Young	2	1992	Ray Buchanan	4
1973	Norman Heard	4		Tom Cavallo	4
1974	A.J. Jacobs	7	1993	Anthony Bridges	7
1975	Mike Anderson	2	1994	Tony Bethel	2
	David Bradshaw	2		Tyrus McCloud	2
	Don Harold	2	1995	Sam Madison	5
	Don Pomeroy	2	1996	Sam Madison	6
1976	Wilbur Boggs	2	1997	Don Bibb	3
	Fred Hackett	2	1998	Bud Herring	2
1977	Zarko Ellis	4		Rashad Holman	2
1978	Otis Wilson	6		Antonio Roundtree	2

Anthony Bridges

138

Cardinal Football

SACKS (FROM 1989)

Year	Name	Sacks
1989	Mike Flores	13
1990	Mike Flores	14
1991	Jeff Hayes	8
1992	Joe Johnson	6
1993	Joe Johnson	17
1994	Kendrick Gholston	4
1995	Kendrick Gholston	8
1996	Carl Powell	11
1997	Kendrick Gholston	10
1998	Rashad Harris	3
	Reggie Hargrove	3

Mike Flores

Joe Johnson

Cardinal Football

PUNTING

Year	Name	No.	Yds.	Avg.	Year	Name	No.	Yds.	Avg.
1965	Al MacFarlane	44	1820	41.4	1982	Phil Ellis	69	2461	35.7
1966	Wally Oyler	38	1454	38.3	1983	Phil Ellis	44	1510	34.3
1967	John Waller	35	1174	33.5	1984	Danny Cerione	39	1514	38.8
1968	Cookie Brinkman	33	1229	37.2	1985	Kirk Kennedy	57	2300	40.4
1969	Cookie Brinkman	67	2419	36.1	1986	Kirk Kennedy	60	2196	36.6
1970	Scott Marcus	57	2085	36.6	1987	Kirk Kennedy	63	2313	36.7
1971	Scott Marcus	79	3175	40.2	1988	Klaus Wilmsmeyer	53	1944	36.6
1972	Scott Marcus	60	2235	37.2	1989	Klaus Wilmsmeyer	41	1585	38.6
1973	Wilbur Summers	83	3517	42.3	1990	Klaus Wilmsmeyer	48	2062	42.9
1974	Wilbur Summers	81	3302	40.7	1991	Klaus Wilmsmeyer	46	1848	40.2
1975	Wilbur Summers	72	3101	43.0	1992	Brandon Brookfield	60	2501	41.7
1976	Rich Pennella	63	2444	38.7	1993	Brandon Brookfield	59	2332	39.5
1977	Rich Pennella	72	2878	40.0	1994	Brandon Brookfield	64	2655	41.5
1978	Nick Gagel	40	1481	37.0	1995	Jeremy Borseth	61	2399	39.3
1979	Dave Betz	53	1982	37.4	1996	Jeremy Borseth	69	2800	40.6
1980	Mark Blasinsky	76	2949	38.8	1997	Jeremy Borseth	68	2746	40.4
1981	Mark Blasinsky	89	3579	40.2	1998	Jeremy Borseth	49	1908	38.9

Scott Marcus

Klaus Wilmsmeyer

140

Cardinal Football

ALL-PURPOSE YARDAGE

Year	Name	Rush	Rec.	Ret.	Total	Year	Name	No.	Yds.	Avg.
1965	Al MacFarlane	358	524	3	885	1982	Mark Clayton	68	1112	7	1187
1966	Jim Zamberlan	5	747	0	752	1983	Willie Shelby	447	212	43	702
1967	Herbie Phelps	254	186	579	1019	1984	Ernest Givins	18	689	275	982
1968	Herbie Phelps	468	216	527	1211	1985	Ernest Givins	204	577	955	1736
1969	Lee Bougess	1064	16	0	1080	1986	Keith Stephens	34	10	1162	1206
1970	Bill Gatti	981	135	0	1116	1987	Keith Stephens	48	8	691	747
1971	Howard Stevens	1429	168	144	1741	1988	Keith Stephens	367	288	859	1514
1972	Howard Stevens	1294	221	618	2133	1989	Carwell Gardner	595	614	111	1320
1973	Walter Peacock	1294	139	401	1834	1990	Ralph Dawkins	542	373	36	951
1974	Walter Peacock	827	37	457	1321	1991	Ralph Dawkins	622	297	258	1177
1975	Walter Peacock	1013	0	671	1684	1992	Ralph Dawkins	416	506	305	1227
1976	Calvin Prince	1028	20	220	1268	1993	Aaron Bailey	30	531	752	1313
1977	Calvin Prince	1050	46	185	1281	1994	Anthony Shelman	1084	73	0	1157
1978	Nathan Poole	1394	36	0	1430	1995	Calvin Arrington	1016	257	0	1273
1979	Greg Hickman	648	4	0	652	1996	Donnell Gordon	433	200	18	651
1980	Don Craft	687	74	13	774	1997	Arnold Jackson	0	687	296	983
1981	Don Craft	475	207	0	682	1998	Arnold Jackson	33	1165	131	1545

Ralph Dawkins

Cardinal Football

TOTAL OFFENSE

Year	Name	Rush	Pass	Plays	Total	Year	Name	Rush	Pass	Plays	Total
1965	Benny Russell	141	1791	325	1932	1982	Dean May	-112	2034	374	1922
1966	Benny Russell	273	2016	427	2289	1983	Dean May	-71	1609	302	1538
1967	Wally Oyler	256	1039	297	1295	1984	Ed Rubbert	-112	2465	387	2353
1968	Wally Oyler	249	1410	325	1659	1985	Ed Rubbert	-185	1475	287	1290
1969	Gary Inman	262	843	244	1105	1986	Ed Rubbert	-199	1304	243	1105
1970	John Madeya	-200	1750	323	1550	1987	Jay Gruden	-190	2481	453	2291
1971	Howard Stevens	1429	0	252	1429	1988	Jay Gruden	-182	2605	438	2423
1972	John Madeya	-152	1709	341	1557	1989	Browning Nagle	-121	2503	386	2382
1973	Walter Peacock	1294	0	290	1294	1990	Browning Nagle	-50	2150	306	2100
1974	Walter Peacock	827	0	237	827	1991	Erik Watts	-144	1294	143	1150
1975	Walter Peacock	1013	0	262	1013	1992	Jeff Brohm	-41	2008	396	1967
1976	Calvin Prince	1028	64	221	1092	1993	Jeff Brohm	45	2626	263	2671
1977	Calvin Prince	1050	5	224	1055	1994	Marty Lowe	-64	2091	258	2027
1978	Nathan Poole	1394	0	212	1394	1995	Marty Lowe	-59	2268	395	2209
1979	Stu Stram	-29	806	169	777	1996	Chris Redman	-148	1773	309	1625
1980	Pat Patterson	-161	933	246	772	1997	Chris Redman	-121	3079	492	295
1981	Dean May	-70	589	137	529	1998	Chris Redman	-33	4042	513	4009

Marty Lowe

Jay Gruden

Cardinal Football

UNIVERSITY OF LOUISVILLE
ALL-AMERICANS

1998
Ibn Green | TE | Sporting News, Second Team
Football News, Second Team
Associated Press, Third Team

1996
Sam Madison | CB | Football News, First team
Gannett News Service, Third team
Associated Press, Third team

Tyrus McCloud | LB | Sporting News, Second team
Associated Press, Third team

1995
Roman Oben | OT | College Sports, Second team
Football News, Second team
Associated Press, Third team

Sam Madison | CB | College Sports, Third team

1994
Jamie Asher | TE | United Press, First team
Football News, First team
Sporting News, Honorable Mention

Roman Oben | OT | Gannett News Service, First team

1993
Anthony Bridges | CB | Associated Press, Second team
United Press, Second team
Football News, Second team
Joe Johnson | DT | United Press, Honorable Mention
Ralph Dawkins | RB | Football News, Honorable Mention

1992
Ray Buchanan | CB | Football News, Second team
Associated Press, Honorable Mention
Ralph Dawkins | RB | Football News, Honorable Mention

1991
Ray Buchanan | CB | Associated Press, Honorable Mention

1990
Mark Sander | LB | Associated Press, Third team

1989
Mark Sander | LB | Associated Press, Honorable Mention

1988
Mark Sander | LB | Associated Press, Honorable Mention
Ted Washington | DT | Sporting News, Honorable Mention

1985
Matt Battaglia | LB | Associated Press, Honorable Mention

1979
Otis Wilson | LB | NEA, First team
Sporting News, First team

1972
Howard Stevens | RB | Walter Camp, Second team
Associated Press, Second team
United Press, Second team
Gridiron News, Second team
Football News, Second team

Tom Jackson | LB | Walter Camp, First team
Associated Press, Second team
Football News, Third team
United Press, Honorable Mention

Scott Marcus | P | Gridiron News, Third team
John Madeya | QB | Associated Press, Honorable Mention
Gary Barnes | WR | Associated Press, Honorable Mention
Frank Gitschier | C | Associated Press, Honorable Mention

1963
Ken Kortas | T | Dell Sports, First team

1957
Lenny Lyles | RB | AP Little All-America, First team

1952
Otto Knop | C | College Little All-America, First team

1949
Tom Lucia | RB | AP Little All-America, Second team

1948
Bob Bauer | End | AP Little-All-America, Honorable Mention

1941
Charles Isenburg | RB | AP Little All-America, Honorable Mention

1939
Lou Zimlich | End | Williamson's Little All-America, First team

1930
Tom Thompson | RB | Williamson's Little All-America, First team

Guy Shearer | LB | Williamson's Little All-America, HM

UNIVERSITY OF LOUISVILLE
BOWL GAMES

1958 SUN BOWL

Louisville 34, Drake 20

January 1, 1958
El Paso, Texas

The University of Louisville made its first bowl appearance Jan. 1, 1958, as Frank Camp's squad battered Drake 34-20 in the Sun Bowl.

The victory over the Drake Bulldogs capped a near-perfect season for the Cardinals. U of L finished with a 9-1 record, the best in school history. The only blemish was a 13-7 setback at Kent State University.

Louisville's squad was headed by Lenny Lyles, the nation's leading rusher. Unfortunately, Lyles went down in the first quarter with an injury. He managed just six yards on two carries.

In Lyles' absence, Ken Porco and Pete Bryant stepped forward offensively. Porco ran for a game-high 119 yards on 20 carries.

"Porco ran wild that day," Camp said. "He was just a freshman and I hadn't planned on using him much as a ball carrier during the game. But when Lyles was hurt we had to go with Porco, and I guess it's a good thing we did. Drake couldn't stop him."

Bryant added 80 yards on 14 carries, while also tossing a 20-yard scoring pass. His four-yard run in the second quarter gave the Cardinals a 21-14 advantage that they did not yield.

SUMMARY

	Drake	U of L
First Downs	16	14
Rushing Yards	176	228
Passes	10-33	6-10
Passes Int.	1	0
Passing Yards	140	148
Total Offense	316	316
Punts-Avg.	4-25.8	5-34.2
Penalties-Yards	5-51	5-75
Fumbles-Lost	3-2	1-0

Drake	7	7	0	6	-20
Louisville	7	14	7	6	-34

Drake: Labrasca, 2-yard run (Leeman kick)
Louisville: Cain, 4-yard run (Young kick)
Drake: Newell, 17-yard run (Leeman kick)
Louisville: Young 37-yard pass from Orem (Young kick)
Louisville: Bryant, 4-yard run (Young kick)
Louisville: Porco, 2-yard run (Young kick)
Drake: Kinzell, 55-yard pass from Labrasca (kick failed)
Louisville: Young, 20-yard pass from Bryant
(kick failed).

1970 PASADENA BOWL

Louisville 24, Long Beach St. 24

December 19, 1970
Pasadena, Calif.

In 1970, the University of Louisville's Missouri Valley Conference Championship team tied Long Beach State 24-24 at the Pasadena Bowl to close the season.

Long Beach trailed the Lee Corso's Cardinals almost the entire game after John Madeya scored a pair of touchdowns.

On the strength of a safety and some nifty running by fullback Leon Burns, LBSU managed to forge a fourth-quarter tie.

A strange play near the end of the game had the Louisville faithful thinking they just might secure a victory.

Madeya threw a screen pass to tailback Tom Jesukaitis, who was supposed to go out of bounds. Instead Jesukaitis put the ball in the air again, throwing a pass to Cookie Brinkman who went in for a touchdown.

The rulebook prohibits more than one pass on a single play, however, and U of L was penalized five yards.

"It was definitely an ad lib play," Jesukaitis said. "It seemed like the thing to do. I was running for the sidelines, but I saw Cookie out there all alone."

Louisville's Paul Mattingly was named Defensive Player of the Game. He blocked a 32-yard field goal attempt in the fourth quarter and was in on a game-high 17 tackles.

SUMMARY

	LBSU	U of L
First Downs	16	20
Rushing Yards	243	210
Passes	9-17	12-27
Passes Int.	1	1
Passing Yards	148	90
Total Offense	391	300
Punts-Avg.	6-30.0	8-39.0
Penalties-Yards	4-44	4-36
Fumbles-Lost	3-3	2-0

Louisville	14	7	3	0	-24
Long Beach	7	7	2	8	-24

Long Beach: Burns, 4-yard run (Logue kick)
Louisville: Madeya, 4-yard run (Marcus kick)
Louisville: Welch, 65-yard interception return
(Marcus kick)
Louisville: Madeya, 1-yard run (Marcus kick)
Louisville: Marcus, 24-yard field goal
Long Beach: Safety, Gatti tackled in end zone
Long Beach: Burns, 4-yard run (Matthews pass from Graves).

Attendance: 20,472

1977 INDEPENDENCE BOWL

Louisiana Tech 24, Louisville 14

Shreveport, La.
December 17, 1977

The 1977 Louisville team, coached by Vince Gibson, ended a seven-year bowl drought, and took a 24-14 setback from Louisiana Tech at the Independence Bowl.

To even appear in a bowl game would have seemed remote at the beginning of the season.

"We fooled 'em," Gibson said. "We played our hearts out the last month of the season, and we deserved to go to the bowl. It was a big reward for the kids and a great honor for the university."

Louisiana Tech, the Southland Conference champion, took the thrill out of the trip for U of L, handing the Cards a 10-point loss.

Kevin Miller provided the spark offensively for U of L, electrifying the crowd with a 60-yard first quarter punt return for a touchdown.

In the third quarter, Miller scored again on a 13-yard run to cap a 13-play, 58-yard scoring drive.

Tech quarterback Keith Thibodeaux, the offensive player of the game, countered Miller's heroics with two touchdown passes.

Miller nearly came up with another TD, but he mishandled a pass in the end zone from Stu Stram. Another potential Cardinal touchdown was called back by a holding penalty.

Linebacker Otis Wilson was selected as the game's outstanding defensive player.

SUMMARY

	La. Tech	U of L
First Downs	25	11
Rushing Yards	48	100
Passes	19-39	9-23
Passes Int.	2	1
Passing Yards	287	61
Total Offense	335	161
Punts-Avg.	6-32.0	8-38.0
Fumbles-Lost	6-3	8-3

La. Tech	21	3	0	0	-24
Louisville	7	0	7	0	-14

Louisville: Miller, 60-yard punt return (Posadas kick)
La. Tech: Lewis, 1-yard run (Swiley kick)
La. Tech: Pree, 41-yard pass from Thibodeaux (conversion failed)
La. Tech: McCartney, 8-yard pass from Thibodeaux (Lewis run)
La. Tech: Swiley, 21-yard field goal
Louisville: Miller, 13-yard run (Posadas kick).

Attendance: 18,500 (est.).

UNIVERSITY OF LOUISVILLE
BOWL GAMES (Continued)

1991 FIESTA BOWL

Louisville 34, Alabama 7

Tempe, Ariz.

January 1, 1991

Playing in its first bowl game in 13 years, the Louisville football team felt it had something to prove at the 1991 Fiesta Bowl. The squad proved its point to the tune of a 34-7 thrashing of Alabama.

Browning Nagle threw for a Fiesta Bowl record 451 yards, including 223 during a 25-point first-quarter explosion. He completed 20-of-33 passes and had three scoring passes.

"We took this game for everything it was worth," Nagle said. "We wanted to come out here and gain respect, and that's what we did. It's a great tribute to the coaches for getting us focused."

"We prepared exceptionally well for this game, and Browning had a superhuman performance," Head Coach Howard Schnellenberger said. "He had us in the right play practically every down. No way in my wildest dreams did I expect us to be in this situation. Just coming here was a quantum leap for us. Winning this was another quantum leap for our program."

The Crimson Tide allowed just 5.4 points per game in their previous seven contests before running into the Cardinal juggernaut.

Alabama's offense did not experience much more success. For the game the Tide rolled for just 189 yards of total offense.

U of L defensive back Ray Buchanan was tabbed as the game's defensive most valuable player. He recorded five tackles, recovered a fumble, broke up a pass and picked up a blocked punt for a touchdown.

SUMMARY

	U of L	Ala.
First Downs	25	10
Rushing Yards	113	95
Passes	21-39	12-35
Passes Int.	3	2
Passing Yards	458	94
Total Offense	571	189
Punts-Avg.	3-41.0	8-40.2
Penalties-Yards	10-87	7-40
Fumbles-Lost	3-1	3-1

Louisville	25	0	7	2	-34
Alabama	0	7	0	0	- 7

Louisville: Ware 70-yard pass from Nagle (Wilmsmeyer kick)
Louisville: Dawkins 5-yard run (kick blocked)
Louisville: Cummings 37-yard pass from Nagle (pass failed)
Louisville - Buchanan recovered blocked punt (pass failed)
Alabama: Gardner 49-yard interception return (Doyle kick)
Louisville: Cummings 19-yard pass from Nagle (Bell kick)
Louisville: Safety.

RUSHING
Louisville: Bynm 8-48, Dawkins 5-38, Lipsey 9-23, Hall 2-12, Ware 3-11, Gardner 2-6, Jones 1-0, G. Brohm 1-(-2), J. Brohm 2-(-3), Nagle 6-(-20)
Alabama: Turner 6-49, Anderson 7-26, Sewell 5-25, Woodson 8-17, Houston 1-0, Lassic 1-0, Etter 1-(-7), Hollingsworth 4-(-15)

PASSING
Louisville: Nagle 33-20-1-451, Lipsey 1-1-0-7, Brohm 3-0-2-0, Watts 2-0-0-0
Alabama: 23-10-1-59, Woodson 10-2-1-35, Etter 2-0-0-0

RECEIVING
Louisville: McKay 5-110, Lipsey 4-65, Cummings 3-69, Dawkins 3-32, Jones 2-89, Ware 1-70, Broomfield 1-11, Nagle 1-7, Bynm 1-5
Alabama: Turner 4-35, Lassic 2-35, Houston 2-4, Finkley 1-15, Russell 1-7, Busky 1-3, Sewell 1-(-5)

Attendance: 69,098

UNIVERSITY OF LOUISVILLE
BOWL GAMES (Continued)

1993 LIBERTY BOWL
Louisville 18, Michigan State 7
Memphis, Tenn.
December 28, 1993

The 1993 Cardinals put a cap on an 8-3 regular season with an 18-7 victory over Michigan State at the Liberty Bowl. Howard Schnellenberger's squad registered the first win ever by the Cardinals over a Big Ten foe.

The conditions were hardly ideal for an aerial display, but quarterback Jeff Brohm checked in with one of the guttiest efforts in the history of Cardinal football. Brohm, playing with two steel pins and one steel plate in the index finger of his throwing hand completed 19-of-29 passes for 197 yards and a touchdown amidst 20-degree temperatures and freezing rain.

Most of that courage was shown in the fourth quarter. Entering the final frame, Louisville trailed 7-3. With 12:05 remaining, Brohm connected on a 25-yard strike to Reggie Ferguson to put the Cardinals in front for good.

Just over three minutes later, it was the defense's turn to make a big play. Pinned back to their one-yard line, the Spartans were merely looking to get some breathing room for their offense. Running back Craig Thomas took the handoff and was immediately met by All-American defensive end Joe Johnson and reserve linebacker Tyrus McCloud for a safety.

On the ensuing possession, the Cardinals marched down the field for an insurance touchdown when Anthony Shelman bolted into the end zone from 11 yards out.

The Cardinal defense put the clamps on the MSU offense for the remainder of the contest, as it had for most of the game.

SUMMARY

	MSU	U of L			
First Downs	18	20			
Rushing Yards	114	172			
Passes	15-28	19-31			
Passes Int.	1	0			
Passing Yards	193	197			
Total Offense	307	369			
Punts-Avg.	5-29.0	5-36.2			
Penalties-Yards	5-60	6-45			
Fumbles-Lost	0-0	1-0			
Michigan State	7	0	0	0	- 7
Louisville	3	0	0	15	-18

Michigan State: Goulbourne 1-yard run (Stoyanovich kick)
Louisville: Akers 31-yard field goal
Louisville: Ferguson 25-yard pass from Brohm (Akers kick)
Louisville: Safety
Louisville: Dawkins 11-yard run (PAT fails).

RUSHING
Michigan State: Thomas 10-57, Goulbourne 19-63, Holman 1-1, Miller 1-(-7)
Louisville: Dawkins 14-88, Shelman 17-59, Brohm 9-25

PASSING
Michigan State: Miller 28-15-1-193
Louisville: Brohm 29-19-0-197, Lowe 2-0-0-0

RECEIVING
Michigan State: Coleman 6-100, Greene 4-49, Goulbourne 3-11, Outlaw 1-18, Abrams 1-15
Louisville: Dawkins 8-68, Asher 4-15, Ferguson 3-68, Fitzpatrick 2-17, Bailey 1-16, Cooper 1-13

Attendance: 21,097

146

Cardinal Football

UNIVERSITY OF LOUISVILLE
BOWL GAMES (Continued)

1998 MOTOR CITY BOWL

Marshall 48, Louisville 29

Pontiac, Mich.
December 23, 1998

The Cardinals ran into a second half buzzsaw as Marshall scored 24 unanswered points to take control of the second annual Motor City Bowl. The loss, however, could not dampen the metamorphosis of the Louisville football team during the 1998 season.

Opening the year 0-2 and being outscored 113-56, the Cardinals won seven of their last nine regular season games to secure their third bowl appearance in the 1990's and record the top turnaround in Division IA in 1998.

U of L held serve with Marshall through the first 30 minutes holding a 21-21 deadlock with the Thundering Herd behind the offense of junior running back Leroy Collins and quarterback Chris Redman.

Redman showed little ill effects from a knee sprain which caused him to miss the regular season finale with Army. The junior from local Male High who watched Browning Nagle and Jeff Brohm guide the Cards to bowl wins as a youngster, completed 35 of 56 throws for 336 yards and a second-quarter TD to Charles Sheffield. The outing was a fitting end to a junior season which saw him finish second nationally in total offense and become the 13th quarterback in I-A history to throw for 4,000 yards.

Collins found the end zone three times in the bowl loss to cap a record-setting season. The junior college transfer hit paydirt 19 times during the regular season to break Lenny Lyles 40-year-old mark.

U of L showed the spark which guided them to the top offense in the nation in 1998 but for every Cardinal action, there was an equal and opposite Marshall reaction.

Herd quarterback Chad Pennington set virtually every MCB record completing 18 of 24 passes for 411 yards and four touchdowns as Marshall exploited an injury-riddled U of L defense.

Following the contest, the Cards two main contributors also made headlines as Redman announced he would remain at U of L for his senior season while Collins declared himself eligible for the NFL Draft.

SUMMARY

	U of L	MU
First Downs	26	27
Rushing Yards	66	202
Passes	34-54	18-24
Passes Int.	1	0
Passing Yards	336	411
Total Offense	402	613
Punts-Avg.	4-49.3	1-58.0
Penalties-Yards	13-109	14-123
Fumbles-Lost	3-0	2-0

Louisville	0	21	0	8	- 29
Marshall	7	14	17	10	- 48

MU: Williams 29 pass from Pennington (Malashevich kick)
UL: Collins 2 run (Hilbert kick)
MU: Washington 14 pass from Pennington (Malashevich kick)
UL: Sheffield 21 pass from Redman (Hilbert kick)
MU: Williams 26 pass from Pennington (Malashevich kick)
UL: Collins 13 run (Hilbert kick)
MU: Long 50 pass from Pennington (Malashevich kick)
MU: Chapman 1 run (Malashevich kick)
MU: Malashevich 22 field goal
MU: Chapman 1 run (Malashevich kick)
UL: Collins 1 run (Hilbert kick)
MU: Malashevich 32 field goal

RUSHING
UL: Collins 14-94, Cooper 2-0, Redman 5-(-28)
MU: Turner 13-94, Chapman 26-76 Pennington 3-34, Leftwich 3-(-4), Baxter 0-2

PASSING
UL: Redman 54-35-1-336
MU: Pennington 24-18-4-411

RECEIVING
UL: Jackson 8-96, Boyd 8-84, Sheffield 8-75, Collins 4-10, Green 3-38, Parker 3-27, Cooper 1-6.
MU: Cooper 5-67, Williams 3-68, Chapman 2-69, Long 2-57, Colcough 2-56, Washington 2-35, Kellett 1-59, Turner 1-0

Attendance: 52,016

UNIVERSITY OF LOUISVILLE
NFL DRAFT SELECTIONS

Player	Team	Pick
1997		
Sam Madison-DB	Miami Dolphins	2nd Round, 44th pick
Tyrus McCloud-LB	Baltimore Ravens	4th Round, 118th pick
Carl Powell-DE	Indianapolis Colts	5th Round, 156th pick
Leland Taylor-DT	Baltimore Ravens	7th Round, 238th pick
1996		
Alan Campos-LB	Dallas Cowboys	5th Round, 167th pick
Roman Oben-OT	New York Giants	3rd Round, 66th pick
1995		
Jamie Asher-TE	Washington Redskins	5th Round, 137th pick
1993		
Deral Boykin-S	Los Angeles Rams	6th Round, 149th pick
Ray Buchanan-CB	Indianapolis Colts	3rd Round, 65th pick
Joe Johnson-DL	New Orleans Saints	1st Round, 13th pick
1992		
Klaus Wilmsmeyer-K	Tampa Bay Buccaneers	12th Round, 311th pick
1991		
Jerry Crafts-OL	Indianapolis Colts	11th Round, 292nd pick
Mike Flores-DE	Philadelphia Eagles	11th Round, 298th pick
Browning Nagle-QB	New York Jets	2nd Round, 34th pick
Ted Washington-DT	San Francisco 49ers	1st Round, 25th pick
1990		
Carwell Gardner- FB	Buffalo Bills	2nd Round, 42nd pick
1987		
Bruce Armstrong-OT	New England Patriots	1st Round, 23rd pick
1986		
Ernest Givins-WR	Houston Oilers	2nd Round, 34th pick
1985		
Ron Davenport-RB	Miami Dolphins	6th Round, 167th pick
1984		
Tom Andrews-OT	Chicago Bears	4th Round, 98th pick
Dean May-QB	Miami Dolphins	5th Round, 119th pick
1983		
Mark Clayton-WR	Miami Dolphins	8th Round, 223rd pick
Richard Tharpe-OL	Buffalo Bills	10th Round, 260th pick
1982		
Donnie Craft-RB	Green Bay Packers	12th Round, 314th pick
1981		
Eddie Johnson-LB	Cleveland Browns	7th Round, 187th pick
1980		
Ricky Skiles-LB	Green Bay Packers	11th Round, 283rd pick
Otis Wilson-LB	Chicago Bears	1st Round, 19th pick
1979		
Nathan Poole-RB	Cincinnati Bengals	10th Round, 250th pick
Dwayne Woodruff-S	Pittsburgh Steelers	6th Round, 161st pick
1978		
Calvin Prince-RB	Cincinnati Bengals	11th Round, 293rd pick
1976		
Wilbur Summers-P	Denver Broncos	15th Round, 418th pick
1975		
A.J. Jacobs-DB	Los Angeles Rams	13th Round, 332nd pick
Marty Smith-DT	Pittsburgh Steelers	15th Round, 390th pick
1974		
Richard Bishop-DT	Cincinnati Bengals	5th Round, 127th pick
1973		
Tom Jackson-LB	Denver Broncos	4th Round, 88th pick
John Mayeda-QB	Atlanta Falcons	14th Round, 351st pick

Player	Team	Pick
1972		
Amos Martin-DE	Minnesota Vikings	6th Round, 154th pick
1971		
Larry Ball-TE	Miami Dolphins	4th Round, 91st pick
Horace Jones-DT	Oakland Raiders	12th Round, 305th pick
1970		
Lee Bouggess-RB	Philadelphia Eagles	3rd Round, 59th pick
Cleo Walker-LB	Green Bay Packers	7th Round, 172nd pick
Dave Sanks-OL	San Diego Chargers	17th Round, 431st pick
1969		
Wally Oyler-QB	Atlanta Falcons	6th Round, 137th pick
1968		
Ed Harmon-LB	Dallas Cowboys	3rd Round, 71st pick
John Neidert-LB	Cincinnati Bengals	6th Round, 145th pick
Wayne Patrick-RB	Cincinnati Bengals	10th Round, 247th pick
Clarence Spencer- TE	San Francisco 49ers	15th Round, 395th pick
1967		
Bill Downs-OT	Philadelphia Eagles	13th Round, 334th pick
Tom Holzer-OT	San Francisco 49ers	2nd Round, 39th pick
1966		
Doug Buffone-LB	Chicago Bears	4th Round
	San Diego Chargers	8th Round
Al McFarlane-RB	Buffalo Bills	13th Round
Benny Russell-QB	Buffalo Bills	11th Round
	St. Louis Cardinals	17th Round
1964		
Ken Kortas-OT	St. Louis Cardinals	1st Round
	Kansas City Chiefs	3rd Round
Dick Schott-OT	Minnesota Vikings	19th Round
	Buffalo Bills	24th Round
1963		
Mario Cheppo	Kansas City Chiefs	3rd Round
	Chicago Bears	18th Round
1960		
Larry Caldwell	Houston Oilers	4th Round
Howard Turley	Pittsburgh Steelers	19th Round
	Denver Broncos	27th Round
	Minnesota Vikings	50th Round
1959		
Ed Young	Pittsburgh Steelers	26th Round
1958		
Lenny Lyles	Baltimore Colts	1st Round
1956		
Maury Woodford	Los Angeles Rams	9th Round
1955		
Johhny Unitas	Pittsburgh Steelers	9th Round
1953		
Jim Williams	Pittsburgh Steelers	19th Round
1942		
Clure Mosher	Pittsburgh Steelers	14th Round

*-The AFL held a draft from 1960-66. The first combined NFL-AFL draft beganin 1967.

**-Compiled from information provided by the NFL.

UNIVERSITY OF LOUISVILLE
CARDINALS IN THE PROS

David Akers— Berlin Thunder, NFLE (1999), Washington Redskins (1998)

Tom Andrews—Seattle Seahawks (1987); Chicago Bears (1984-85)

Bruce Armstrong—New England Patriots (1987-present)

Jamie Asher—Philadelphia Eagles (1999-present); Washington Redskins (1995-1998)

Aaron Bailey—Indianapolis Colts (1994-1999)

Larry Ball—Miami Dolphins (1977-78; 1972-74); Tampa Bay Buccaneers (1976); Detroit Lions (1975)

Matt Battaglia—Philadelphia Eagles (1987)

Dave Betz—Washington Federals,USFL (1983)

Richard Bishop—Los Angeles Rams (1983); Miami Dolphins (1982); New England Patriots (1976-81); Ottawa Roughriders, CFL (1975); Hamilton Tiger-Cats, CFL (1974)

Deral Boykin—Philadelphia Eagles (1996); Jacksonville Jaguars (1995); Los Angeles Rams (1993-94)

John Brewer—Philadelphia Eagles (1952-53)

Jeff Brohm—Denver Broncos (1999-present); Tampa Bay Buccaneers (1998; San Francisco 49ers (1995-1997); San Diego Chargers (1994)

Ray Buchanan—Atlanta Falcons (1997-present); Indianapolis Colts (1993-96)

Doug Buffone—Chicago Bears (1966-80)

Lee Calland—Pittsburgh Steelers (1969-72); Chicago Bears (1969); Atlanta Falcons (1966-68); Minnesota Vikings (1963-65)

Alan Campos—Scottish Claymores, NFLE (1999); Dallas Cowboys (1996)

Rico Clark—Indianapolis Colts (1997-present)

Mark Clayton—Green Bay Packers (1993); Miami Dolphins (1983-92)

Anthony Copeland—Washington Redskins (1987)

Donald Craft—Houston Oilers (1982-84)

Jerry Crafts—Amsterdam Admirals, WLAF (1996-present), Green Bay Packers (1995); Buffalo Bills (1992-94)

Ron Davenport—Miami Dolphins (1985-89)

Ralph Dawkins—Amsterdam Admirals, WLAF (1995-present); New Orleans Saints (1994)

Mike Flores—Cincinnati Bengals (1995); Philadelphia Eagles (1991-94)

Kevin Gaines—London Monarchs (1997-present)

Carwell Gardner—San Diego Chargers (1997); Baltimore Ravens (1996); Cleveland Browns (1995); Buffalo Bills (1990-94)

Bill Gatti—San Antonio Wings (1975); Florida Blazers, WFL (1974)

Kendrick Gholston—Berlin Thunder, NFLE (1999)

Ernest Givins—Jacksonville Jaguars (1995); Houston Oilers (1986-94)

Ernie Green—Cleveland Browns (1962-68)

Jim Hanna—New Orleans Saints (1994)

Ed Harmon—Cincinnati Bengals (1969)

Tom Jackson—Denver Broncos (1973-86)

Joe Jacoby—Washington Redskins (1980-93)

Charlie Johnson—San Francisco 49ers (1966-68)

Eddie Johnson—Cleveland Browns (1981-91)

Joe Johnson—New Orleans Saints (1994-present)

Horace Jones—Seattle Seahawks (1977); Oakland Raiders (1971-75)

Ken Kortas—Chicago Bears (1969); Pittsburgh Steelers (1965-68); St. Louis Cardinals (1964)

Marty Lowe—Texas Terror, AFL (1997)

Lenny Lyles—Baltimore Colts (1961-69, 1958)

Pete McCartney—New York Jets (1987)

Tyrus McCloud—Baltimore Ravens (1997-present)

Sam Madison—Miami Dolphins (1997-present)

Amos Martin—Seattle Seahawks (1977); Minnesota Vikings (1972-77)

Dean May—Philadelphia Eagles (1984)

Kevin Miller—Minnesota Vikings (1979-80)

Frank Minnifield—Cleveland Browns (1984-92); Chicago Blitz, USFL (1983-84)

Clure Mosher—Pittsburgh Steelers

Browning Nagle—Orlando Pedators, AFL (1999-present); Atlanta Falcons (1995); Indianapolis Colts (1994); New York Jets (1991-93)

John Neidert—Chicago Bears (1970); New York Jets (1968-69); Cincinnati Bengals (1968)

Roman Oben—New York Giants (1996-present)

Wayne Patrick—Buffalo Bills (1968-72)

Nathan Poole—Denver Broncos (1987, 1985, 1982-83); Cincinnati Bengals (1979-80)

Carl Powell—Rhein Fire, NFLE (1999), Indianapolis Colts (1997-present)

Steve Reese—Tampa Bay Buccaneers (1976), New York Jets (1975)

Terry Rice-Locket—Scottish Claymores, NFLE (1999)

Ed Rubbert—Miami Dolphins (1989); Washington Redskins (1987-88)

Benny Russell—Buffalo Bills (1969)

Mark Sander—Scottish Claymores, WLAF (1995); Miami Dolphins (1991-93)

Joey Smith—British Columbia Lions, CFL (1995); New York Giants (1992-93)

Marty Smith—Buffalo Bills (1995)

Howard Stevens—Baltimore Colts (1975-77); New Orleans Saints (1973-74)

Wilbur Summers—Detroit Lions (1977)

Leland Taylor—Baltimore Ravens (1997-present)

Chris Thieneman—Birmingham Barracudas, CFL (1995); Sacramento Goldminers, CFL (1993-94), San Antonio Riders, WLAF (1992); Saskatchewan Roughriders, CFL (1991).

Johnny Unitas—San Diego Chargers (1973); Baltimore Colts (1956-72)

Cleo Walker—Atlanta Falcons (1971); Green Bay Packers (1970)

Ted Washington—Buffalo Bills (1996-present); Denver Broncos (1994-95); San Francisco 49ers (1992-93)

Carl Williams- Tampa Bay Buccaneers (1985)

Klaus Wilmsmeyer—Carolina Panthers (1999-present); Miami Dolphins (1998); New Orleans Saints (1995-1997); Tampa Bay Buccaneers (1994); San Francisco 49ers (1992-94)

Otis Wilson—Chicago Bears (1980-90)

Dwayne Woodruff—Pittsburgh Steelers (1979-90)

Key—AFL (Arena Football League); CFL (Canadian Football League); NFLE (National Football League Europe); WFL (World Football League); WLAF (World League of American Football)

Super Bowl Service

Name	Team	Years
Tom Andrews	Chicago Bears	1986
Bruce Armstrong	New England Patriots	1997
Ray Buchanan	Atlanta Falcons	1999
Jerry Crafts	Buffalo Bills	1992, 93
Larry Ball	Miami Dolphins	1973, 74
Jeff Brohm	San Diego Chargers	1995
Mark Clayton	Miami Dolphins	1985
Ron Davenport	Miami Dolphins	1985
Carwell Gardner	Buffalo Bills	1990, 91, 92, 93
Tom Jackson	Denver Broncos	1978, 87
Joe Jacoby	Washington Redskins	1983, 84, 88, 91
Amos Martin	Minnesota Vikings	1974, 75, 77
John Neidert	New York Jets	1969
Johnny Unitas	Baltimore Colts	1969, 71
Klaus Wilmsmeyer	San Francisco 49ers	1995
Otis Wilson	Chicago Bears	1986
Dwayne Woodruff	Pittsburgh Steelers	1980

BRUCE ARMSTRONG
OFFENSIVE TACKLE 1983-86

From the minute he joined the New England Patriots, Bruce Armstrong was an impact player. He was a consensus all-rookie selection in 1987, and Associated Press tabbed him as the National Football League's Offensive Rookie of the Year.

After the promising rookie campaign, Armstrong only got better. In 1991, 1992 and 1996 he was selected to the Pro Bowl.

There was a time when playing offensive tackle at any level seemed remote to Armstrong. As a freshman and sophomore at U of L, he played tight end. His numbers were pretty respectable: seven catches for 103 yards as a freshman and 26 catches for 289 yards and three touchdowns as a sophomore.

When Howard Schnellenberger came to U of L, however, he asked Armstrong to make the change to the line.

"I wasn't happy about it to say the least," Armstrong said of his initial reaction to the switch.

Nobody is complaining now, however.

Armstrong came to Louisville after a standout career at Miami's Central High.

DOUG BUFFONE
LINEBACKER/CENTER 1962-65

Maybe the finest tribute to how good Doug Buffone was came in the 1965 University of Louisville media guide.

Veteran coach Frank Camp said Buffone was "... the most complete ball player I've ever coached." A pretty strong testimony from a man who coached National Football League stars like Johnny Unitas, Lenny Lyles, Ernie Green, Lee Calland and Ken Kortas.

Buffone saw action on both sides of the football during his three seasons as a Cardinal. A center on offense and a linebacker on defense, Buffone became the first player in Louisville history to lead the team in tackles three consecutive seasons.

His biography raved of his 138 unassisted tackles in 1964 but it's a wonder how his 201 total tackles in 1965 would have been summed up.

The son of coalmining family from Yatesboro, Pa., Buffone became a fourth-round draft choice of the Chicago Bears.

Buffone went on to legendary status with the Bears playing 15 seasons in the Windy City at a linebacker spot in three different decades. He ranks sixth all-time on the Bears interception list with 24.

MARK CLAYTON
WIDE RECEIVER 1979-82

During the 1980s, no passing combination in the NFL was more feared than the Miami Dolphins'. The sight of quarterback Dan Marino throwing strike after strike to wide receivers Mark Duper and former U of L standout Mark Clayton was enough to scare defensive coordinators around the league.

Miami certainly was not counting on Clayton to make it big. The Dolphins made him an eighth-round selection in 1983, but he overcame the odds to become a Pro Bowl performer in 1984, 1985, 1986, 1988 and 1991. The 18 touchdown passes he caught in 1984 were an NFL record (since broken).

"He's one of the smartest guys we've ever had come in here," Miami Head Coach Don Shula said.

Clayton still ranks among Louisville's all-time leading receivers. His 2,004 yards still rank first on U of L's career receiving charts, and his 20.9 yard per catch average is also the best ever. When Miguel Montano caught 50 passes last year, he joined Clayton as the only Cardinal wide receivers to catch 50+ passes in a season.

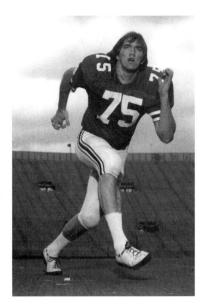

ERNEST GIVINS
WIDE RECEIVER 1984-85

Louisville football fans can only stop and wonder what might have been had the Cardinals had Ernest Givins for four years. The elusive wideout spent his first two seasons at Northeast Oklahoma.

Nonetheless, Cardinal faithful saw Givins account for 67 catches and 1266 yards in 1984 and 1985.

A second-round selection of the Houston Oilers in 1986, Givins stepped in to contribute 61 catches and 1062 yards en route to all-rookie accords. He was just the ninth rookie ever to record in excess on 1,000 yards receiving.

He went on to play in the Pro Bowl three different times—1991, 1992 and 1993.

Givins attended Lakewood High School in St. Petersburg, Fla. Growing up, Givins pondered a career in another sport—baseball. One particular encounter in high school convinced him to concentrate on the gridiron.

After a pitcher threw two fastballs past him, Givins worked the count to 2-2. A sharp breaking ball sent him back to the dugout as a strikeout victim. He was not the only player that pitcher victimized. The hurler was Dwight Gooden.

"I think that's when I decided to play football," Givins said.

ERNIE GREEN
RUNNING BACK 1958-61

It is considered part of the job these days for a running back to be a large part of the passing offense, but that was not always the case in football. Ernie Green was a pass-catching fullback long before players like Roger Craig and John L. Williams made their marks professionally.

Green was the Green Bay Packer's 14th choice in the 1962 draft, but was shipped to Cleveland during his first training camp. He initially played halfback, and he posted respectable numbers. A move to fullback in 1966, however, made him one of the game's elite.

That first season at fullback, Green ran for 750 yards while catching 45 passes for 445 yards. A year later, the league took notice as he was named to the Pro Bowl after rushing for 710 yards and catching 39 passes for 369 yards.

In addition to his on-field accomplishments, Green also acted as the Browns' player representative and secretary of the NFL Players Association.

He was the Cardinals' leading ground gainer in 1959 and 1960. He bypassed a chance to play professional baseball to play in the NFL.

Green attended Spencer High in Columbus, Ga.

JOE JACOBY
OFFENSIVE TACKLE 1978-80

Joe Jacoby has more Super Bowl rings (three) than any other former Cardinal player. The former Washington Redskins' standout also had four Pro Bowl berths to his credit (1983, 1984, 1985 and 1986).

Early in his professional career, though, Jacoby considered giving up the game of football. In 1981, his mother died and he thought about pursuing another line of work.

The Redskin organization is elated that his brother, Charlie, talked him out of the career change.

"I didn't want to look back later and feel I'd missed something," Jacoby said.

He would have missed being a part of one of the most renowned offensive lines in the history of the NFL. Jacoby joined Jeff Bostic, Mark May and Russ Grimm to form "The Hogs."

A late-bloomer, Jacoby did not start until his junior year. As a senior, he was a co-captain. Not drafted, Jacoby considered offers from the Seattle Seahawks and the Washington Redskins before inking a pact with Washington.

"I saw the Capitol, the Washington Monument, and the White House and knew Washington was where I wanted to play," Jacoby said.

Jacoby attended Western High in Louisville.

Cardinal Football

FRANK MINNIFIELD
CORNERBACK 1979-82

Frank Minnifield had a knack for proving people wrong.

Coming out of high school, no Division I university felt that he warranted a scholarship. At 5-9, most deemed him too small to be an effective performer.

A desire to excel and a 44-inch vertical jump helped Minnifield prove otherwise.

He became a standout defensive back and kickoff/punt returner for the Cardinals while earning that scholarship nobody thought he deserved coming out of high school.

Upon completing his eligibility, Minnifield opted to sign with the fledgling United States Football League's Chicago Blitz in 1983. He was projected as a second-round selection in the NFL Draft, but no club wanted to take a chance on him after he had signed with the Blitz.

After two seasons, Minnifield signed with the Cleveland Browns as a free agent. He teamed with Hanford Dixon to give the Browns one of the premier cornerback tandems in the mid-to-late 1980s.

In 1986, 1987, 1988 and 1989, he was named to the Pro Bowl.

Minnifield attended Henry Clay High in Lexington, Ky.

OTIS WILSON
LINEBACKER 1977-79

After spending one season at Syracuse where he was the varsity's Most Valuable Defensive Player, Otis Wilson brought his considerable football talents to the University of Louisville, and he will go down as one of the Cardinals' all-time greats.

"There may be other linebackers as good as Wilson, but I don't see how they could be any better," Louisville Courier-Journal Sports Editor Earl Cox said during Wilson's senior year.

Wilson was selected in the first round of the 1980 National Football League Draft by the Chicago Bears.

While playing for the Bears afforded him the opportunity to win a Super Bowl championship in 1986, at times it deprived him of the individual attention a player of his caliber warranted.

After all, Wilson was surrounded by standouts such as Mike Singletary, Dan Hampton, Richard Dent and Wilbur Marshall among others.

He felt he warranted a trip to the Pro Bowl after the 1984 season, but he was denied. After declaring he was on a mission to make the Pro Bowl, he was named to the squad after the 1985 campaign, and he returned after the 1988 season.

Wilson attended Thomas Jefferson High in Brooklyn, N.Y.